"DON'T HIT MY MOMMY!"

A Manual for Child–Parent Psychotherapy With Young Children Exposed to Violence and Other Trauma

SECOND EDITION

Alicia F. Lieberman, Chandra Ghosh Ippen, and Patricia Van Horn

"DON'T HIT MY MOMMY!"

A Manual for Child–Parent Psychotherapy With Young Children Exposed to Violence and Other Trauma

SECOND EDITION

Alicia F. Lieberman, Chandra Ghosh Ippen, and Patricia Van Horn

ZERO TO THREE
Early connections last a lifetime

Washington, DC

Published by

ZERO TO THREE
1255 23rd St., NW, Ste. 350
Washington, DC 20037
(202) 638-1144
Toll-free orders (800) 899-4301
Fax: (202) 638-0851
Web: http://www.zerotothree.org

The views contained in this book are those of the authors and do not necessarily reflect those of ZERO TO THREE: National Center for Infants, Toddlers and Families, Inc.

These materials are intended for education and training to help promote a high standard of care by professionals. Use of these materials is voluntary and their use does not confer any professional credentials or qualification to take any registration, certification, board or licensure examination, and neither confers nor infers competency to perform any related professional functions.

The user of these materials is solely responsible for compliance with all local, state or federal rules, regulations or licensing requirements. Despite efforts to ensure that these materials are consistent with acceptable practices, they are not intended to be used as a compliance guide and are not intended to supplant or to be used as a substitute for or in contravention of any applicable local, state or federal rules, regulations or licensing requirements. ZERO TO THREE expressly disclaims any liability arising from use of these materials in contravention of such rules, regulations or licensing requirements.

The views expressed in these materials represent the opinions of the respective authors. Publication of these materials does not constitute an endorsement by ZERO TO THREE of any view expressed herein, and ZERO TO THREE expressly disclaims any liability arising from any inaccuracy or misstatement.

Cover design: Jennifer Paul
Text design and composition: Design Consultants, Inc.

Library of Congress CIP data on file.

10 9 8 7 6 5 4 3

ISBN 978-1-938558-52-8

Printed in the United States of America

Suggested citation: Lieberman, A. F., Ghosh Ippen, C., & Van Horn, P. (2015). *Don't hit my mommy!: A manual for Child–Parent Psychotherapy with young children exposed to violence and other trauma*. Washington, DC: ZERO TO THREE.

To Selma Fraiberg,

who understood the magic of the early years

TABLE OF CONTENTS

ACKNOWLEDGMENTS TO THE SECOND EDITION

TEN YEARS HAVE PASSED SINCE THE FIRST EDITION of *Don't Hit My Mommy!* was published by ZERO TO THREE. As we read the Acknowledgments section in the 2005 edition, we find that there are many continuities as well as much change. The practice of Child–Parent Psychotherapy (CPP) has expanded to most states as well as several countries. A group of more than 50 CPP national trainers maintains an active exchange of ideas and mutual support in the shared goal of helping young children and their families heal from the impact of traumatic experiences. Clinicians rostered as CPP therapists are now in the hundreds. We continue to rejoice in productive partnerships with cherished colleagues through a variety of organizations, salient among them the Substance Abuse and Mental Health Services Administration (SAMHSA) National Child Traumatic Stress Network—where, since 2001, we have had the privilege of leading the Early Trauma Treatment Network collaborative with our sister programs at Boston Medical Center, Louisiana State University Medical Center, and Tulane University. We continue to find a nurturing home at the University of California San Francisco Medical Center and the San Francisco General Hospital, and we are proud of our long-standing association with the San Francisco Department of Public Health in promoting trauma-informed systems in the Bay Area. We are fortunate to have the support of foundations whose values we cherish and share: the Coydog Foundation, the Irving B. Harris Foundation, the John and Lisa Pritzker Family Fund, the Tauber Foundation, and the Tipping Point Community. Our team at the Child Trauma Research Program feels like an extended family: Laura Castro, Nancy Compton, Miriam Hernandez Dimmler, Markita Mays, Griselda Oliver Bucio, Vilma Reyes, and Maria Augusta Torres as clinicians and supervisors, and Dione Johnson, Emily Cohodes, Luisa Rivera, Helen Chen, and Efraim Dacuma as administrative staff. Only Patricia Van Horn is missing. Her untimely death in

January 2014, just as she had finished giving a masterful class to CPP students in her beloved Israel, brings a wistful note to the richness of the work. Her memory kept us loving company while updating this manual, and we continue to remember her and derive inspiration from her in every aspect of our work. In her spirit, we remember the Biblical commandment to Choose Life, and we offer our gratitude to those whose love supports us in doing trauma work: our husbands David Richman and Erich Ippen, and Raiden Ippen, who shares his mama with the work, knowing all the while that he comes first.

Alicia F. Lieberman and Chandra Ghosh Ippen
San Francisco, August 2015

ACKNOWLEDGMENTS

FIRST EDITION

THIS MANUAL IS THE PRODUCT OF MANY YEARS of providing Child–Parent Psychotherapy to young children and their parents as they struggle to change the violence and hopelessness of their family bonds and find more security, pleasure, and love within themselves and in each other. We thank the countless parents who trust us as allies in their efforts, allowing us into the privacy of their closest relationships. We are particularly grateful to the children, who are our persistent teachers in showing us what they need until we finally understand and are able to respond.

The development of this manual involved an active collaborative process. Drafts of the work were discussed monthly over the course of 2 years during our case review at the Child Trauma Research Program (CTRP), and the feedback from our colleagues and students spurred us toward greater specificity in the description of intervention strategies. The clinical examples, derived from their detailed narrative session notes, owe much to their talent and creativity. Our program faculty—Nancy Compton, Chandra Ghosh Ippen, Laura Castro, and Laura Mayorga—has been steadfast in providing us with a sturdy, secure base where the challenges of treating families experiencing violence can be shared as we search together for a helpful course of action and where the joys of progress can be jointly celebrated. Donna Davidowitz, Robin Silverman, Edie Walden, and Maria Augusta Torres participated in shaping our direction during the earlier years of the program, and their contributions continue to be valued.

We learn much from the interns and postdoctoral fellows who spend 1, 2, or 3 years with us, bringing us their unique outlooks and skills. There are now more than 50 graduates of the program, and their sheer number precludes our naming them individually. They know, however, that they constitute our extended family and continue to be remembered and appreciated for their commitment to the children, the families, and the work.

Being part of the University of California–San Francisco (UCSF) and San Francisco General Hospital is an integral part of our programmatic and professional identities. We could not have written this manual without the inspiration and support of Robert L. Okin, who, as chief of the Department of Psychiatry at San Francisco General Hospital, invited us to launch the CTRP in 1996 and gave us the impetus to develop and evaluate evidence-based approaches to the treatment of traumatic stress in young children. His unwavering commitment to the underserved has transformed the landscape of mental health services in San Francisco, and we are among the many beneficiaries of his vision. Craig Van Dyke, chair of the UCSF Department of Psychiatry, is an exemplary leader in promoting the individual academic pursuits of the faculty while fostering a spirit of collaboration within a large and diverse department.

We are grateful to our present and past funders for providing both financial support and opportunities for constructive dialogue. The cornerstone of the CTRP consists of an agreement between San Francisco General Hospital, the Department of Public Health, and the Department of Human Services (DHS). We thank Sai-Ling Chan-Sew as well as DHS managers, supervisors, and child welfare workers for many years of productive partnership on behalf of traumatized young children that provide the groundwork for this manual. The National Institute of Mental Health supported our pilot randomized trial of manual-guided Child–Parent Psychotherapy through an R21 Exploratory/Development grant. Our scientific review administrator, Victoria Levin, is legendary among grantees for integrating extraordinary knowledge with unmatched selflessness in sharing it.

This institutional support has been buttressed by the generosity of private foundations and individual donors. Irving Harris was quick to recognize both the urgency and the obstacles involved in addressing the effects of trauma in the early years, and his ongoing contribution underwrites the infrastructure and training components of our program. The Coydog Foundation and William Harris are enabling us to explore new angles in the interface between trauma and attachment through the beneficial effect of loving experiences in guiding the restoration of healthy bonds. The Miriam and Peter Haas Fund enabled us to develop productive collaborations with Child Protective Services and with the courts, and Cheryl

Polk shared her talent and expertise in program development. The A. L. Mailman Foundation and the Nathan Cummings Foundation supported the inclusion in the manual of intervention strategies developed for the first 2 years of life. The Pinewood Foundation, the Francis S. North Foundation, and the George Sarlo Foundation made possible the development of intervention strategies geared specifically to the experiences of immigrant and minority families facing violence. Gifts from Jonathan and Kathleen Altman, from Aubrey and Beverly Metcalf, and from the Isabel Allende Foundation allow us to respond to unanticipated needs. Our sense of indebtedness to all of them gives substance to Felix Frankfurter's observation that "gratitude is one of the least articulate of emotions, especially when it is deep."

The manual profited immensely from the input of cherished colleagues and friends. Dante Cicchetti, Scott Henggeler, Arietta Slade, and Sheree Toth reviewed an early draft and were generous with their clinical insights and editorial skills. Elizabeth Power contributed her expertise with manual development. Our participation in the National Child Traumatic Stress Network (NCTSN) of the Substance Abuse and Mental Health Services Administration (SAMHSA) enabled us to establish the Early Trauma Treatment Network as a collaborative among our program and three groundbreaking programs working with young children exposed to interpersonal violence at Boston Medical Center, Louisiana State University Health Science Center, and Tulane University. We thank their directors and our partners in this collaborative, Betsy McAlister Groves, Joy Osofsky, Julie Larrieu, and Charles Zeanah, for their thoroughness and zeal in implementing the manual in their training and treatment protocols and for sharing their extensive experience and valuable clinical insights with us. Our understanding of traumatic stress was greatly enhanced through the seminal work of other members of the NCTSN, including Robert Pynoos, Bessel van der Kolk, Judy Cohen, and Steven Marans. Our deep thanks for their readiness to make their knowledge available to us. We have also learned a great deal from local collaborators. Our colleagues at the San Francisco Unified Family Court, at the Safe Start Initiative, and in the domestic violence advocacy community all gave us their valuable perspectives on the families that we serve. Their contributions greatly enriched our work.

Work is done best when supported by a sustaining home life. We thank our partners, David Richman and Verlene Perry, for many things: their love, their unfaltering support during this project, and, perhaps above all, their forbearance during the long hours we spent in bringing it to fruition.

Alicia F. Lieberman and Patricia Van Horn
San Francisco, July 2003

INTRODUCTION

"My daddy makes my mommy cry, and my mommy makes me cry, and that's how it works."—Sandra, 3 years old

"Even a fist was once an open palm with fingers."
—Yehuda Amichai

THE ORIGINS OF AN AGGRESSIVE STANCE toward other people can be traced to the earliest years of childhood, to experiences of helplessness and pain that instill in the child a conviction that being on the offensive is the best defense. Witnessing violence and being the victim of violence shatter the child's confidence that his well-being matters and that adults will take care of him. Little Sandra, at 3 years old, displayed a philosopher's analytical skills when she concluded, on the basis of her family experience, that making somebody cry is the way of the world. At the same time, she strenuously protested this state of affairs when she screamed, "Don't hit my mommy!" in a frantic but futile effort to protect her mother by stopping her father's violence. Millions of children who are exposed to family violence share Sandra's internal dilemma of yearning for safety while simultaneously learning that the people she loves make each other cry. The question left unspoken is: Will Sandra also make someone cry someday? Will she become the next link in the crying chain? Or is it possible to reach her before her hand becomes a fist, while it is still "an open palm with fingers?"

Child–Parent Psychotherapy (CPP) is designed to repair the behavioral and mental health problems of infants, toddlers, and preschoolers whose most intimate relationships are disrupted by experiences of maltreatment, violence, and other forms of trauma that shatter the child's trust in the safety of attachments. Over the years, working with hundreds of families across the United States and other countries, we have witnessed the urgent desire of many mothers and fathers to engage with their children in a safe new start free of prevailing conflict and fear. This manual provides CPP implementation guidelines. Although the primary focus is on children exposed to domestic violence, the intervention strategies described also apply to many other forms of child maltreatment and trauma, including emotional, physical, and sexual abuse; exposure to community violence; accidental injuries; and painful illnesses and medical procedures.

The focus on interpersonal violence as a specific and particularly destructive form of early trauma is warranted by three converging factors: the shocking frequency of violence in young children's daily experience, the enormous impact of such exposure on children's well-being, and the persistent and widespread misconception among service providers and the general public that young children are inherently resilient and do not remember early traumatic events. The data show otherwise. Infants, toddlers, and preschoolers are more likely than older children to die or be injured by maltreatment, and they are disproportionately represented among children in foster care (Finkelhor, Ormrod, Turner, & Hamby, 2005; U. S. Department of Health and Human Services, 2010). For the past 20 years, there has been a steady accumulation of studies showing that witnessing or experiencing interpersonal violence interferes with the mastery of age-appropriate developmental milestones and leaves children at risk for conduct disorder, posttraumatic stress disorder (PTSD), anxiety, and depression (Crusto et al., 2010; Margolin, 1998; Osofsky & Scheeringa, 1997; Pynoos, 1993; Rossman, Hughes, & Rosenberg, 2000; Scheeringa & Zeanah, 1995; for a review, see Lieberman, Chu, Van Horn, & Harris, 2011).

It is by now an inescapable conclusion that babies and young children remember what happens to them and show us what they learned from their experiences through their physiological profiles, the emotional quality of their relationships, and their approach to the challenges of exploring the world and learning. In spite of extensive data documenting the risks of exposure to trauma—and in spite of evidence that infants, toddlers and preschoolers are at greater risk than older children (Fantuzzo & Fusco, 2007)—early childhood mental health interventions do not usually include a systematic assessment of child exposure to traumatic events and continue to focus largely on enhancing the quality of parent–child interactions and promoting secure attachment. Important as these goals are, unidentified and unaddressed child trauma exposure poses a powerful obstacle to their achievement and leaves children at risk for repeated maltreatment.

In spite of considerable data on the prevalence and impact of family violence, there are still few bridges between this research knowledge and its clinical application. In many ways, the statement made by John Bowlby in his 1983 Karen Horney Lecture at the Association for the Advancement of Psychoanalysis is still relevant:

> It seems to me that as psychoanalysts and psychotherapists we have been appallingly slow to wake up to the prevalence and far-reaching consequences of violent behavior between members of a family… Yet there is now abundant evidence not only that it is much commoner than we had hitherto supposed but that it is a major contributory cause of a number of distressing and puzzling psychiatric syndromes. Since, moreover, violence breeds violence, violence in families tends to perpetuate itself from one generation to the next." (Bowlby, 1988, p. 77)

In his characteristically straightforward fashion, he goes on to state that among clinicians, it is "extremely unfashionable to attribute psychopathology to real-life experiences" (Bowlby, 1988, p. 78).

This attitude remains the norm among many mental health professionals, institutions, and training programs in spite of numerous efforts for change that include a statement by Steve Sharfstein (2006), who announced the formation of an American Psychiatric Association task force on the effects of violence on children, saying, "Interpersonal violence, especially violence experienced by children, is the largest single preventable cause of mental illness. What cigarette smoking is to the rest of medicine, early childhood violence is to psychiatry." The Substance Abuse and Mental Health Services Administration (SAMHSA)–funded National Child Traumatic Stress Network (NCTSN) has numerous resources documenting the impact of violence on young children and links practitioners to trainings for trauma-informed interventions (see www.nctsn.org). The Childhood Adversity Narratives (CAN) is a free online resource developed and distributed by Putnam, Harris, Lieberman, Putnam, and Amaya-Jackson and has had thousands of downloads since it was launched in May 2015 (see www.canarratives.org).

We strongly believe that assessing for trauma exposure in young children and tailoring treatment to the manifestations of early traumatic stress should become a standard component of best practice in early childhood mental health. This conviction is consistent with the recommendations of the American Academy of

Child and Adolescent Psychiatry (AACAP, 2010) article "Practice Parameter for the Assessment and Treatment of Children and Adolescents With Posttraumatic Stress Disorder", which highlighted the centrality of trauma exposure as a pathogenic event and recommended the routine inclusion of questions about trauma exposure and symptoms of PTSD in the clinical assessment of children and adolescents. This manual has the purpose of providing practitioners from a variety of disciplines with a comprehensive treatment approach that integrates clinical and research knowledge from developmental psychopathology, attachment theory, and the field of trauma and offers concrete intervention strategies to identify and address the consequences of traumatic experiences for young children and their families.

This manual is divided into five sections. Section I describes the theoretical premises that guide CPP; provides an overview of the treatment; and explains how this form of treatment is used with infants, toddlers, and preschoolers exposed to traumatic events. Section II describes the phases of CPP, specifies the main domains of intervention, and describes therapeutic strategies that are unique and essential to CPP. Section III describes the conceptual framework used to ensure fidelity to the model and provides clinical examples of the different fidelity strands. Section IV describes the procedures recommended when the intervention needs to include case management, particularly contacts with child protective services and the judicial system. Section V provides a list of items that are essential but not unique to CPP as well as a list of items that are incompatible with this treatment model, as recommended by Waltz, Addis, Koerner, and Jacobson (1993).

Although we describe specific therapeutic strategies and provide illustrative examples, this manual does not prescribe a step-by-step treatment approach. Development is never linear—and least so in the first years of life. Young children's profound individual differences in personality, adaptation styles, and cognitive, social, and emotional maturation are accompanied by unexpected discontinuities, accelerations, and lapses in the unfolding of the child's developmental timetable. Moreover, parents present a broad range of psychological vulnerabilities as well as strengths, both as individuals and as caregivers. CPP involves the flexible tailoring of therapeutic interventions to those specific aspects of the child–parent relationship that interfere with the child's healthy development while also supporting the growth-promoting aspects of the relationship. Because not all clinical problems encountered in situations of trauma are necessarily trauma-related, therapeutic strategies are informed by the clinician's appraisal of which domain of intervention might be most conducive to positive change in the moment and may entail a focus on early childhood development, the parent's developmental stage and current circumstances, child and adult psychopathology, intersubjective processes, and/or cultural–ecological factors in the sociology and psychology of violence-related trauma.

We believe that, at its best, therapeutic intervention is co-created by the clinician and the recipient(s) of the treatment, which in CPP comprise at the very least the child and one parent and may include, depending on the clinical need, both parents and perhaps siblings as well. For this reason, we offer alternative strategies for addressing common therapeutic quandaries, with the knowledge that each clinician's creativity, individual style, and sense of timing will guide and enrich her use. Throughout the text, we use the term "parent" to mean any primary caregiver who serves as an attachment figure for the child because of the emotional immediacy of this term in evoking safety and loving commitment—the attitudes that are at the root of what we are trying to promote and repair.

SECTION I

CHILD-PARENT PSYCHOTHERAPY: A RELATIONSHIP-BASED, TRAUMA-INFORMED TREATMENT MODEL

THIS SECTION PROVIDES AN OVERVIEW of the foundational facets of Child–Parent Psychotherapy (CPP), including the conceptual premises, the historical roots, cultural and developmental considerations in framing treatment, intervention modalities and objectives, and the empirical evidence supporting the efficacy of CPP through randomized studies with diverse populations.

Basic Conceptual Premises

CPP is based on six conceptual premises that organize the therapeutic approach to promoting young children's mental health. We describe these premises here.

PREMISE 1: THE ATTACHMENT SYSTEM IS THE MAIN ORGANIZER OF CHILDREN'S RESPONSES TO DANGER AND SAFETY IN THE FIRST 5 YEARS OF LIFE (AINSWORTH, 1969; AINSWORTH, BLEHAR, WATERS, & WALL, 1978; BOWLBY, 1969/1982). From the perspective of attachment theory, traumatic experiences—such as witnessing domestic violence and enduring maltreatment—damage the child's developmentally appropriate expectation that the parents will be reliably available as protectors. In these conditions, parents themselves become the sources of danger rather than the child's protectors from it. Young children exposed to interpersonal stressors learn that the people dearest to them may be unable or unwilling to protect them and may also be the ones who cause the greatest hurt.

Arietta Slade (2014) has restored much-needed attention to the central role of fear, in Bowlby's (1969/1982) thinking, as a foundational motivation that guides the moment-to-moment balance between attachment and exploration and the formation of working models of the attachment figure and of the self.

When unmanageable fear becomes an ever-present feature of everyday experience, the child's sense of self and others becomes permeated with mistrust, apprehension, hypervigilance, and anger—responses that are in conflict with age-appropriate strivings for closeness and safety with the parents (Lieberman & Van Horn, 1998; Main & Hesse, 1990; Pynoos, Steinberg, & Piacentini, 1999).

These responses are particularly notable in the period from birth to preschool because during this developmental stage, children learn primarily from observing and imitating the behavior of cherished adults (Kagan, 1981). Children who observe and imitate aggression from an early age are more likely to become aggressive adolescents and adults and are more likely to use aggression as a way of coping with stress in intimate relationships (Kalmus, 1984). Research evidence suggests that toddlers and preschoolers with a combination of risk factors that include early aggression, high family stress, and negative parenting are most likely to show patterns of maladjustment as they enter school (Campbell, Shaw, & Gilliom, 2000). CPP has the goal of helping children modulate negative emotions, express feelings in socially acceptable ways, and learn age-appropriate ways of recognizing and respecting the parents' motivations and feelings.

PREMISE 2: EMOTIONAL AND BEHAVIORAL PROBLEMS IN INFANCY AND EARLY CHILDHOOD ARE BEST ADDRESSED IN THE CONTEXT OF THE CHILD'S PRIMARY ATTACHMENT RELATIONSHIPS (FRAIBERG, 1980; LIEBERMAN, SILVERMAN, & PAWL, 2000; LIEBERMAN & ZEANAH, 1995). Enhancing the physical and emotional security of attachment relationships is the most effective vehicle for promoting the child's healthy development because the child's sense of self evolves in the context of those relationships.

CPP strives to create a safer and more protective caregiving environment by identifying and addressing the immediate and enduring impact on feelings and behaviors of past and present threats to child and parent safety; encouraging protective, loving, and development-promoting interactions and appropriate discipline; and targeting for change patterns of aggression, punitiveness, and emotional withdrawal in the parent–child interaction. These goals are pursued by helping the parent and the child become more accurately attuned and appropriately responsive to the needs, feelings, and motivations of the other.

The interactive mutuality of attunement and responsiveness between parent and child becomes increasingly more salient as the child grows from infancy to the toddler and preschool years. During the first year of life, the baby's signals of need have center stage as an organizer of parental responsiveness, with the baby's crying as an archetypal mobilizer of the parental caring response. As the child becomes increasingly autonomous through mobility and language, socialization takes on an important place as a component of healthy parenting in response to cultural expectations of prosocial behavior, including sharing, turn-taking, waiting, tolerating frustration, using words instead of impulsive actions to express affect, and complying with adult directives. Goal-corrected partnership is the most mature stage of attachment relationships, involving an empathic willingness to find an accommodation between one's needs and desires and the needs and desires of the loved other (Bowlby, 1969/1982). Reflective function and mentalization (Fonagy, 2010) serve in this process as underpinnings of secure attachment, which is promoted both by responsiveness to the young child's signals and by parental expectations of culturally sanctioned, age-appropriate behavior from the child.

PREMISE 3: THE CULTURAL AND SOCIOECONOMIC ECOLOGY OF THE FAMILY MUST BE AN INTEGRAL COMPONENT OF CLINICAL FORMULATIONS AND TREATMENT PLANS. Risk factors in the first 5 years of life, including disorders of attachment, operate in the context of the transactions between the child and her environment, including the family, neighborhood, community, and larger society (Cicchetti & Lynch, 1993).

The child's parents or surrogate attachment figures may live in circumstances that tax their resources and that may be beyond their control, such as poverty; low education; unemployment; violent neighborhoods; pollution and toxic environmental products that increase the incidence of chronic ailments such as asthma; inadequate access to healthy and affordable food, adequate housing, reliable transportation, and health services; and historical trauma. Racism and discrimination remain potent, malevolent forces that marginalize and endanger millions of children and families from racial, ethnic, and religious backgrounds who are disproportionately the victims of these adverse sociological factors. These conditions affect young children's development both directly and through the negative environmental conditions that are created.

Violence in the home is often multidetermined by a variety of risk factors that include the sociological circumstances described previously. Faced with these stressors, parents are often unable to support their children's development unless the intervention includes a concerted effort to improve parents' own circumstances and well-being (Fraiberg, 1980; Henggeler, Schoenwald, Borduin, Rowland, & Cunningham, 1998; Lieberman & Van Horn, 2008). Parents exposed to traumatic events often experience an unsettling derailment in their capacity for affect regulation, comfort with body sensations, trust in interacting and problem solving with others, and feelings of safety in exploration and learning. In these situations, clinicians need to direct specific attention to the impact of trauma on all aspects of parental functioning, including parents' competence in attending and responding to the concrete demands of everyday life that in turn affect the child's safety and the predictability of daily routines. CPP has the goal of improving the parent's psychological functioning and parenting competence by offering the therapeutic relationship as an agent of active assistance with problems of living as well as a vehicle for psychological exploration and emotional growth. This may involve active practice with problem solving to address issues such as homelessness, food insufficiency, unemployment, unsafe housing, access to educational opportunities for parent and child, and other material needs that are foundations of physical and psychological well-being. The therapeutic stance of CPP is compatible with the premises outlined in the Tenets of Infant Mental Health (St. John et al., 2012), which issue a call to incorporate an attitude of respectful interest, willingness to learn, and inclusiveness toward the diverse cultural and sociological configurations of families.

PREMISE 4: INTERPERSONAL VIOLENCE IS A TRAUMATIC STRESSOR THAT HAS SPECIFIC PATHOGENIC REPERCUSSIONS ON THOSE WHO WITNESS IT AND THOSE WHO EXPERIENCE IT (PYNOOS ET AL., 1999). Young children are disproportionately more exposed to maltreatment and domestic violence than older children, with children in the first 5 years of life overrepresented among victims of child abuse (Fantuzzo & Fusco, 2007; U.S. Department of Health and Human Services, 2010). Moreover, different sources of violence tend to coexist. For example, children who witness domestic violence are much more likely to also be physically abused (Ghosh Ippen, Harris, Van Horn, & Lieberman, 2011; Osofsky, 2004).

These experiences are unfortunately all too common in the lives of young children, but there is a persistent failure in mental health settings to assess for their occurrence. In a study demonstrating the underidentification of trauma exposure in early childhood, Crusto and colleagues (2010) screened children 3 to 6 years old who were referred to mental health community agencies. The majority of these children were referred due to social, emotional, and behavioral concerns (42.9%); only 13% were referred as the result of exposure to violence or abuse. Using the Traumatic Events Screening Inventory–Parent Report Revised (Ghosh Ippen et al., 2002), the authors discovered a previously unidentified high prevalence of trauma exposure: 42% of the children had seen people in the family assaulting each other, 18% had been assaulted or beaten, close to 6% had been forced to see or do something sexual, 27% had witnessed physical assault between non–family members, and nearly 15% had experienced the death of someone close to them. In addition, traumatic exposure did not, as a rule, occur as a single, discrete event. The children had been exposed to an average of 4.9 different types of traumatic and stressful events, with more than 48% of the children experiencing five or more of these types of events. Trauma exposure had concrete repercussions on child functioning. Clinically significant posttraumatic stress scores were shown by 23.4% of the children using the Trauma Symptom Checklist for Young Children (Briere, 2005), and another 16.2% were in the subclinical but problematic range. These children would not typically be identified as needing trauma-informed treatment if their initial assessment did not include screening for trauma exposure. This study demonstrates the deleterious consequences of the routine failure to screen for trauma exposure in mental health assessment and treatment planning.

Maltreated children can become overwhelmed by intense multisensory stimulation, including physical pain, terrifying visual images, loud screaming, crashing objects, the smell of gunpowder or blood, and frantic movement—what Pynoos et al. (1999) described as "the traumatic moment," characterized by a multiplicity of overpowering sensations coupled with helplessness in stopping them from happening. Domestic violence and maltreatment often consist of multiple episodes that occur unpredictably over an extended time span, so that the child is confronted with many compounded images and may be unable to create a coherent narrative of the frightening events. This is particularly the case if the young child is at different developmental stages when the different episodes of violence take place—ranging, for example, from the preverbal period to the toddler or preschool years.

Many of the traumatic stress responses shown by young children exposed to interpersonal violence are also manifested in response to accidents, injuries, painful illnesses, and intrusive medical procedures. Car accidents, dog bites, near-drownings, accidental ingestion of dangerous substances, falls, and other frightening experiences may result in traumatic sequelae that alter the child's perception of the world and trust in the parents' capacity to provide safety. How severe, pervasive, and prolonged the child's responses might be to these kinds of events may depend on a variety of factors, including the intensity and the discrete versus repetitive nature of the event, the sequence of secondary stressors set in motion by the trauma (e.g., being separated from the parent during the ambulance ride on the way to the hospital following a car accident), the child's constitutional makeup such as temperamental characteristics, the quality of the child's attachment prior to the traumatic event, and the parents' response to the trauma. A relational model of the factors that predict, mediate, and moderate the child's responses to trauma was developed by Scheeringa and Zeanah (2001) and is a valuable tool to guide clinical formulation.

Once an experience of trauma occurs, pre-established expectations of danger and safety may be dramatically altered. Everyday stimuli that were previously emotionally neutral can now become fraught with perceptions of threat if they are construed as resembling some aspect of the traumatic event. Interoceptive sensations and interpersonal cues may be misinterpreted as threats when they bear a subjective or objective resemblance to those experienced during the traumatic event. Traumatic reminders may affect the quality of the child–parent relationship by triggering traumatic stress responses that are misconstrued by the recipient when the behavior appears unconnected with its origins in the traumatic moment. CPP uses a dual attachment lens and a trauma lens to address these distortions in the perceptions that the child and the parent may have of each other following trauma. The dual lens enables the clinician to attend to the effect of trauma on the child–parent relationship and to enhance the relationship as a protective mechanism to help the child manage the fear and dysregulation associated with traumatic reminders.

PREMISE 5: THE THERAPEUTIC RELATIONSHIP IS A FUNDAMENTAL MUTATIVE FACTOR IN TREATMENT. As Sameroff and Emde (1989) pointed out, relationships affect relationships. The clinician's efforts to bring about positive change can succeed only if the clinician's interactions with the parent and the child are based on sensitivity, empathy, transparency, and respect for their experience. By reflecting together on the child's and the parent's real-life experiences, motivations, feelings, and needs, the clinician and the parent develop a collaborative agenda in which they work together toward jointly held intervention goals.

When the child has experienced one or more traumatic events, creating a working alliance on behalf of the child includes helping the parents understand how these events may be causally related to the child's presenting problems. A core component of CPP is the creation of a trauma frame, giving the parents compassionate, nonjudgemental explanations that (a) frightening events cause strong emotions of fear and anger at all ages; (b) young children and parents may express these emotions through behaviors such as aggression, dysregulation, or withdrawal; and (c) the clinician wants to help the parent create safe conditions and support the parent and the child in practicing ways of tolerating and transforming difficult emotions.

This "triangle" of explanations linking traumatic event, behavioral consequences, and treatment guides the clinician's approach to the therapeutic relationship. Different aspects of the collaborative agenda may be explicitly articulated or implicitly shared, depending on the parent's and child's receptiveness versus defensiveness and types of communication styles, but the working relationship must reflect an agreement between parent and clinician to work toward alleviating threats to safety; increasing areas of harmony, competence, and well-being; and decreasing areas of conflict and stress. The parent's cultural values—influenced by race, ethnicity, and socioeconomic circumstances—must be incorporated in the intervention as essential components in building a therapeutic alliance. Throughout this manual, references are made to the role of cultural factors in shaping specific intervention strategies.

Contrary to the commonly accepted belief that the clinician must wait until a therapeutic working relationship is formed before acknowledging and exploring consciously known traumatic experiences, CPP holds that the clinician actively fosters the formation of the therapeutic working relationship by describing the trauma as a causal factor in the child's and the parents' emotional and relational difficulties that can improve with treatment. Issues of timing and therapeutic tactfulness remain key principles in good psychotherapy of any kind, but the clinician's emphasis on acknowledging and normalizing the responses to trauma is a core part of the foundational phase of treatment because hope rooted in knowledge of the emotional landscape is the most important ingredient of all effective psychotherapy.

PREMISE 6: TREATMENT INCLUDES "SPEAKING THE UNSPEAKABLE" WHILE PROMOTING SAFETY AND HOPE. CPP includes the tactful but open exploration and acknowledgment of the adversities, stressors, and traumatic events that the child and the caregivers experienced and their possible links to the presenting problems. This supportive, nondidactic psychoeducation is consistent with trauma-informed intervention guidelines advocating that intervenors should change their approach to assessment and treatment from a stance of asking themselves, "What is wrong with this person?" to a stance of asking the client, "What happened to you?" At the same time, interventions actively incorporate the promotion of positive emotions through playfulness and enjoyable activities. Trauma narratives are always bracketed with protective narratives that affirm a therapeutic commitment to safety and repair.

The emphasis on speaking openly about traumatic events represents a r/evolution in therapeutic attitude but remains a work in progress. Clinicians are trained not to rush their clients into revealing aspects of their lives that may be experienced as shameful or emotionally unbearable. Here, we must pose the pivotal question raised by Roth and Fonagy (2014) in their influential book, *What Works for Whom?* There continues to be great value in offering adult clients a therapeutic holding environment where they can move at their own pace in exploring their inner lives. Unhurried free association can lead to unexpected and transformational links between previously fragmented experiences and affects that may be suppressed, repressed, or subjected to other psychological defenses as mechanisms to fend off the pain associated with them. Elucidating the presence and impact of experiences that are unavailable to conscious retrieval must be undertaken with the utmost clinical caution because psychological defenses have an important function in personality structure and in protecting the person's adaptation to the past and the present.

The clinical situation, however, is very different when the traumatic event is recent, current, and available to conscious recollection. This is particularly the case for young children, who need adult acknowledgment of their experience in order to develop an accurate perception of reality. Over the course of many years and in different venues, Bowlby spoke and wrote about the pressure that adults exert on children to hide or deny to themselves and others the adversities and traumas that happened to them. In his seminal work, "On knowing what you are not supposed to know and feeling what you are not supposed to feel," Bowlby (1988) wrote:

> [C]hildren not infrequently observe scenes that parents would prefer they did not observe; they form impressions that parents would prefer they did not form; and they have experiences that parents would like to believe they have not had. Evidence shows that many of these children, aware of how their parents feel, proceed then to conform to their parents' wishes by excluding from further processing such information as they already have, and that, having done so, they cease consciously to be aware that they have ever observed such scenes, formed such impressions, or had such experiences. Here, I believe, is a source of cognitive disturbance as common as it is neglected. (pp. 101–102)

Bowlby goes on to link this phenomenon to adult experiences of depersonalization, dissociation, amnesia, and unreality.

There is extensive evidence that correcting negative self-attributions and false assumptions about the world (i.e., *pathogenic beliefs*) is a therapeutic intervention shared by effective clinicians across different theoretical orientations (Weiss, 1993). Many of these pathogenic beliefs may involve traumatic expectations that originated in childhood experiences of unmanageable stress when the child was not helped to feel safe after enduring frightening circumstances. Clinicians in early childhood mental health have an invaluable opportunity to prevent the distortions of cognition and personality structure that stem from the pressure on the young child to not know and to not feel. At least some of the stresses and traumatic events endured by young children in the first 5 years of life are usually known to the caregivers and to the child. If we ask, they will tell us what happened and how they feel about it. Their story may be incomplete or inaccurate and may need clarification, expansion, and corrections as treatment proceeds, but, in our experience, parents and children most often feel relief that the clinician is interested and able to tolerate the pain, worry, confusion, guilt, and shame of their experience starting from the beginning of the therapeutic relationship.

Upholding the curative power of recognizing the emotional pain of trauma does not divert therapeutic attention from the equally powerful healing powers of physical pleasure, playfulness, supportive relationships, beauty, spirituality, and all human endeavors that promote well-being. The concept of "angels in the nursery" (Lieberman, Padron, Van Horn, & Harris, 2005) emerged from the realization that the intergenerational transmission of relational patterns includes not only unresolved childhood conflicts but also early experiences of feeling completely loved, cherished, and safe in the company of an adult who cared. As the physicist Niels Bohr is quoted as saying, "The opposite of a profound truth may well be another profound truth" (as cited in Rozental, 1967, p. 328). Remembering goodness is as important to healing as remembering hurt. Psychoanalysis recognizes that the integration of opposites holds the most mature solution to psychological conflict, just as in painting the discovery of the chiaroscuro as a technical interplay of light and shadow opened new dimensions in the evolution of art. Wolfenstein (1966) noted that young children have a short sadness span. This is as it should be. Children need to protect their emotional energy to grow, explore, discover, and derive pleasure and meaning from being alive. The same may be said of parents of young children, who need support in their forward-looking developmental stage. The therapist must meet parent and child in their sadness, anger, and fear but also help to make these feelings one part of their emotional experience, a darker tone in a symphony of emotional colors that includes also the brightness of joy and the sustaining light of hope. This attitude also has personal value for the clinician because placing trauma in the broader perspective of life's many possibilities can help protect against vicarious traumatization, burnout, and compassion fatigue.

The six conceptual premises guide the clinician's intervention at every stage of treatment.

Historical Roots and Evolution of Child–Parent Psychotherapy

CPP is a relationship-based treatment that focuses on the child–parent interaction and on each partner's perceptions of the other, with a particular focus on safety and trust versus danger and fear as the core intersubjective domain that is transacted between parent and child during the first years of life. The theoretical framework represents an integration of psychoanalytic, attachment, and developmental psychopathology perspectives. Goals include increasing the parent's and child's age-appropriate capacity to form a *goal-corrected partnership* (Bowlby, 1973), defined as the ability to be emotionally attuned and flexibly responsive to each other's motivations and needs; transforming mutually reinforcing negative interactional patterns that generate fear, mistrust, and alienation; and identifying and addressing traumatic triggers as causal factors in child and parent dysregulated affect and maladaptive responses.

The theoretical target of CPP is the web of jointly constructed meanings in the child–parent relationship, which emerge from each partner's mental representations of themselves and of each other (Lieberman, 2004). In this sense, the intervention targets the parent's and child's maladaptive mental representations and fosters the motivation to understand and respect their own and each other's internal worlds. When parent or child behaviors are addressed directly, the intervention is informed by the context in which the behavior occurs and by the meaning that the behavior may hold for the parent and for the child.

CPP originated in *infant–parent psychotherapy* (Fraiberg, 1980), a psychoanalytic treatment that uses the metaphor of "ghosts in the nursery" to prevent the intergenerational transmission of psychopathology from parent to child in the first 3 years of life. Infant–parent psychotherapy is described in exquisite detail in the book *Clinical Studies in Infant Mental Health: The First Year of Life* (Fraiberg, 1980), the first in a planned series of three books that was expected to also include a volume on the second year and a volume on the third year of life. Selma Fraiberg's premature death in 1981 at 63 years old prevented her from completing what would have surely become an extraordinary contribution to psychotherapy with toddlers and young preschoolers, but she left an enduring legacy of clinical wisdom that continues to inform later generations of infancy and early childhood mental health clinicians. Adaptations of Fraiberg's model to toddler–parent psychotherapy were conceptualized by Lieberman (1992) and empirically supported in randomized studies by Lieberman, Weston, and Pawl (1991) and by Cicchetti, Toth, and Rogosch (1999); Cicchetti, Rogosch, and Toth (2000); and Toth, Rogosch, Manly, and Cicchetti (2006).Further adaptations for the treatment of preschoolers and their parents were introduced by Toth, Maughan, Manly, Spagnola, and Cicchetti (2002); Lieberman, Van Horn, and Ghosh Ippen (2005); and Lieberman and Van Horn (2005, 2008).

The need for a single nomenclature to describe the treatment of infants, toddlers, and preschoolers rooted in Fraiberg's "ghosts in the nursery" (1980) model became apparent from the substantial conceptual overlaps in child–parent interventions across the first 5 years of life. It also became apparent that advances in knowledge brought about by attachment theory, developmental psychopathology, and other fields needed to be incorporated in the conceptualization and practice of this approach during infancy and early childhood. In addition, the specific developmental characteristics of toddlers and preschoolers called for significant therapeutic adaptations to the classic infant–parent psychotherapy model of addressing the child's mental health symptoms and pathogenic mother–child interactions primarily through the lens of the mother's unresolved childhood conflicts. Even more than babies, toddlers and preschoolers bring their own urgent expressions of individuality to the therapeutic setting. The meaning of these individual behaviors cannot always be understood through the lens of negative parental attributions, although such attributions are often expressed in responses to the child that exacerbate and perpetuate the child's maladaptive behaviors. For example, a 2-year-old with a very high activity level and intense emotional style may respond to witnessing his father battering his mother by becoming aggressive and may be perceived by his father as a "real boy" and by his mother as "an abuser just like his father." Neither the mother nor the father would, in this case, understand the child's aggression as a last-ditch effort to cope with his fear of the father's anger by identifying with him in a classic example of "identification with the aggressor" (A. Freud, 1936/1966).

Children of all ages, including unborn children and newborns, can become a transference object to their parents, but their individual characteristics and their unique adaptations to their parents' attributions need to be integral components of a comprehensive therapeutic approach. In the previous example of the aggressive toddler, interpreting each of the parent's attributions is not likely, by itself, to result in decreases in the child's aggression: It is also essential to help parents and child learn and implement age-appropriate interventions to identify anger and practice nonaggressive ways of expressing it. As they grappled with specific clinical dilemmas in the treatment of infants, toddlers, and preschoolers, Lieberman and Toth discussed the developmental issues involved in the treatment of young children and their parents and agreed to adopt the term *Child–Parent Psychotherapy* (CPP) to describe the therapeutic interventions that originated in Fraiberg's infant–parent psychotherapy and that were extended to include children in the first 5 years of life (Alicia Lieberman & Sheree Toth, personal communication, February 2004). *Child–Parent Psychotherapy* (CPP) is now the standard term used to describe the relational treatment of infants, toddlers, and preschoolers and their parents using an integrated psychoanalytic, attachment, and developmental psychopathology perspective (e.g., Cicchetti, Rogosch, Toth, & Sturge-Apple, 2011; Lieberman, 2004; Lieberman, Ghosh Ippen, & Van Horn, 2006; Lieberman et al., 2005; Lieberman & Van Horn, 2005, 2008; Osofsky, 2005; Osofsky & Lederman, 2004; Toth, Gravener-Davis, Guild, & Cicchetti, 2013; Toth, Manly, & Nilsen, 2008).

Although CPP is based on a theoretical integration of psychoanalysis, attachment theory, and developmental psychopathology, it also includes body-centered and behavior-based techniques derived from developmental theory, trauma theory and clinical practice, cognitive–behavioral approaches, and social learning theory, particularly as it relates to affect regulation, psychogenic beliefs, and the links between coercive parenting and aggressive and defiant child behavior (Cohen, Mannarino, & Deblinger, 2006; Patterson, 1982; Reid & Eddy, 1997; van der Kolk, 2014; Webster-Stratton, 1996).

The intervention supports and reinforces perceptions, attitudes, and behaviors that promote safety and foster positive affect, reciprocal play, joint exploration of the world, age-appropriate socialization, and constructive conflict resolution. It targets for change punitive parenting practices and unmodulated and dysregulated parental and child behaviors, with a specific focus on manifestations of traumatic stress that may include externalizing problems—such as aggression, defiance, noncompliance, recklessness, and excessive tantrums—and internalizing problems— such as multiple fears, inconsolability, separation anxiety, difficulties sleeping, and social and emotional withdrawal.

Although the intervention focuses on family processes and most specifically on the child–parent relationship, every effort is made to tailor these strategies to the family's cultural values and socioeconomic and educational circumstances. For this reason, the model incorporates active assistance with the family's problems of living as a basic ingredient in establishing a collaborative stance with the family. Parents who are immersed in family turmoil, which may include cultural dislocation and socioeconomic hardship, often find it difficult to remain emotionally attuned to their children's needs. In fact, they may perceive their children's bids for attention as one more source of strain on their depleted personal resources. In these circumstances, concrete assistance with problems of living is often an essential step in enlisting the parent's willingness to participate in the intervention because it conveys the clinician's ability and willingness to incorporate the parent's perspective into the work.

CPP can be used in any situation where the relationship between a young child and the parent is negatively affected by the family's difficult circumstances, including parental depression or other mental illness, bereavement, or chronic stress; child constitutional or developmental characteristics that interfere with the formation of a secure attachment; and "poorness of fit" (Chess & Thomas, 1984) in the temperamental styles of parent and child. Each set of factors calls for individually tailored interventions. The fundamental difference between CPP and psychodynamically informed infant/early childhood mental health treatments is CPP's focus on identifying and addressing traumatic events and their psychological sequelae. Because of the dearth of trauma-informed treatments in the field of early childhood mental health, this manual highlights the specific therapeutic strategies employed when the child–parent relationship and the child's mental health and developmental momentum are damaged by the experience of violence.

Developmental Considerations in Children and Parents

All psychotherapies should consider development as a process that encompasses the entire life span and involves momentum toward healthy growth as well as unmet milestones, distortions, delays, and pathological patterns. CPP incorporates the conceptual principles of *developmental psychopathology*, a multidisciplinary field that uses a life-span perspective to understand the many processes at work in the origins, development, and consolidation of psychopathology. Developmental psychopathology integrates a variety of disciplines, including developmental, clinical, social, and experimental psychology; psychiatry; psychoanalysis; sociology; cultural anthropology; embryology; genetics; neuroscience; and epidemiology in an effort to create a unified conceptual framework for the study of individual differences, the continuity or discontinuity of adaptive and maladaptive patterns of functioning, and the emergence and life course of psychopathology. Knowledge generated by developmental psychopathology theory and research has clinical applications of great value. For example, this field has contributed to a better understanding of causality in psychopathology by replacing the search for single, individual risk factors with an understanding of the interplay between risk and protective factors and the importance of context in the understanding of normative and atypical behavior. It has also contributed the concept of developmental pathways that are associated with specified outcomes, including the phenomenon of *equifinality* (the same condition may be the result of different antecedents for different people) and the phenomenon of *multifinality* (the same risk factors may be associated with different outcomes in different people). Another contribution of great clinical value is a focus on the single and cumulative impact of risk factors. Therapists informed by a developmental psychopathology perspective are well prepared to make clinical formulations and use therapeutic strategies that take into account the different risk and protective factors that may be at work in influencing the child and family functioning at the biological, psychological, sociological, and anthropological levels of analysis.

When the child is exposed to trauma, the critical link between the stress experienced as the result of a traumatic situation and the child's personality development is the formation of trauma-related expectations that shape the biology of the developing child and that are expressed through perceptions, feelings, thoughts, and behavior (Pynoos, Steinberg, & Goenjian, 1996). These traumatic expectations alter the child's developmental trajectory and can last a lifetime. The level of disturbance is determined by a complex interaction between the child's constitutional characteristics and previous experience; the objective and subjective features of the traumatic experience(s); subsequent reminders of the experience; comorbid conditions; secondary stresses; and environmental supports before, during, and after the traumatic experience (Pynoos, Steinberg, & Wraith, 1995). When the trauma consists of family violence, an extra layer of complexity is added as the child's traumatic expectations interact with the expectations of the parents who inflicted and/or were themselves traumatized by the violence.

Violence is particularly traumatizing when it is long-lasting and when it occurs in the context of intimate relationships, where safety and protection are preconditions for a sense of personal integrity. Even if its impact is not manifested in a diagnosable psychiatric condition, violence among family members routinely results in alterations of self-perception, affect regulation, relationships with others, and systems of meaning (Herman, 1992; Horowitz & O'Brien, 1986; Pynoos et al., 1999; van der Kolk, 1996, 2014). Each of these disturbances has damaging repercussions on the adult's capacity to parent and on the quality of the parent–child relationship that they are able to establish. Regardless of age, the experience of trauma bypasses the individual's capacity to use advanced intellectual faculties such as purposeful planning and logical reasoning to process the traumatic event as it occurs. The biologically driven mechanisms to cope with overwhelming stress in the moment—flight, fight, freeze—comprise the wisdom of the body in enhancing the chances of survival (Cannon, 1932) but become maladaptive when they remain fixed as chronic patterns of response (Sapolsky, 1994). Among young children, predominant manifestations of these responses involve fleeing toward the attachment figure; fighting sources of danger to the attachment figure (e.g., physically coming between the parents during a marital fight and hitting the perceived attacker while saying, "Stop!"); and staying very still, averting gaze, or remaining with the eyes glued on the source of danger. When the danger is past, the intense sensations experienced at every level of the organism (visual, auditory, olfactory, tactile) leave an enduring mark that was aptly described by Bessel van der Kolk (2014) as "the body keeps the score," and reminders of the trauma may set in motion a version of the original trauma response that has physiological, emotional, and behavioral manifestations (Pynoos et al., 1999; Sapolsky, 1994).

In infants, toddlers, and preschool children, the experience of violence frequently leads to a disruption of normative developmental processes. As van der Kolk (1987) noted, "the earliest and possibly most damaging psychological trauma is the loss of a secure base" (p. 32). The empirical literature supports this insight, with findings that young children exposed to violence have high levels of internalizing and externalizing problems that include affect dysregulation, difficulty establishing relationships, play re-enactment of the traumatic experience, sleep disturbances, bouts of intense fear and uncontrolled crying, regression in developmental achievements, aggression, and noncompliance (Davidson, 1978; Eth & Pynoos, 1985; Gaensbauer, 1994; Parson, 1995; Pruett, 1979; Pynoos & Nader, 1988; Terr, 1981).

Young children are in a period of rapid developmental change, and their responses to trauma exposure are influenced by their developmental stage (Marans & Adelman 1997; Osofsky, 1995; Pynoos & Eth, 1985). During the first year of life, infants respond to perceived danger with sensorimotor disorganization and disruption of biological rhythms in the forms—for example—of intense and prolonged crying; unresponsiveness to soothing; movement problems such as flailing, muscular rigidity, restlessness, and agitation; eating disorders such as lack of appetite or excessive eating; sleeping disorders such as difficulty falling asleep, frequent night wakings, and night terrors; and elimination problems such as constipation and diarrhea without apparent organic causes. Numbing of affect may be manifested in the form of sadness, a subdued demeanor, and unresponsiveness to age-appropriate stimulation (Drell, Siegel, & Gaensbauer, 1993). At the deepest levels, trauma is experienced and manifested through the body.

Toddlers and preschoolers—who can use autonomous mobility—engage in fight-or-flight mechanisms in response to the perception of danger. These mechanisms may involve recklessness and accident proneness, inhibition of exploration, and precocious competence in self-care—patterns that can be seen as distortions of the normative pattern of secure base behavior that is characteristic of the second and third years of life (Lieberman & Zeanah, 1995).

Toddlers and preschoolers also make increasing use of language and symbolic play to engage in active efforts to understand causality and give meaning to their experiences. They often misattribute the reason for frightening events, blaming themselves when parents are angry or when fights erupt between the adults. The internal conflicts resulting from self-blame and from feeling torn between fear of the parents and longing to be close to them are often manifested in externalizing problems—such as aggression, defiance, and noncompliance—and in internalizing problems—such as excessive fearfulness and withdrawal. Toddlers and preschoolers may also engage in precociously competent and self-protective behaviors when they cannot rely on their parents to feel safe (Lieberman & Zeanah, 1995).

Posttraumatic stress in early childhood. A diagnosis of posttraumatic stress disorder (PTSD) may be called for when the child experiences, witnesses, or learns about an event that involves actual or threatened death or serious injury to the child or others, or a threat to the physical or psychological integrity of the child or others (ZERO TO THREE, 2005). The following manifestations are considered criteria for the disorder:

1. Re-experiencing of the traumatic event through posttraumatic play, recurrent recollections of the event outside of play, repeated nightmares, distress at exposure to reminders of the trauma, and/or episodes with objective features of a flashback or dissociation.
2. Avoidance of reminders of the trauma through efforts to avoid people, places, or activities that serve as reminders of the trauma.
3. Numbing of responsiveness or interference with developmental momentum, as expressed through increased social withdrawal, restricted range of affect, temporary loss of previously acquired developmental skills, and/or decrease or constriction of play.
4. Increased arousal, as manifested through night terrors, difficulty going to sleep, repeated night wakings, attentional difficulties, hypervigilance, and exaggerated startle responses.

Children who have been exposed to traumatic events may demonstrate very serious disturbances of functioning even when they do not meet criteria for a diagnosis of PTSD. Carrion, Weems, Ray, and Reiss (2002) reported that maltreated children had similarly poor scores in performance regardless of whether they met full criteria for a PTSD diagnosis. In addition, children exposed to traumatic events may respond with symptoms of other clinical disorders, such as depression, in keeping with the developmental psychopathology principle of multifinality. They may also develop new symptoms that were not present before the traumatic event, such as aggression toward peers, adults, or animals; separation anxiety; fear of toileting alone; fear of the dark or other new fears; somatic symptoms; motor re-enactments; and/or precociously sexualized behavior.

These behavioral problems do not exist in an individual vacuum. They not only reflect the impact of trauma on the child but may also be the outcome of stresses in the parent–child relationship and the emotional climate of the family and the larger environment, including risks and supports in the neighborhood. Traumatized children often have traumatized parents, and the impact of trauma on parents needs to be the focus of sustained clinical attention and care.

Parenting as a developmental stage. Development is an ongoing process that continues throughout one's lifetime. Becoming a parent ushers in an adult developmental stage that offers new opportunities for reworking long-standing maladaptive patterns and finding more satisfying ways of relating to oneself and others (Benedek, 1959). At the same time, the daily demands of being a parent can constitute a relentless challenge to the adult's identity by testing his or her nurturing capacity and sense of personal competence.

Family violence and domestic violence represent formidable risk factors to the healthy development of the capacity to parent. Under the best of circumstances, being a parent is an emotionally demanding task. The ordinary stresses of life, compounded by lack of knowledge about an infant's or toddler's capacity for compliance and self-control, can lead parents to react harshly when children behave in ways that are annoying or burdensome.

Parents who are prone to violence and/or the victims of violence are even more ill-equipped to respond to challenging or unmodulated child behaviors because they themselves have difficulty regulating strong emotion and because they are often anxious, depressed, or suffering from PTSD. The parents may tend to misperceive their child's behavior as indications that the child is intrinsically "bad," disrespectful, or unloving (Lieberman, 1999); they may see their children's age-appropriate behavior as harmful or dangerous based on their own trauma-based expectations that the world and the people in it are dangerous (Pynoos et al., 1996).

Even parents who are usually able to remain emotionally attuned to their children in spite of their personal difficulties may find themselves at a loss in knowing how to respond when their children engage in challenging behaviors. They may react with helpless efforts to placate the child or with impulsive punishment. These responses confirm the child's sense, derived from witnessing domestic violence, that the parent cannot provide a sense of safety and protection. As a result, the parent's responses may unwittingly exacerbate the child's sense of helplessness, anger, and fear. CPP is designed to help both parent and child understand and modulate their responses to traumatic reminders, to help them find ways to calm and soothe themselves when faced with upsetting feelings, to restore their trust in one another, and to address these misattunements between the parent and the child.

Cultural Considerations

Intimate relationships are regulated by cultural mores, which dictate if, how, and when feelings can be displayed. This is the case for intimate relationships between adults as well as between adults and children. All intimate relationships exist in a cultural context that influences their expression. All cultures have developed mechanisms to contain and modulate the expression of emotions that, left unchecked, can become destructive to the social fabric.

Anger is such an emotion. Different cultures have different tolerance levels for the expression of anger, the channels used to express it, and the people toward whom it may be expressed. An action that is considered violent in one society may well be seen as a normative expression of displeasure in another. This does not mean that a specific culture can be equated with a specific, monolithic attitude toward the expression of anger or any other emotion. Cultures are nuanced and multifaceted, with a wide range of individual differences within a culture. One would be stereotyping a culture if he made sweeping generalizations that did not allow for intracultural differences, which may be due to a diversity of factors, including ethnicity, socioeconomic status, educational background, acculturation, generational differences, age, temperamental style, and family history.

Clinicians must strive to learn about the cultural traditions of the families with whom they work and to understand how specific child-rearing practices give expression to the prevailing values of a cultural group. At the same time, this basic stance might have to be modified under certain conditions. For example, there might be child-rearing practices that are common in a particular cultural context but may not be legally or morally acceptable in the United States. Such practices need to be addressed in the course of the intervention. The fact that such practices are culturally normative in a different country does not exempt these practices from thoughtful discussion about their function and their effects on the child as seen from the perspective of prevailing values in the United States.

Cultures and the individuals who represent them evolve over time in response to changing circumstances, and they can become more or less tolerant or intolerant of diversity as the result of historical processes and social and economic change. The changing social status of women, children, and minorities are cases in point. These groups have been historically the targets of violence and abuse, but their position within different cultures has changed, both for better and for worse, as the cultures have changed over time in response to historical, sociological, political, and economic circumstances.

A decrease in aggression from those in power toward the less powerful is a moral and therapeutic goal that transcends narrowly defined cultural considerations. Cultural sensitivity should not become a reason for a cultural relativism that condones the infliction of pain by the strong on the weak. In the United States, there is a social consensus that domestic violence and harsh physical punishment of children are harmful and often against the law. The frequent personal and institutional failures to hold perpetrators accountable should not detract from appreciating the enormous advance in public attitudes represented by laws against child abuse and domestic violence. From this perspective, neither practice can be overlooked by the clinician or dismissed as an expression of cultural tradition.

When the clinician believes that a parent's child-rearing practice is harmful, the intervention can be couched in an acknowledgment that different cultures have different child-rearing practices. This can be followed with a conversation in which the clinician explains why the practice in question is not acceptable in this country and elicits the parent's viewpoint so that the topic can be thoughtfully considered in all its complexity. In elucidating the cultural roots of a specific child-rearing practice or value, clinicians must remember that there is much intracultural variation in child-rearing, not least as the result of socioeconomic factors, and that intracultural differences may exceed cross-cultural differences in this area (van IJzendoorn & Kroonenberg, 1988). When necessary, a referral to child protective services should be made to protect the child.

Goals and Mechanisms of Treatment in Recovery From Traumatic Experiences

A prerequisite for the treatment of traumatic responses, both for children and adults, is the establishment of a safe environment, both in real life and in the therapeutic setting. This goal can be particularly challenging when the trauma consists of overwhelming exposure to violence that can recur unpredictably in the family or in the neighborhood. Battered women may be unable to appraise signals of danger realistically because of their own traumatization, leaving them and their children vulnerable to repetition of traumatic experiences. The therapist needs to focus on developing and mobilizing the parent's capacity for self-protection and protection of the child as a cornerstone of the treatment.

Recognition of the traumatic impact of violence is also a prerequisite to the recovery process. Parents tend to underestimate both the extent to which their children were witnesses to the violence and the damaging impact of the violence on the child (Peled, 2000). CPP enables the child and the parent to overcome the taboo against speaking about the violence. The clinician acts as a safe mediator between the parent and the child, both of whom are often unable or reluctant to name the violence for fear that acknowledging it will trigger overwhelming feelings of guilt, shame, blame, and loss.

Different approaches to the treatment of trauma, for children as well as adults, share many commonalities in their goals and the mechanisms proposed to achieve them (Marmar, Foy, Kagan, & Pynoos, 1993). The common features target the main symptoms of traumatic response and are described here.

1. *Return to normal development, adaptive coping, and engagement with present activities and future goals.* Healthy normative development is the overarching goal of treatment, both for children and for adults. A central component of the intervention is a focus on the continuity of daily living. The child–parent psychotherapist provides support for developmentally appropriate achievements and for daring to try new and adaptive ways of functioning as a mechanism to achieve this goal.

2. *Increased capacity to respond realistically to threat.* Safety is based on the ability to evaluate whether a situation may involve danger. Traumatized children and adults are often impaired in their ability to appraise and respond to cues of danger. They may either minimize or exaggerate danger, and sometimes they do both, overreacting to minor stimuli and overlooking serious threats. In children, this tendency is manifested in an alternation of recklessness and accident proneness. On the one hand, they may react aggressively to perceived slights, such as a toy being taken away. On the other hand, they might rush into dangerous situations, such as darting across the street or approaching a stranger. Therapeutic strategies focus on fostering more accurate perceptions of danger and appropriate responses to it.

3. *Maintaining regular levels of affective arousal.* Traumatic events impair the ability to regulate emotion. This impairment creates a "biopsychosocial trap" because neurophysiological disruptions in the regulation of

arousal affect other self-regulatory healing mechanisms. For example, numbing, avoidance, and hyperarousal may interfere with the spontaneous extinction of learned conditioning and with the ability to rely on the help of others as a way of restoring a sense of safety (Shalev, 2000). Children appear to be especially prone to sleep disturbances after trauma, including somnambulism, vocalization, motor restlessness, and night terrors (Pynoos, 1990). Sleeplessness can make children more prone to overreact and respond to mild aversive events with anger and aggression. These changes in physiological reactivity are a behavioral analogue of traumatic expectations (Pynoos et al., 1996). Therapeutic strategies include identifying and implementing ways of anticipating and preventing damaging levels of arousal and implementing actions that help with affect regulation in response to hyperarousal.

4. _Reestablishing trust in bodily sensations._ The body is the primary stage where affects are experienced and where the memory of the trauma lives on. As a result, the body itself, by "keeping the score" (van der Kolk, 1996), may become something to be feared and avoided, defensively shutting down sensations and closing off the possibility of intimacy and pleasure with another. For young children, for whom touching and being touched are essential building blocks for a healthy relationship to themselves and others, the recovery of trust in one's body and the body of the caregiver is an essential component of developmental progress.

The intervention must give the message that one can safely touch and be touched, and that the pleasure of safe touching is something to be cherished. This message can be given by encouraging expressions of affection between the parent and the child, by accepting naturally but without excessive enthusiasm the expressions of physical affection of the child to the therapist, and by not recoiling from casual physical contact in the context of play or other activities.

5. _Restoration of reciprocity in intimate relationships._ If the loss of a secure base is the earliest and most damaging consequence of psychological trauma, its reconstruction is essential to recovery. Secure attachments are built on the caregiver's ability to respond contingently to the young child's signals (Ainsworth et al., 1978). Conversely, violence-related traumatization involves the most extreme disruption of mutuality through

the creation of helplessness in one partner by the domination of the other (Benjamin, 1988). Battered women are often impaired in their ability to foster an emotionally reciprocal relationship with their children because of emotional numbing and hyperarousal, which may lead them to ignore or overreact to their children's behavior. Children exposed to violence, for their part, may engage in internalizing and externalizing behavioral problems that are likely to exacerbate the mother's maladaptive responses. The intervention must involve a search for solutions to failures of reciprocity that are both developmentally appropriate and within the scope of the psychological resources of the parent and the child.

The child–parent therapist must also attend to failures of reciprocity that flow from the complicated and sometimes very different feelings that the battered mother and her child experience toward the father. Both of them may alternately fear and love him, and, if he is gone, yearn for his return. But they may not experience these feelings at the same time or with the same intensity. Failures of reciprocity can occur when the child is longing for the father's return at a time when the mother is focused on her fear of him and her need to protect herself and her child from him. The intervention must involve the search for resolutions to these lapses of reciprocity, helping the parent and child understand one another's perspectives.

6. *Normalization of the traumatic response.* Traumatized adults often worry that they are "crazy"; children harbor fantasies that they are "bad" and "unlovable" when their behaviors evoke negative responses from others. Both may feel guilty because they could not stop the traumatic event from occurring or because they harbor sometimes very graphic and violent wishes for revenge. For adults as well as for children, treatment focuses on establishing a frame of meaning and validating the legitimacy and universality of the traumatic responses. Revenge fantasies can become manageable when they are reframed as an understandable desire to restore a feeling of fairness by undoing the painful consequences of an aggressive act.

7. *Increasing differentiation between reliving and remembering.* Being flooded by intrusive recollections is one of the frequent sequelae of trauma. In children, it is manifested in repeated re-enactment of the

traumatic scenes either through action or through play. Treatment involves helping the adult or the child realize the connection between what they are doing and feeling in the moment and the traumatic experience, stressing the difference between the past and present circumstances, and increasing the person's awareness of the current, safer surroundings.

8. *Placing the traumatic experience in perspective.* Treatment focuses on helping the adult or the child to gain control over the uncontrolled emotions evoked by the memory of the trauma. Children and adults are encouraged to achieve a balance where the memory of the trauma is not eradicated, but there is a marked decrease in being preoccupied by it. Instead, the person is encouraged to take pleasure in rewarding life events and personal characteristics and to make space to appreciate the positive and enriching aspects of life.

Intervention Modalities

A particular challenge for CPP is that the intervention goals and mechanisms of change described previously need to be cultivated simultaneously for at least two partners (parent and child) who are at different developmental stages and who process trauma differently. Sometimes paradoxically, CPP relies on the traumatized (and sometimes abusive) parent to be an active partner in the process of promoting the psychological healing of the child. When both parents as well as siblings are present, the challenge is even greater because the needs of several participants must be taken into account. Nevertheless, the difficulties of this approach are more than compensated by its therapeutic potential because healing the child–parent relationship holds the promise of individual healing both for the parent and for the child (Lieberman et al., 2006). A growth-promoting child–parent relationship can then support the ongoing healthy development of the child long after the intervention itself has ended.

As described in the previous section, the goals and mechanisms of treatment for trauma are characterized by the belief that the negative effects of trauma in infancy and early childhood can be relieved when the child is able to integrate body-based sensations, feeling, and thinking into reassuring expectations, described as follows:

- Stressful bodily experiences can be alleviated through the help of others and through active coping strategies on the child's part;
- Adults can support and protect the child from danger and fear;
- The child did not make the bad event(s) occur and is not to blame for them;
- Strong negative feelings can be processed and transformed instead of enacted through harmful behavior; and
- Life contains elements of pleasure, mastery, and hope.

CPP makes use of six major intervention modalities to accomplish these goals. Within each modality, there is emphasis on legitimizing the affective experience and promoting a sense of competence in both the parent and the child. The six intervention strategies are described here.

Promoting developmental progress through play, physical contact, and language. Healthy development in the early years is based on the child's ability to engage in trusting relationships, explore and learn, contain overwhelming affect, clarify feeling, and correct misperceptions. Sensitive responsiveness to the child's signals, safe and supportive physical contact, age-appropriate play, and the use of language to explain reality and put feelings into words are basic competence-building strategies to promote these capacities. These strategies are even more crucial for infants, toddlers, and preschool children whose behavior is dysregulated and whose perception of relationships is damaged as the result of exposure to violence. Play and language are used as vehicles to explore themes of danger and safety and to build a vocabulary for feelings that can replace the child's use of destructive action to express anger, fear, and anxiety. The books *Your Child at Play* (Segal, 1998a, 1998b) are valuable resources for clinicians who want to learn how to encourage age-appropriate play activities geared to children from birth to 5 years old.

Offering unstructured reflective developmental guidance. This intervention modality is used to provide the parent with information about age-appropriate children's behavior, needs, and feelings as these emerge spontaneously in the course of the sessions. The therapist links the child's behaviors, needs, and feelings to the circumstances of the family's life and how these circumstances, including the experience of family violence, may influence the child's experience. The developmental guidance is "unstructured" because it does not follow a prescribed curriculum, and it is "reflective" because it promotes "reflective functioning"

(Fonagy, Gergely, Jurist, & Target, 2002) by encouraging the parents to attend to their own internal experiences as well as to how their children are likely to understand and respond to a particular situation.

An unstructured and reflective approach to providing developmental information is individually tailored to the particular impasses, struggles, or conflicts that emerge in the child, the parent, or their relationship in the course of the intervention. It also addresses areas of pleasure, competence, and mastery. Whenever possible, the parent's own life experiences are used to frame the developmental guidance and increase the parent's understanding of what the child might be going through. Information and reflection about developmental processes, reframing, empathy, and appropriate limit-setting are emphasized in this modality.

Providing developmental guidance involves not only giving information but also helping the parent appreciate young children's construction of the world (Fraiberg, 1959; Lieberman, 1993). Twelve common developmental themes are listed here:

1. Crying and proximity-seeking are the young child's most basic communication tools, and children develop a healthy sense of competence and self-esteem when the parent responds by offering comfort.
2. Young children have a strong desire to please their parents, although parents are often unaware of it.
3. Separation anxiety is an expression of love and fear of loss rather than a manipulative ploy.
4. Young children fear losing their parent's love and approval.
5. Young children imitate their parents because they want to be like them.
6. Children blame themselves when their parent is angry or upset or when something goes wrong. This tendency is an emotional by-product of the cognitive egocentrism of young children, which leads them to overestimate their role in the relation between cause and effect (Piaget, 1959).
7. Young children believe that the parents are always right, know everything, and can do anything they wish. This belief in the parents' omnipotence goes hand in hand, often paradoxically, with children's belief in their own power and their determination to assert it.
8. Children feel loved and protected when parents are confident about their child-rearing practices and enforce their rules about what is safe and what is dangerous, right and wrong, allowed, and forbidden.

9. Toddlers and preschoolers use the word "no" as a way of establishing a sense of autonomy, not out of disrespect for the parents.
10. Babies and young children remember. They have well-developed memories from an early age, and their capacity to remember precedes their capacity to speak about their memories. Memory is particularly vivid for events that evoke strong emotions, such as joy, anger, or fear. The memories may not be completely accurate because they are influenced by the child's affective state and cognitive level, including their understanding of cause–effect relations. Children are keen observers of what happens around them and may remember it for a long time afterward.
11. Babies, toddlers, and preschool children feel intensely but do not yet know how to regulate their emotions. Intense crying, tantrums, and aggression are not expressions of the child's intrinsic nature but manifestations of distress that the child is too immature to express in socially acceptable ways.
12. Conflicts between parents and children are inevitable due to their different goals, personalities, and developmental agendas. Conflicts can serve a valuable developmental function when they are used to highlight the separate but equal legitimacy of the partners' goals and wishes and to mobilize collaboration for the purpose of resolution.

These common developmental themes come as a surprise to many parents, but most particularly to parents whose upbringing has been characterized by stress, pain, and unpredictability. In learning how their children interpret the world, parents often find new meaning in their childhood memories, and, in this process, they can acquire a richer and more compassionate understanding of themselves.

Modeling appropriate protective behavior. This modality involves taking action to stop dangerously escalating behavior, such as retrieving a child who is engaged in self-endangering behavior or stopping a child from hurting others. Modeling by the clinician is always followed by an explanation about the reasons for the action and an invitation to the parent (and the child, if it is appropriate) to reflect on what happened and to understand the danger potential and the importance of protective action. Emphasis is placed on how much the parent and the child care for each other, and how important it is to be safe from danger. The clinician also models appropriate protective behavior geared to the parent's safety by outlining sources of concern and suggesting alternatives when the adult engages in risky activities.

Interpreting feelings and actions. At its best, interpretation allows the parent and child to experience an increased sense of inner and interpersonal coherence by giving meaning to disorganized feelings and inexplicable responses and behaviors. In this sense, interpretation involves speaking about the unconscious, unspoken, or symbolic meaning of the parent's or the child's behavior in a way that increases self-understanding in the parent or the child.

Interpreting children's behavior: The four primordial anxieties.

Young children experience the sequential unfolding of four universal anxieties in the first 5 years of life: (a) fear of loss/abandonment, (b) fear of losing the parent's love, (c) fear of body damage, and (d) fear of not living up to the expectations of the self and others (called *superego condemnation* by S. Freud, 1926/1959). Each of these anxieties signals a new achievement in the child's capacity to understand danger. The transition from fear of abandonment and loss (manifested in separation anxiety and becoming particularly salient between 8 and 18 months old) to fear of losing parental love and approval marks a transition from reliance on the parent's physical presence to feel safe to a keen awareness of the parent's emotional availability during the toddler years. The second and third years of life also witness the emergence of fear of body damage, which serves as a survival-promoting counterbalance to the toddler's recently acquired mobility. The fear of not living up to expectations of the self and others (fear of "being bad"), which is predominant in the preschool years, demonstrates the child's increasing internalization of social standards and the emergence of a moral conscience.

Each of these normative anxieties is accentuated or relieved by the child's sense of self in relation to the parents. Parental responses to the child's curiosity about the genitals, for example, may be punitive or supportive, and the child in turn may interpret these responses of approval or disapproval as indications of being good or bad, loved or unloved, accepted or rejected.

Trauma exacerbates all of these normative anxieties for the young child. Children see themselves as the cause of the important events in their surroundings (Piaget, 1959), and, starting in the second year, they tend to blame themselves when something goes wrong that affects them or their family. Many seemingly irrational behaviors in early childhood become understandable when one interprets them in the context of family circumstances as manifestations of the child's fear of being sent away, not being loved, getting hurt, or being bad. Traumatic expectations, at their root, involve fear that one of these cataclysmic events will come about. Speaking them aloud and reassuring the child that these fears are unfounded can have a rapid positive effect in unburdening the child from these heavy apprehensions. For example, a 4-year-old said to his teacher, "I was bad, and now I can't live with my mom anymore." The teacher responded, "You are a little boy, and you are not bad. You are not living with your mom because she did not learn to take care of little children like you." The child looked visibly surprised. From then on, whenever the child misbehaved in class, the teacher told him, "You are a little boy, and you are not bad. I need to teach you how to do things like a 4-year-old." The child's behavior improved significantly in a period of 2 weeks.

Using interpretation with parents.

A frequent form of interpretation in CPP is making explicit the links between the parents' perception of their life experiences, their feelings for their children, and their parenting practices. For example, parents who were routinely physically punished, criticized, and neglected may unconsciously repeat these patterns in relation to their children (Fraiberg, 1980; Lieberman & Pawl, 1993). In cases of domestic violence or maltreatment, the battered parent may see an unsettling resemblance between the child and the abusive partner or an abusive caregiver from the past, or the parent may view the child's motives or behavior through the lens of trauma and anticipate aggression and victimization. In these cases, the parent might make negative attributions that are internalized by the child and that deeply influence the child's sense of self (Lieberman, 1999; Silverman & Lieberman, 1999).

Using timely interpretations can help parents become aware of the unconscious repetition of their past in the present, correct their distorted perceptions of the child, and free them to learn developmentally appropriate child-rearing practices. Interpretation can also help the child become more aware of maladaptive unconscious beliefs and defense mechanisms.

Interpreting unconscious processes calls for the utmost tact and a well-honed sense of timing. The therapist needs to be quite sure that the parent's character structure is sufficiently solid to tolerate the new and sometimes unsettling hypotheses presented by an interpretation. This is particularly the case when the therapist feels the need to interpret the parent's behavior in the presence of the child. In the case of preverbal, presymbolic infants and toddlers, interpreting the parent's behavior can usually take place in the child's presence because the child, not having mastered receptive language, is less likely to be burdened by an understanding of the parent's painful experiences. Older toddlers and preschoolers present a challenge to the use of interpretation geared to adults because they claim greater participation in the therapeutic interaction and because they have greater understanding of what the parent and the clinician are saying (Lieberman, 1991).

Speaking in front of the child about highly emotionally charged topics can compound the child's stress and worry about the parent's and child's safety and well-being. Many children are routinely exposed to inappropriately difficult topics because adults often carry on conversations as if children are not present or are not able to understand what the adults were saying. For children who are present when their parents or other adults discuss disturbing topics, not addressing those same topics in the therapeutic setting is tantamount to conveying the message that there are subjects that cannot be discussed with the therapist. In such situations, the clinician faces a difficult dilemma: What is more conducive to the child's mental health? To discuss, in her presence, topics that are not appropriate for her age as a way of presenting a more balanced view of situations that the child witnesses in the course of her daily life? Or, alternatively, to model for the parent a protective stance where children are shielded from topics that are stressful to them?

The answer is usually highly specific to individual situations. As a result, the clinician must weigh whether and when it is appropriate to elicit from the parent information about emotionally laden experiences in the presence of the child. If the clinician decides that speaking in front of the child would be threatening or harmful to the child, three different strategies that involve modifying the dyadic format of the sessions may be used:

- The session may be divided into two sections: one that is adult-centered and another that is child-centered. Such an arrangement is often welcomed by parent–child dyads who find themselves at odds with each other because each wants time alone with the clinician.

- Occasional or regular collateral individual meetings with the parent may be used when direct intervention with the parent is important to bring about improvement in the child–parent relationship and the child's development.
- Referrals for concurrent individual or group psychotherapy can also be implemented when the parent is in ongoing need of such services.

The use of interpretation is often associated with bringing awareness about the origins of negative feelings such as anger and sadness. The model of "ghosts in the nursery" (Fraiberg, 1980) has become the classic representation of the intergenerational transmission of trauma from parent to child through abusive and neglecting relationship patterns. In this model, the child is freed from engulfment in parental conflicts when the parent is able to gain insight into the early origins of his or her feelings of rejection, anger, and alienation toward the child. It is equally important, however, to help parents identify and integrate into their sense of self forgotten or suppressed beneficial influences in their life experience. These "angels in the nursery" (W. Harris, personal communication, April 23, 2003) serve as harbingers of hope by upholding the possibility of goodness within the parent, the child, and the parent–child relationship (Lieberman, 2004).

Providing emotional support and empathic communication. All effective therapeutic interventions are built on a foundation of trust that develops through the clinician's emotional availability. In CPP, parental emotional support and empathic communication with the child are facilitated by the presence of these qualities in the clinician's way of relating to the parent and the child. Supportive and empathic interventions take the form of conveying, through words and actions, a realistic hope that the treatment goals can be achieved; sharing in the satisfaction of achieving personal goals and developmental milestones; helping to maintain effective coping strategies; pointing out progress; encouraging self-expression; and supporting reality testing (Luborsky, 1984).

Providing crisis intervention, case management, and concrete assistance with problems of living. This modality consists of taking appropriate action to prevent or remedy the consequences of a family crisis or stressful circumstances. Although listed last, this strategy is often the first to be used when intervention begins because victims of domestic battering are often faced with a variety of real-life stresses that require immediate attention. Helping the parent in concrete ways can be the primary building block in forming a solid working relationship because the parent perceives the clinician as actively involved and receptive to her or his plight. This modality of intervention might involve advocacy for the family with the housing authorities to prevent an eviction, consultation with the child care provider to prevent expulsion of the child for inappropriate behavior, mediation between the mother and child protective services if questions of abuse or neglect arise, or referral to other needed services.

Families in which there is domestic violence often face difficult legal issues. Child custody decisions, filing and enforcement of restraining orders, dealings with attorneys, depositions, court appearances, and other aspects of the legal system are bewildering in their own right and can be even more stressful for battered women who are suffering from the psychological sequelae of the violence and who continue to fear for their own and their children's safety. Clinicians must be reasonably knowledgeable about the relevant laws and regulations in their states, and they need to provide appropriate referrals as well as assist parents in coping with the stresses inherent in their legal difficulties. This may include assuming the role of advocates and intermediaries in dealing with the legal system when this is necessary to protect the parent's or the child's safety. These issues are discussed more fully in Section IV of this manual.

Children exposed to violence often enact their emotional difficulties in the child care environment. Consultation with the child care provider, "shadowing" of the child, and promoting communication between the parent and the child care provider around the child's needs are often integral components of CPP.

What Is Unique About CPP?

None of the six individual modalities described previously is, in itself, unique to CPP. The uniqueness of CPP resides in the integrated use of these modalities, which are flexibly deployed according to the family's needs. In this sense, CPP is truly cross-disciplinary, combining elements of social work, mental health intervention, teaching, and advocacy.

Two features distinguish how the different therapeutic modalities are used in CPP:

1. The integrated use of all the modalities toward the therapeutic goal of promoting a more secure and growth-promoting relationship between the child and the parent(s).
2. Selecting the use of each modality for the specific purpose of changing the damaging mental representations that the child and the parent have of themselves and of each other, and changing the harmful behaviors through which these mental representations are enacted.

These two features and the general trauma treatment goals already described guide the treatment plan and the choice of intervention modalities. The integration of different intervention modalities conveys a powerful message to the parents about the therapist's commitment to the totality of their experience. This includes not only problems in feeling and thinking (the conventional loci of mental health intervention) but also everyday dilemmas, concrete circumstances, and problems of living. All of these modalities are needed because neither empathy nor insight are sufficient in and of themselves to bring about therapeutic change. Empathy and insight need to be linked to appropriate behavior in order to help the child and the parent, both individually and in their relationship to each other. This encompassing therapeutic stance maximizes the chances for the "moments of meeting" (i.e., authentic interpersonal connections that reorganize the way patient and therapist know each other) that add "something more" to psychodynamic interpretations and promote therapeutic change (Stern et al., 1998).

CPP is unchanging in its goals but versatile in its choice of therapeutic strategies. Depending on the particular needs of the child and the parent, different intervention modalities can be added to those already described. For example, infant massage can be used to help a motorically disorganized infant achieve better state regulation. Breathing techniques can be used to help a mother who is in a state of acute anxiety regain her calm. Therapeutic sessions may be videotaped for joint review in the next session. Reading books, singing songs, practicing yoga poses, making collages or family albums—the decision to introduce these and other interventions is guided by clinical need and by the therapist's creativity and repertoire of intervention skills.

As the field of mental health intervention in infancy and early childhood accumulates experience with successful forms of intervention, these strategies will be incorporated to the modalities currently used by CPP. Referrals to alternative forms of intervention—such as individual psychotherapy for the parent or the child, stress and anger management groups, trauma groups, a spiritual community, massage, meditation, exercise classes, and other activities—are made on the basis of relevance and appropriateness to the needs of the family.

The versatility of CPP lends it some resemblance to the multisystemic treatment (MST) of antisocial behavior in children and adolescents (Henggeler et al., 1998). MST, influenced by the seminal contributions of Bateson (1972) and Bronfenbrenner (1979) to the understanding of family systems and social ecology, emphasizes the multidetermined nature of serious antisocial behavior. MST involves the flexible deployment of a variety of intervention strategies designed to target the factors that were jointly identified by the therapist and the family as contributing to the problem. CPP shares the philosophy that problem behaviors in children are multidetermined and that intervention must be informed by an understanding of how the multiple systems in which the child and the family are embedded influence each other. However, within this broad ecological perspective, CPP gives particular salience to the nature of the transactions between parent and child because primary caregiving relationships are seen as a powerful common pathway through which diverse environmental influences affect children in the first 5 years of life.

Ports of Entry for the Intervention: Building From Simplicity

Young children are endlessly spontaneous. They are never more authentic and at ease than when they set the tone for what they will do. Following instructions is a painstakingly acquired skill that does not come easily for them. These developmental characteristics are built into the structure of CPP, which does not rely on a session-by-session curriculum but, rather, takes advantage of the opportunities that the child and the parent offer through their moment-to-moment spontaneous activities and interactions. Stern (1995) spoke of "ports of entry" as the component of the child–parent system that is the immediate object of clinical attention—the avenue through which the clinician enters into the system to create change. Once a port of entry emerges, the clinician must choose the specific therapeutic modality through which constructive change is most likely to occur.

Simple interventions are often the best. Many parents lack elementary developmental information. Once they learn it, they are able to implement it without much trouble. Telling a parent that pediatric advice now recommends that babies sleep on their backs rather than on their tummies in order to prevent sudden infant death syndrome (SIDS) is one example. Most parents need to hear this advice only once in order to heed it. Well-timed information, advice, and showing by example—when offered tactfully and placed in the context of the parent's cultural values—are time-honored methods for helping parents learn rapidly and well.

Only when these methods are not effective should the clinician consider forms of intervention geared to the parent's resistance, mistrust, or other psychological obstacles. CPP does not rely on a single, conceptually determined port of entry, such as the maternal representation of the child. Rather, there are various possible ports of entry, and the port of entry is chosen on the basis of the presence, appropriateness, and modulation of child and parent affect. The specific port of entry may vary from family to family or, within a family, from session to session or from one time frame to another within a session. This variety of ports of entry adds versatility, flexibility, and emotional richness to the intervention. The clinician needs to use clinical judgement to determine which port of entry is most likely to be conducive to therapeutic change on the basis of timing and receptiveness of the parent and child.

Regardless of the port of entry selected by the clinician, one guiding principle must always be followed. Whenever speaking directly to the parent or directly to the child, the clinician must keep the parent–child relationship in mind. Even experienced clinicians sometimes make the mistake of focusing on one member of the dyad to the exclusion of the other when first learning to use this model. This unilateral focus of attention can go on for several minutes or for entire sessions, with the result that the parent and child are encouraged to form intimate individual relationships with the clinician rather than cultivate and enrich their relationship with one another. Although the clinician's relationship with the parent and the child is an important vehicle for healing, the child–parent psychotherapist seeks primarily to serve and support the relationship between the parent and the child and makes that relationship the focus of the intervention. When clinicians choose a port of entry that involves speaking directly to the parent or to the child, it is critical that they consider how the other member of the dyad will hear and experience that intervention. Clinicians who hold both members of the dyad in mind create an atmosphere that promotes emotional proximity between the parent and the child because their relationship is assumed to be chiefly responsible for supporting the child's development.

Ports of entry and intervention strategies must be geared to the child's developmental stage. In general, the less verbal the child, the more effective it is to intervene using direct action. An inconsolably crying baby needs to be picked up and soothed; a toddler who is running away needs to be retrieved and held back; a young child who is about to do something forbidden needs to be distracted and redirected to a different activity. Taking effective action does not preclude using language as an intervention tool. For preverbal children, children who are delayed in their use of language, or children who are so distraught that they cannot pay attention to speech, the adult's use of verbalization is a useful adjunct to action because it helps the child to associate behavior with symbolic meaning. However, unambiguous action is the primary vehicle for intervention in these situations. Whenever possible, the clinician will support the parent in taking action. Where safety demands it, however, the clinician may first take action and then discuss that action with the parent and child.

Although action-based interventions are appropriate for the very young child, the same interventions are insufficient or even inappropriate for an older child who is able to use language. A preschooler must learn to restrain aggressive impulses as a first step in acquiring a reliable moral conscience that enables him to understand that it is wrong to hurt others. For example, a scarcely verbal 24-month-old child can be redirected to bite a teething ring rather than another child when the urge to bite takes over. Much more is expected of a preschool child: A verbally fluent 4-year-old, for example, needs to recognize when the anger is about to spill out into biting, and he must learn to leave the situation or to put the anger into words rather than into biting. He must conjure up the realization, before he bites, that biting hurts and that hurting others is wrong. The interventions for such a child must aim at helping him construct a sense of self in relation to others that includes this sense of moral accountability. For older children, the use of language to explain feelings and how the world works becomes an increasingly salient form of intervention.

Action and language are essential tools that the clinician brings to the therapeutic situation, but the child communicates most freely through play. That is the reason for choosing play as the first domain of the intervention in Section II of the manual. Winnicott (1971) pointed out that psychotherapy involves two people "playing together"—in other words, sharing a game without rules in which the players create a spontaneous dialogue with no predetermined goal or conclusion.

In CPP, it is at least three people who play together: the child, the parent, and the therapist. Turn-taking and giving others the space to play become more complex because the parent may want to direct the child's play or take over the play space. The therapist's role is to be a guardian of the child's freedom to play, facilitating the fluidity of the exchanges and moving tactfully to prevent either the parent or the child from monopolizing or becoming coercive in directing the flow of the play. Optimally, the child and the parent build a new freedom to play both individually and together in CPP. They find ways of balancing out the urge to be the main actor in the play with understanding and respect for the other's urge to do the same. Through playing together and with the therapist, they learn to take turns without feeling obliterated or abandoned.

The clinician's understanding of developmental stages and individual differences in the early years is essential in guiding developmentally appropriate interventions. There are a number of excellent books and papers that describe early childhood development. Clinicians should strive to integrate this conceptual knowledge with their experience-based knowledge of young children and their parents.

The Intervention Setting: Office Playroom or Home Visiting?

CPP can be conducted in a variety of settings. The two most frequent settings are the office playroom and the home, and each of these settings has its advantages and limitations. When the treatment is conducted in an office playroom, the predictability of the setting serves as a safe container in which the parent and child can enact their difficulties and practice more adaptive conflict-resolution strategies without external distractions. At the same time, many of the immediate stresses that impinge on the day-to-day child–parent relationship may remain unnoticed and unaddressed.

Home visiting, however, has a different set of advantages and disadvantages. Home visiting can be a remarkably effective vehicle for intervention for at least three primary reasons. First, it reaches out to parents who lack the internal or external resources to come to the clinician's office. Second, it provides an unparalleled opportunity to understand and appreciate the family's circumstances and the child's environment. Third, it gives the parents the message that the clinician is willing to share in their circumstances, however strained those circumstances might be (Fraiberg, 1980). As a result, it is not surprising that there is solid empirical evidence supporting the effectiveness of home visiting as a format for intervention (Olds & Kitzman, 1993).

Although offering unique opportunities, home visiting also presents special challenges. One primary challenge is how to maintain a focus on the clinical goal in the face of often changing external circumstances. In this sense, home visiting calls for remarkable self-discipline on the clinician's part because what happens in the home is completely unpredictable, from the time of the home visitor's arrival to the time of departure. Such unpredictability starts from very concrete questions prior to the beginning of the visit (How will traffic be at that time? Will there be a parking space? Will the family be there, and if not, how long should one wait? How safe is the neighborhood, and what should one say if a neighbor asks about one's identity and reason for being there?) and continues throughout the visit, which might pose such dilemmas as what to do if one is offered food or drink; how to respond to cultural traditions such as the custom of removing one's shoes at the door; or what the appropriate response is if unexpected visitors are present, if the TV is loudly on, or if the parent spends a large portion of the session talking on the phone.

These questions and dilemmas highlight the first task of home visitors: finding a balance between their identity as professionals with a particular set of goals in mind and their simultaneous role as guests in the parents' home. The inherent tension between these two disparate social roles is at the root of much uncertainty about what constitutes appropriate clinician behavior during a home visit. As professionals, the home visitors need to tactfully take the lead in shaping what is happening during the session. As guests, they need to respect and abide by the parents' sense of what is appropriate or inappropriate in their home.

If the professional identity prevails, the home visitor runs the risk of coming across as authoritarian, unfeeling, and rude, as if saying, in effect, "When I am in your home, this living room becomes my office, and I decide what needs to be done" (and, for example, unilaterally turning off the TV). Such an approach takes away from the parents their sense of dignity and psychological authority over their surroundings and reduces them to the status of children who must be told what to do in their own homes.

If, however, the home visitor overemphasizes the social aspects of the situation, there is a risk of forgetting the reason for the home visit. Coffee drinking or partaking of a snack can then become a social occasion, rather than a social ritual that signals hospitality and cordiality as the by-product of a professional relationship rather than as an end in itself. These tensions can be discussed with the parent during the early stages of treatment so that both the intervener's and the parent's expectations are clarified and conflict can be resolved in a collaborative way.

Each home visitor must find a personal balance between the professional role and the social role, but doing so calls for self-scrutiny and an empathic awareness of the parents' experience in having a visitor in their personal space. Some clinicians have no qualms about helping a parent wash the dishes, sweep up rice spilled from a box, or participating in hanging the laundry while simultaneously pursuing the goals of the intervention. Other home visitors dislike doing these chores in their own homes, let alone in someone else's, and are punctilious about not participating in everyday routines in their clients' homes. Such variability is inevitable, but respect for the parents' authority in their own home is an essential ingredient of effective intervention.

Sessions can be conducted in settings other than the home or the office playroom. Beleaguered and disempowered families often need help with transportation for important appointments or in running errands essential to the household. Assistance with problems of living involves the clinician's willingness to help out in these matters. When this happens, the car, the street, the supermarket, the pediatrician's waiting room, or the housing authority offices may become settings for the intervention.

A *therapeutic setting* can be defined most succinctly as any place where the parent, the child, and the clinician spend time together and interact with each other because any of these settings can offer the opportunity for transformative action. At the same time, the question of clinical focus should guide the reliance on alternative settings as adjuncts to the intervention. The clinician must be aware of the danger that running errands or helping with concrete problems can easily become ends in themselves, blurring the clinical goal of achieving sustained improvement in the parent–child relationship and the child's emotional functioning.

Clinician Safety

Clinician safety is a central question in determining the appropriate location of the intervention. Prior to establishing whether the sessions can take place in the home, it is important to discuss the issue of safety with the parent whenever there is uncertainty about the neighborhood or the home circumstances. Many parents are only too aware of the danger in their surroundings and are appreciative of the clinician's candor and explicit reliance on the parent's input.

This is particularly crucial when domestic violence is a problem, even if the perpetrator is no longer living in the home but might still have access to it or has stalked the partner or violated restraining orders in the past. In raising the question of safety, the clinician is modeling an initial attitude of protectiveness toward herself, the parent, and the children—protectiveness that will be demonstrated repeatedly in the course of the intervention.

On occasion, a clinician's deep commitment to the family and to the therapeutic process may result in his or her overlooking or minimizing clues to danger in the environment. At other times, the clinician may be keenly aware of the danger but decide to brave it as a form of solidarity with the client. Such situations can be understood as "parallel processes" where the clinician risks self-endangerment through identification with the endangered parent. When this happens, the clinician is missing an opportunity to demonstrate to the client that it is possible to take decisive action to avert violence and protect oneself and one's children.

Programs that address domestic violence must create an atmosphere of trust where clinicians can disclose their fears, anger, and anxiety to each other and where colleagues can feel free to be outspoken when issues of safety are at stake. Reflective supervision, staff meetings, and weekly case reviews need to be used as a forum to bring up clinical difficulties as well as worries about possible danger. Changing the site of the intervention from home visiting to an office-based setting in order to forestall danger can be the clinician's most eloquent expression of commitment to safety as an overriding goal of the treatment.

Clinician Self-Care

The Jewish sage Hillel used three questions to simultaneously ask and answer the apparent contradiction between caring for oneself and striving to do good in the world: "If I am not for myself, who will be for me? And if I am only for myself, then who am I? And if not now, then when?"

Therapist safety must begin with self-care, and the moment is always now. Trauma work is at different times draining, frustrating, confusing, exhausting, and overwhelming—although it can also be stimulating, enriching, and transformative. A reflective attitude about one's personal well-being can help the clinician identify early signs of burnout, vicarious traumatization, or compassion fatigue. Including self-care activities into regular routines should become an integral part of the clinician's therapeutic attitude: "Do for yourself the good that you do for others," and "treat yourself the way you would like others to treat you."

Strategies for self-care are as varied as the tastes, preferences, and personalities of the therapists doing this work and may include attending to the body, the mind, and the soul. Whatever the specific activity—from eating to singing to praying—the common denominators are cultivating time-out, not letting the work invade all aspects of one's life, protecting one's private life, and cherishing the gift of a good present moment.

Self-care must also be built in the workplace. Two important strategies are seeking out consultation or supervision in demanding situations and building support systems at work. Just as it takes a village to raise a child, it takes a communal approach to protect and support clinicians working with trauma. The administrative structure of agencies should include respect for the clinicians as well as for the clients by creating a supportive and collaborative atmosphere, time for consultation and supervision, and clear lines of differentiation between administrative supervision and clinical supervision to ensure that clinicians do not feel unduly threatened by disclosing difficulties with the work. Mature self-advocacy is a form of self-care. Agencies and programs function better, and children and families receive better care when their clinicians are treated well.

Empirical Evidence of CPP Efficacy

CPP is listed as an evidence-based treatment in the Substance Abuse and Mental Health Services Administration National Registry of Evidence-Based Programs and Practices (see http://nrepp.samhsa.gov) on the basis of five randomized studies that have consistently found improved outcomes relative to control groups. The empirical evidence is described in this section.

Quality of attachment in recently immigrated Latino toddler–mother dyads (Lieberman et al., 1991). This study tested the hypothesis that CPP would improve the relationship quality of anxiously attached toddler–mother dyads ($n = 34$) relative to a control group of anxiously attached toddlers not receiving intervention ($n = 25$) and that the CPP group would be comparable to a securely attached control group ($n = 34$) after the end of treatment. Quality of attachment was assessed when the children were 12 months old, and anxiously attached toddler–mother dyads were randomly assigned to a CPP group or a nonintervention control group. Securely attached toddler–mother dyads comprised a second control group. Treatment lasted 1 year and ended when the child was 24 months old. Posttreatment assessments showed that the intervention group toddlers were significantly lower in avoidance, resistance, and anger and were significantly higher in goal-corrected partnership when compared with the anxiously attached control group. Mothers in the CPP group had higher scores in empathy and higher levels of interaction with their children than mothers in the anxiously attached control group. There were no differences at outcome between the CPP intervention group and the securely attached control group. Within the CPP intervention group, the mother's score on a measure of therapeutic involvement was significantly positively correlated with adaptive scores in child and mother outcome measures, with greater maternal empathy and interactiveness with the child, higher goal-corrected partnership, and lower child avoidance upon reunion.

Quality of attachment, cognitive development, and family climate in toddlers of depressed mothers. Toth et al. (2006) examined the effects of CPP on the attachment security of toddlers with predominantly White middle-class mothers who met *Diagnostic and Statistical Manual of Mental Disorders 4th ed*; (DSM-IV; American Psychiatric Association, 1994) criteria for depression. Dyads were randomly assigned to a CPP group ($n = 27$) and a no-treatment comparison group ($n = 36$). The CPP group received weekly sessions for an average of 45 weeks. A nondepressed control group was also recruited ($n = 45$). The Beck Depression Inventory (Beck, Ward, Mendelson, Mock, & Erbaugh, 1961) and the Diagnostic Interview Schedule (3rd. ed.; Robins et al., 1985) were used to assess maternal symptoms pre- and postintervention, and the Attachment Q-set (Teti, Nakagawa, Das, & Wirth, 1991) was used as a measure of attachment. Children were approximately 36 months old following the intervention period. Toddlers of depressed mothers in both the CPP and comparison groups showed higher rates of insecure attachment relative to the nondepressed control group. Following the intervention, toddlers in the CPP group demonstrated significant improvements in attachment security (74.1% of the CPP group members were rated as secure compared with 52.8% of the comparison group members). No differences in attachment security were found between the CPP treatment group and nondepressed controls.

Cicchetti et al. (2000) examined the efficacy of CPP in promoting toddlers' cognitive development in this sample (Toth et al., 2006). At baseline, children in all three groups (CPP, comparison, and nondepressed control) showed no differences in cognitive or motor development on the Bayley Mental Development Index (Bayley, 1969). Postintervention results, at 3 years old, showed a relative decline in IQ for the comparison group, with the CPP and nondepressed control group showing an increase in cognitive performance in both the WPPSI-R Full Scale and Verbal IQ scales (Wechsler, 1989).

In a follow-up study of this sample, Peltz, Rogge, Rogosch, Cicchetti, and Toth (2015) explored whether CPP had a long-term positive influence on the family system after 159 depressed mothers and their toddlers received CPP. Longitudinal associations between depressive symptoms and marital satisfaction over 3 years were analyzed to examine whether the benefits of CPP on quality of toddler–mother attachment might generalize within the family and indirectly benefit marital relationships. Hierarchical linear modeling revealed significant associations between depressive symptoms and marital functioning. Specifically, shifts in mothers' depressive symptoms within specific waves of follow-up were associated with corresponding shifts in both their husbands' and their own relationship satisfaction in those same waves. After controlling for demographics and the dynamic association between depressive symptoms and relationship satisfaction, the findings indicated that mothers who received CPP reported increases in relationship satisfaction (β = .299, $p \leq$ .001) in comparison with the two control groups of depressed mothers not receiving intervention and nondepressed mothers, both of which, on average, evidenced drops in their marital satisfaction.

Self- and maternal representations among maltreated preschoolers. Toth et al. (2002) conducted a randomized controlled trial with 122 low-income, multiethnic families (87 maltreating and 35 nonmaltreating) examining the relative efficacy of CPP (n = 23), psychoeducational home visitation (PHV; n = 34), or community standard (CS; n = 30). A low-income normative comparison group (NC; n = 43) was also included. Families with documented histories of maltreatment were recruited through the Department of Social Services, and low-income controls were randomly recruited from a state list of Temporary Assistance for Needy Families (TANF) recipients. The MacArthur Story Stem Battery (MSSB; Bretherton, Oppenheim, Buchsbaum, Emde, & the MacArthur Narrative Group, 1990) was administered to children at baseline and following intervention completion and was coded for adaptive and maladaptive maternal representations, negative self-representation, and mother–child relationship expectations using the *MacArthur Narrative Coding Manual, Rochester Revision* (Robinson, Mantz–Simmons, Macfie, & the MacArthur Narrative Working Group, 1996). Change scores for these outcomes were calculated for children pre- and postintervention, and group differences were assessed through analysis of variance (ANOVA). Children in the CPP group demonstrated significant declines in maladaptive maternal representations relative to the PHV and CS children as well as greater decreases in negative self-representations than did children in the CS, PHV, and NC groups. Mother–child relationship expectations of CPP children showed significant positive changes over the intervention period relative to the NC group and showed a positive trend relative to PHV participants.

PTSD, behavior problems, and maternal symptoms in preschooler–mother dyads exposed to domestic violence (Lieberman et al., 2005). The sample consisted of 75 multiethnic preschoolers exposed to domestic violence (mean age = 4.06 years) and their mothers. Forty-one percent of families were below the federal poverty level, and mothers had an average of 12 years of education. Dyads were randomly assigned to receive either CPP (weekly dyadic sessions for 1 year) or community services plus case management. Dyads were assessed for child behavioral and emotional problems using the Child Behavior Checklist (Achenbach, 1991; Achenbach & Edelbrock, 1983) and the Structured Clinical Interview for DC:0-3 (Scheeringa, Zeanah, Drell, & Larrieu, 1995; Scheeringa, Zeanah, Myers, & Putnam, 2003), and for maternal general psychiatric and PTSD symptoms using the Symptom Checklist-90 (Derogatis, 1994), and the Clinician-Administered PTSD Scale (Blake et al., 1990) at three time points: pre-treatment, after 1 year of treatment, and at a 6-month follow-up. Repeated measures analysis of variance (RM ANOVA) revealed that the CPP group showed significant improvements in children's total behavior problems, traumatic stress symptoms, and diagnostic status. In addition, significant improvements in maternal avoidance symptoms as well as trends toward significant improvements in maternal PTSD symptoms were noted after 1 year.

In a follow-up 6 months after termination of treatment, Lieberman et al. (2006) found that treatment effects persisted. Children who had received CPP continued to show greater reductions in total behavior problems, and mothers in the CPP group continued to improve, now showing significantly greater reductions in general distress than the control group.

Further analysis of the sample to examine the efficacy of CPP by level of child exposure to traumatic and stressful life events showed that children with four or more traumatic and stressful life events who received CPP showed significantly greater improvements in symptoms of PTSD and depression, PTSD diagnosis, number of co-occurring diagnoses, and behavior problems, compared to children with similar exposure in the control group. These effects were maintained at the 6-month follow-up. Mothers of children with four or more traumatic or stressful events in the CPP group also showed greater reductions in symptoms of PTSD and depression than those randomized to community services. In addition, children with fewer than four risks in the CPP group also showed greater improvements in symptoms of PTSD than did those in the community group (Ghosh Ippenet et al., 2011.

Quality of attachment and physiological regulation in maltreated infants. Cicchetti, Rogosch, and Toth (2006) compared the relative efficacy of three interventions on the development of secure attachment in 137 maltreated infants who were randomly assigned to CPP group, a psychoeducational parenting intervention (PPI) group, or a community standard (CS) group. In addition, a fourth group consisting of 52 nonmaltreated infants and their mothers comprised a low-income normative control (NC) group. Infants were predominantly ethnic minority 1-year-olds (mean age = 13.31 months) and were recruited through child protective services reports. Quality of attachment was measured using the Strange Situation (Ainsworth et al., 1978) pre- and postintervention when children were 26 months old. Postintervention, children in the CPP and PPI groups showed significant increases in secure attachment compared with children in the CS and NC groups, who did not experience significant changes in the number of children who were classified as securely attached and who maintained these results when intent-to-treat analyses were conducted.

Cicchetti et al. (2011) examined the effects of maltreatment on daily cortisol patterns in a subsample of the sample used in Cicchetti et al. (2006); the CPP and PPI samples were combined for the purposes of analysis to create one maltreatment intervention (MI) group, consisting of 91 infants (43 boys, 48 girls) and their mothers. Saliva samples were obtained from children at 13 months old (pre-intervention), 19 months old (mid-intervention), 26 months old (postintervention), and 38 months old (1-year postintervention follow-up). Although no differences in morning cortisol were noted between the MI, CS, and NC groups at baseline, significant differences in basal cortisol levels between the NC group and the CS group emerged postintervention and were maintained at the 1-year postintervention follow-up. These results indicated that maltreated infants who received intervention (either CPP or PPI) developed cortisol patterns that resembled those of nonmaltreated infants, with evidence for progressive cortisol dysregulation in the CS maltreated sample that did not receive intervention.

Stronach, Toth, Rogosch, and Cicchetti (2013) conducted follow-up analyses on the maltreated children in this sample to learn whether group differences in attachment security and child behavior problems persisted 12 months after treatment had ended, when children were approximately 38 months old. Children who received CPP continued to have higher rates of secure attachment and lower rates of disorganized attachment than did children in the IPI and CS groups, with no differences in the rates of secure attachment in the CPP and nonmaltreated NC groups. Intent-to-treat analyses found that children in the CPP group continued to have higher rates of secure attachment relative to the PPI and CS groups, but no differences in disorganized attachment were found. Primary and intent-to-treat analyses both found no differences between groups in child behavior problems at follow-up. Although slightly more families in the CS group were unavailable at follow-up, attrition analyses showed no differences in attrition by treatment group.

A further study on this sample—a subsample for which DNA was available—was conducted to examine the role of polymorphisms of the serotonin transporter linked promotor region (5-HTTLPR) and dopamine receptor D4 (DRD4) on attachment style and intervention efficacy (Cicchetti, Rogosch, & Toth, 2011). Investigators found that genetic variation in these regions predicted attachment style only in nonmaltreated infants and that intervention effects held regardless of genetic variation in the maltreated infants. It is hypothesized that high rates of disorganized attachment may supersede the contributions of genetic variation and that early intervention is likely to be effective regardless of genetic differences of these polymorphisms.

SECTION II

PHASES OF CHILD–PARENT PSYCHOTHERAPY

C HILD–PARENT PSYCHOTHERAPY (CPP) USUALLY INVOLVES weekly sessions for a period that may range from 20 to 32 weeks or more, depending on clinical need. Sessions last approximately 60 minutes and may take place in the home or office playroom.

Parent and child are routinely present during the visits, although individual sessions with the parent take place during the Foundational Phase and may also be scheduled later in treatment to discuss issues that are best addressed privately. Exceptions may occur when the parents are so unable to collaborate in the treatment on behalf of the child that their presence becomes damaging—for example, when the parent routinely monopolizes the session in ways that are overstimulating or overwhelming for the child. In these situations, it is often helpful to conduct separate individual sessions with the child and with the parent until the parent's functioning improves to the point of enabling that parent to engage in joint sessions with the child. There are also situations in which individual sessions—either with the child or with the caregiver—are interspersed with dyadic sessions. This format is used when one partner or the other should be protected from exposure to graphic trauma details that would be traumatizing—for example, when a child witnessed his mother's murder and is now in the care of his maternal grandmother, who cannot tolerate the child's enactment of her daughter's final moments.

CPP usually consists of three phases:

1. Foundational Phase: Assessment and Engagement
2. Core Intervention
3. Recapitulation and Termination: Promoting Sustainability of Gains

The five families[1] described here represent a range of clinical presentations and are used as anchors through the rest of the manual to illustrate CPP Foundational Phase strategies and treatment fidelity strands.

Jaylen Fisher

Jaylen was a 32-month-old African American boy referred to treatment after he witnessed the drive-by shooting of another young child while on the way to a neighborhood store with his father. Jaylen's parents, James and Tiana, reported that since the shooting, Jaylen had long and intense temper tantrums and nightly nightmares. He had been very verbal before the shooting but spoke much less and used fewer words and shorter sentences following this event. He also clung to them and would cry whenever he saw that either of them was leaving. Jaylen's father reported feeling overwhelmed by intrusive images of the shooting and by waves of terror that Jaylen could have been the child who was shot. He was also reexperiencing images of his cousin's death. His 15-year-old cousin had been murdered shortly after joining a gang. Jaylen's mother was supportive of her husband but felt that he needed to be strong and try to manage his own reactions in order to help their child.

Susan Chan

Susan, 25 months old, witnessed numerous episodes of domestic violence in the 6 months prior to referral, which began after her father lost his job and began drinking more heavily. In the last incident, Susan's father choked her mother in the child's presence. When Susan got between her parents while screaming, her father pushed her, and she fell down but was not injured. Susan's mother, Nancy, left the house with Susan and moved to her sister's home. A child protective services report was filed by the mother's sister with the mother's consent. Susan's father was from China and came to the United States as an adult to attend college. Susan's mother had immigrated from Cambodia as a young child with her entire family. Both spoke English. Susan's father was pleading for his wife and child to return home,

---

[1]These are composites of families we have seen over the years and are reprinted with permission from Ghosh Ippen et al. (2014).

attributing his violence to the pressures of joblessness and urging his wife not to shame him by abandoning him. Susan's mother was considering going back to him, impelled by a sense of family loyalty, Susan's repeated asking for her father, and economic considerations. Susan was waking up at night, crying "daddy." She was very clingy, and her mother noted that she seemed quiet and withdrawn and spoke much less now. Prior to this, Susan had been a very verbal 2-year-old.

TRAVIS BISHOP JR.

Travis Bishop Jr. ("TJ") was a 39-month-old boy of mixed ethnic heritage (Caucasian, Latino, and Native American) who was seen with both his mother and his great aunt Rosa who TJ called "aunt." TJ's mother, a former substance user, was attempting to reunify with TJ. He had been placed with his aunt 1 year earlier following a child protective services investigation for exposure to domestic violence and child neglect. At intake, his aunt described TJ as extremely aggressive and "a lot like his dad." He had extreme temper tantrums where he flailed on the floor, swung his arms forcefully, and hit himself on the head. He also hit other children. He gorged himself on food and stole food when his aunt told him he could not have another helping. He had difficulty sleeping and had frequent nightmares. He was reckless in his explorations and often got hurt from falls or bumps. His aunt said that she was not sure she could keep the child much longer because of his challenging behavior and expressed the hope that his mother could manage reunification soon.

MARIANNA CHAVEZ

Marianna was a 9-month-old baby who was severely injured in the head while in the care of her day care provider. It was unclear whether the injury was accidental or the result of child abuse. The child was hospitalized for 1 week and was discharged with detailed instructions for the care of the head wounds — instructions that her young mother found difficult to understand and follow. Marianna had become lethargic, sleepy, and unresponsive, and her mother feared that she had endured brain damage in spite of the doctors' reassurances that she would recover completely. Marianna's mother, Aurelia, was a 22-year-old recent immigrant from Mexico who did not have family in this country. She was devastated by her child's injury, particularly because the care provider was a woman from church who had helped Marianna find housing after she had arrived from Mexico and supported her during her pregnancy. Two months before Marianna's birth, her father left Aurelia for another woman, saying that the pregnancy had been a trick to make him stay. The mother began working shortly after Marianna was born, and her job was threatened by the child's medical needs.

....

ANTHONY AND ALYSSA CRAFT

Anthony and Alyssa Craft were 34-month-old White twins referred to treatment by their child protective services worker. They were born premature at 29 weeks' gestation and were removed from their mother at birth due to her substance abuse. Both twins had numerous medical issues and remained in the neonatal intensive care unit (NICU) for 1 month after their birth. Anthony was fed via a nasogastric tube. At 1 month old, they were released from the hospital to a foster family who cared for high-risk babies. They remained in that home until they were 7 months old, when they were returned to their biological mother. They were removed from her care 5 months later (at 12 months old) due to exposure to severe domestic violence. It was reported that the mother's boyfriend stabbed her with a knife and threatened to kill her and the children. Anthony and Alyssa were placed in three different foster homes during the following year and returned again to their mother when they were 2 years old. Six months later, they were removed again after their mother attempted suicide by slashing her wrists. It was unclear whether the children witnessed this event, but there was a great deal of commotion when the mother's sister discovered her, called the ambulance, and left the children with a neighbor to accompany the mother to the hospital. Medical exams done on the children revealed that Anthony had bruises on his body, and an x-ray showed prior tibia trauma. Anthony and Alyssa were placed in foster care with a lesbian couple, Gina and Kerri, who hoped to adopt them, although they, and particularly Kerri, were expressing concern about keeping Anthony because he was very difficult to manage.

Anthony was extremely aggressive, had prolonged and unmanageable temper tantrums, hit, kicked, spat at people, and threw things. He was constantly in motion and had difficulty following any instructions. His speech was delayed, and he was not potty trained. Alyssa was very different from her brother. She was shy and approached people slowly, but once she warmed up, she was talkative and engaging. Her foster mothers reported that Alyssa engaged in sexualized behaviors, trying to kiss them with her tongue and often rubbing her vaginal area. The children's biological mother was still trying to reunify with the children, and it was unclear whether her parental rights would be terminated.

PHASE 1
FOUNDATIONAL PHASE: ASSESSMENT AND ENGAGEMENT

Overview and Goals

All effective treatments begin with a process of engaging the family as motivated participants. While creating a collaborative working relationship with the parents, clinicians also need to find out who the parents and the child are, including the background for the referral to treatment, demographic information, presenting problem, and risk and protective factors in the family constellation. It is imperative to balance the need to gather information needed for clinical formulation and treatment planning with respect for the family's sense of timing in self-disclosure as well as with judicious transparency in sharing with the parent what the clinician may know from other sources about the reasons for the referral. How clinicians conduct themselves during this initial phase of treatment, respond to situational and clinical challenges, and balance attention to adult and child needs will influence the family's ability to engage in and trust the treatment process.

In this sense, the initial assessment represents the foundational engagement phase of the treatment. For the sake of brevity, we abbreviate the language to call it "Foundational Phase" in the sections that follow. Initial goals include the following components:

- Create a therapeutic climate where the caregiver feels supported in speaking about difficult circumstances, including traumatic experiences.
- Convey an attitude of self-competence and hope that improvement is possible.
- Address possible sources of negative transference and resistance, such as mandated treatment.
- Take steps to understand sources of danger and to increase safety.
- Establish a dialogue about cultural values and approaches to child-rearing, including the caregiver's attitudes about mentioning the child's trauma during treatment.
- Develop a joint formulation of the child's presenting problems that incorporates a trauma-informed perspective, sensitivity to the caregiver's psychological functioning, and attention to the family's ecological context.
- Co-create with the parent a treatment plan that includes an agreement about how to address traumatic events, presenting problems, and other difficult topics with the child.

A recurrent concern raised by therapists learning CPP is that asking about traumatic events at the beginning of the assessment may offend, antagonize, or traumatize parents. Establishing comfort in speaking with parents early in treatment about trauma is a core CPP competency that represents a challenge to many therapists. Our experience is that when therapists broach the topic of trauma exposure as an integral and recurrent part of the human experience that can be coped with, parents often feel relieved that events and feelings they deemed as unspeakable are, in fact, amenable to understanding and repair. Crucial in this process is the message that people are not defined by the worst things that happened to them. The trauma frame used in CPP is necessary but not sufficient. The treatment embraces all aspects of the human experience and highlights the centrality of love, play, joy, pleasure, spirituality, and humor in helping the parent and the child connect with the *chiaroscuro* of life. For example, a 4-year-old boy showed his capacity to remember the good things that life has to offer in the midst of pain.

He was telling the therapist how much he missed his mother as the anniversary of her death was approaching and the family was preparing to visit her grave. The therapist affirmed how sad it was that the mother had died, and then she added, "You know, you will not always be sad. There will also be things that make you glad and help you have fun." The boy perked up and asked, "Like chocolate?" The therapist responded, "Like chocolate!" The boy then went on to think of a list of things that he liked, aided by the therapist and by the aunt who had become his caregiver. The therapist and aunt knew then that he was well on his way to recovery.

Procedures

The Foundational Phase usually consists of four to six sessions, although it is not uncommon to conduct several more initial assessment and engagement sessions with families who were not referred of their own volition or who have high safety and stabilization needs. Caregivers may be reluctant to engage in treatment for a variety of reasons. The idea of receiving mental health treatment might not match their cultural attitudes, they may be mandated or feel coerced to seek treatment by child-serving systems (e.g., child welfare, the schools), and/or they may be concerned that sharing information regarding children's exposure to trauma may result in the child's removal and out-of-home placement. In these circumstances, the foundational process is often extended to address obstacles to treatment and to gain the parents' trust as a prerequisite for therapeutic engagement.

As an example, TJ's aunt started the first session by stating "I don't know about therapy, but the preschool is saying that if he doesn't get help, they aren't sure they can keep him. I need to work. He just can't be doing this. If they kick him out, I'm not sure I can keep him." She added, "Anyhow, I'm here for TJ. I'm the only one he's got, but his mom better get it together. I'm worried TJ is a lot like his dad. He just doesn't listen, and he's got quite a temper. Sometimes he's, like, possessed. I'm too old for this. I don't know what I'm going to do with him. I can't take much more of this."

It was clear from the aunt's words and demeanor that therapy was a rather alien concept for her and that she was agreeing to it as a last resort to comply with the preschool's thinly veiled ultimatum that they might expel TJ unless his behavior improved. The therapist's empathic receptiveness to the aunt's anguished uncertainty about her own capacity to keep TJ proved critically important in helping her trust that she had a right to be concerned about her own well-being in light of the challenges posed by the child. When she felt heard and supported, the aunt was able to join the therapist in reflecting about the impact on TJ of the violence and neglect that he had witnessed and experienced, including his worry that nobody loved him or wanted to keep him. As we will see, taking the time to create a solid partnership with the aunt over 8 weeks led to a course of treatment that addressed with TJ what he had been through and how he felt about it and helped him learn and practice more adaptive ways of expressing anger and fear, which resulted in significant improvement.

The *Foundational Phase: Assessment and Engagement Fidelity Form* (see Appendix A) includes a section titled Procedural Fidelity: Assessment and Engagement (see pages 7–10) that describes the procedures used during this phase, including key domains of assessment and topics for psychoeducation, discussion, and reflection. Although the procedures are listed in a specific order on the form, the assessment process should be guided by clinical judgment and the needs of the family. Core activities are specified, but they can be achieved using different methods (e.g., choosing between using a clinical interview or a structured research instrument), and assessment protocols can be tailored to clinical considerations, agency requirements, or research needs.

We offer next a session-by-session outline of how the Foundational Phase is typically conducted at the University of California San Francisco Child Trauma Research Program at San Francisco General Hospital in response to numerous requests for a concrete set of guidelines. Specific tasks and core assessment areas are itemized in the summary box for each session. This outline should be read as illustrative rather than prescriptive. The primacy of clinical judgment is a hallmark of CPP, and clinicians are encouraged to conduct the Foundational Phase in the ways that feel most appropriate to the specific clinical situation and the clinician's own therapeutic style.

Session 1

Session 1: Suggested Tasks and Procedures

❏ Informed consent
❏ Confidentiality
❏ Reporting requirements and ways these requirements are handled (especially important for families mandated to treatment or court-involved families)
❏ Reason for seeking treatment (including, when relevant, differences between the reasons given by the parent and by other involved parties, such as the child welfare system)
❏ Demographic information
❏ Developmental history
❏ Child symptoms

It is recommended that the parent and the therapist meet alone during the first session, which may last between 1 and 2 hours. This format allows for the caregiver and therapist to complete consent forms, discuss the caregiver's concerns, gather basic demographic information, and address any urgent issues related to safety or stabilization. Sufficient time should be allowed so that the parent(s) can express concerns, feel supported, and begin to understand how treatment may be helpful. A core goal for this session involves instilling a sense of hope and positive expectancies for treatment, but, to be authentic, the message of hope must be based on a realistic appraisal of the protective factors, such as the positive steps that the caregiver has already taken or plans to take.

During this first session, CPP therapists may choose to use either a clinical interview or a structured questionnaire to learn about the child's developmental history and the origin and course of current symptoms. In this process, the therapist seeks to understand the parent's views regarding the child's problems and factors that may contribute to these problems (e.g., genetics, developmental challenges, stressful events). The therapist also uses opportunities to explore with the parent possible links between traumatic events and/or adversities described by the parent and the child's presenting problems. In this way, from the first contact, the therapist and caregiver begin to co-construct a framework that connects experience to functioning.

Session 2

Session 2: Suggested Tasks and Procedures

❑ Observation of the parent and child during structured and/or free-play situations
❑ Observation of the child in interaction with the therapist or another assessor during structured and/or free-play situations
❑ Assessment of the child's developmental functioning using clinical observation or structured tools
❑ Assessment of the child's functioning in alternate settings or with alternate caregivers (e.g., day care, preschool, or school) either via observation, interview, or questionnaire

The second session usually involves the parent, child, and therapist. Consistent with best practices for assessing young children (ZERO TO THREE, 2005), the therapist observes the child under a variety of circumstances as described in the box above.

Using multiple observations, the therapist gathers information on the following areas:

- The child's developmental functioning, including achievement of developmental milestones, regulatory capacity, and age-appropriate skills
- The quality of the parent–child relationship
- The ways the caregiver and child typically play and interact together
- The ways the child interacts with other adults
- Areas of strength and areas of challenge
- Possible trauma-related symptoms (e.g., spontaneously playing or talking about traumatic events, hypervigilance, arousal)

Session 3

Session 3: Suggested Tasks and Procedures

❑ Assessment of child trauma history, preferably using a structured instrument such as the Traumatic Events Screening Interview—Parent Report Revised (TESI-PRR; Ghosh Ippen et al., 2002)

❑ Assessment of child trauma symptoms

The primary goal of this session is to learn about traumatic and stressful events that the child may have experienced and to explore possible links between these experiences and the child's symptoms. The session takes place with the parent(s) alone. The therapist introduces the goal of the session by explaining that children's emotional and behavioral problems can often be best understood as a response to the frightening events that happened to them. This rationale sets the trauma frame for the treatment, and the questions that follow enable the parent to entertain possible connections between what happened to the child and how the child is feeling and behaving. It is best to schedule this session alone with the caregiver for the following reasons:

1. Parents may have strong reactions about what happened to their child and may need the therapist's assistance to process these responses. The child's experience of trauma is among the most difficult emotional ordeals that a parent may endure. In addition, parents may have been present during the traumatic event, as in the case of domestic violence or a car accident, and when this occurs, the parents may have trauma-related symptoms that affect their emotional functioning and relationship with the child. Meeting alone with the parent enables the therapist to learn about the parent's emotional functioning and the parent's clarity and reliability as an informer of the child's experience. Meeting alone also gives the clinician the freedom to provide psychoeducation about the normative impact of traumatic events on adults and children, observe how able the parent is to use this information to expand her understanding of the situation, and start building a working relationship based on

an evolving shared understanding of what the child and the parent went through and how they are responding to these events.

2. Parents are sometimes unsure about what their child may have witnessed or remembered and may feel constrained from speaking freely about their questions and worries if the child is present. Meeting alone with the therapist offers them the emotional space to search their memories, entertain possibilities, and engage in an open-ended dialogue with the therapist that includes how the child's presenting problems may be related to the traumatic events and family circumstances.

3. Parents may not be willing initially to acknowledge what the child experienced, especially if they were involved in inflicting the trauma either directly or through failure to protect the child. When it is not yet clear whether the parent can safely care for the child, the therapist may need to discuss events described in the referral materials or reports (e.g., court, police, or child protective services) that the caregiver does not spontaneously bring up. This conversation is geared to exploring the parents' perspective on these reports, perceptions of how the system is treating them, and how these perceptions may extend to the therapist's role and the assessment and treatment process.

4. Safety concerns that need immediate action may come up in the course of describing the child's exposure to trauma, including, for example, the need to make a child abuse report or refer a battered mother to a domestic violence shelter. These issues are easier to address when the child is not present during the session.

When presenting the rationale for screening for trauma, it is helpful to begin by referring to the information about traumatic and stressful events that the parent has already discussed in earlier sessions. In some circumstances, a child may have been referred for one particular traumatic event, and the therapist needs to help the parent understand that other frightening things may have happened that could be affecting the child without anybody realizing it. This was the case for Jaylen Fisher, and an example of the dialogue between the therapist and Jaylen's father is shown beginning on the next page. In the scene, the therapist describes the rationale for trauma screening and then begins the process of screening.

Jaylen Fisher: Rationale for Screening for Child Trauma and Ports of Entry During Screening[2]

Therapist and father had met for two prior assessment sessions. During the first session, the father talked openly about the shooting, detailing what happened and his concerns for Jaylen. During the second session, the therapist observed the father and Jaylen play and did an individual free play with Jaylen. This was the third session.

Therapist: *I know you came here because you want help for Jaylen 'cause of the shooting.*

Dad: *Yeah, I want him to be OK.*

Therapist: *What you saw was awful, and it makes sense that you were both affected by it.*

Dad: *Yeah.*

Therapist: *You told me that it's hard to think about what happened.*

Dad: *Yeah. I don't like to think about it.*

Therapist: *I really want to thank you for being so open and talking to me about it, given how hard it is. When we start working with Jaylen, he might talk or play out what happened, and what you told me helps me start to think about how we can help him.*

Dad: *Do you really think he'll talk about what happened?*

Therapist: *I don't know, but you told me that he brings it up at home and when you go to the playground. It might be good for him to have a place where we can help him with these memories.*

Dad: *OK.*

Therapist: *So I mentioned that today I want to ask you some questions that we use with all families so that we can find out about the different things that often happen to children and think about how this might affect them.*

---

[2] Reprinted with permission from Ghosh Ippen, Van Horn, and Lieberman (2014)

Dad: *What do you mean?*

Therapist: *Well, this is a list of stressful things that kids can go through that can be very hard on them. I already know about the shooting, but I'd like to ask you about other things in this list and think with you about whether there's been anything else that Jaylen's been through. So I'll read an event, and if he hasn't experienced it, you'd just say no, but if he has, it would be good for us to talk about it, so I would know what happened, how old Jaylen was, and whether you think it might have affected him.*

Dad: Looks curious.

Therapist: *For example, the first two questions are about accidents, so you can tell me if Jaylen was ever in a serious accident or saw one. Because even though you are coming because of the shooting, it would be good for me to know about something like this because sometimes when kids talk or play about what happened, they make up a story and mix in all the different things they've been through. It can been confusing to us, and it helps if we've talked about the different things that happened to him before we bring him in. Does that make sense?*

Dad: *I think so.*

Therapist: *Well, so, the first item asks if Jaylen's ever been in a serious accident where someone could have been or actually was severely injured or died? This would be like a car or bike accident, a fall, fire, an incident where he was burned or nearly drowned. Anything like that.*

Dad: *Jaylen's never been in an accident or seen one, but I have.*

Therapist: *Yeah?*

Dad: *Yeah. I was like 11, and I was going to school . . . A car hit this bus right in front of me. The bus went spinning, hit a pole, and flipped over. I remember people screaming. I think they said like two people died. I remember not knowing what to do.*

Therapist: *That sounds so scary.*

Dad: *Yeah it was. There are parts of it I still can't get out of my head.*

Therapist: *That makes sense. It sounds awful. When things like this happen, sometimes they're hard to forget.*

Dad: *Yeah. I still don't like riding the bus. I walk everywhere.*

Therapist: *I wouldn't like the bus either. Did you ever talk to anyone about what you saw?*

Dad: *No. I just tried to forget.*

Therapist: *I think most people would wish they could just forget, but there are things that our brain just holds on to.*

Dad: *I know what you mean.*

Therapist: *Yeah?*

Dad: *Yeah.*

Therapist: *I know that talking about things doesn't make it so that they didn't happen, but it can make you feel less alone with the memories, and it can help you make sense of how these things affected you. Like, it totally makes sense that you don't like buses.*

Dad: *Yeah* (smiles a little).

Therapist: *This is what we're trying to do for Jaylen, to let him know he's not alone, that he can talk about these things, and that, together, we can help him.*

Dad: *Yeah, that's what I want.*

Therapist: *Cool. That's what I want, too. I want to help you help Jaylen, and I'd also like to be able to support you. I was thinking about what we talked about the first time we met. I thought a lot about how you protected Jaylen but how scary it was for you to do that.*

Dad: *Yeah.*

Therapist: *Was it OK talking to me?*

Dad: *Yeah. I guess so. I told Tiana that maybe she was right.*

Therapist: *Yeah?*

Dad: *She told me that we should get help for Jaylen and for me, too.*

Therapist: *What do you think?*

Dad: *You know I'll do anything if it'll help Jaylen.*

Therapist: *I know you would. I'm glad you're here. I think we can both help him.*

Dad: *Yeah. That's good.*

Therapist: *So if it's OK with you, I'll go through this questionnaire, and we'll see if there may be other things that Jaylen's been through or not.*

Dad: *OK.*

Therapist and Dad go through the questionnaire. The dad says no to the first four questions, and then the therapist asks the fifth question.

Therapist: *Has Jaylen ever experienced the death of someone close to him?*

Dad: *Yeah.*

Therapist: *Oh, what happened?*

Dad: *My dad died of a heart attack 'bout last year.*

Therapist: *I am so sorry.*

Dad: *Thanks* (looks down).

Therapist: *Seems like it might have been sudden.*

Dad: *Yeah. None of us expected it.*

Therapist: *I am so sorry . . . . Did Jaylen know him well?*

Dad: *Yeah. He lived just a few blocks from us. Jaylen called him Paw Paw. For a long time, he kept asking where Paw Paw was.*

Therapist: *What did you tell him?*

Dad: *We told him he was up in Heaven with Jesus.*

Therapist: *That's beautiful.*

Dad: *I don't think he understood. He knows about Jesus, but he was mad at Jesus and didn't want Paw Paw to be with him.*

Therapist: *It's hard to understand when you're little . . . sometimes, also when you're big.*

Dad: *Yeah, that's true, but we just gotta trust that it's all for a reason.*

Therapist: *I guess we do . . . . Were you or Jaylen there when your dad died?*

Dad: *No. We just got a call from my sister. They were together. I'm glad she was there.*

Therapist: *Yeah.*

Therapist and Dad sit for a little while.

Therapist: *I know it's hard to talk about, but it's good that I know this. It helps me to know how you've talked to Jaylen about what happens when people die.*

Dad: *Yeah. He's been talking about that.*

Therapist: *Yeah?*

Dad: *Yeah. Jaylen said that Victor (the boy who was shot) is with Jesus and Paw Paw. He said Paw Paw would take care of him.*

Therapist: *That's a pretty amazing thought.*

Dad: *Yes, it is. He's a pretty amazing kid.*

Therapist: *Yes, he is. It was good to see him last week. He really enjoyed playing with you.*

Dad: Smiles.

Therapist: *I know we could talk more about this, and I am hoping that as we continue to get to know each other, we'll continue talking about these things that have affected your family, but I am wondering if for now it's OK if I continue and ask you another question from this form.*

Dad: *Sure. That's fine.*

The therapist continued administering the TESI-PRR questions and completed the trauma screening questionnaire. The only other item that James endorsed for Jaylen was the shooting they had both seen (that he had seen violence in the neighborhood). He explained that 2 months before the referral, he and Jaylen were headed to their neighborhood store. They heard shots, and James pushed Jaylen on the ground behind a car. When they got up, people were screaming. James went toward the screams because he wanted to help. He heard people yelling, "They killed a baby." As they got closer, James saw that a young child was shot and bleeding. The child's mother was screaming and cradling him in her arms. James scooped Jaylen up and turned and ran toward home. The ambulances were coming, and he didn't think it was good for Jaylen to see all of this. He didn't know what to tell Jaylen, so he told him the boy would be OK. Jaylen's mother came home from work later that evening and heard what happened. James and Tiana watched the news after Jaylen went to sleep. Tiana realized in horror that the boy who was killed was an older boy that Jaylen sometimes played with at the park.

In the case of Jaylen Fisher, the trauma screening revealed important sources of stress and grief both for Jaylen and for his father that were influencing how they responded to the shooting. In other families, such as TJ Bishop's and Anthony and Alyssa Craft's, we work with a caregiving relative or foster parent who may not know the child's full history. In these cases, we use the comprehensive trauma screening instrument to guide discussion around what the caregiver knows, what the caregiver wonders about given the way the child behaves, and, if systems permit, what the therapist has learned from other sources (e.g., social workers, prior caregivers, and court reports).

When the reason for referral does not include trauma, as was the case for TJ and so many other children seen in community mental health clinics, the therapist normalizes trauma screening as part of standard clinic procedures and, during early sessions, looks for opportunities to help the caregiver think about stressful situations that the child may have endured, such as being separated from a caregiver, witnessing community violence, or experiencing family conflict that may contribute to the child's difficulties. This often provides a bridge for introducing why we would like to jointly complete the trauma screening instrument.

EXAMPLE.

TJ's aunt initially said that she didn't know anything about what TJ had been through. The therapist acknowledged how difficult this was and then asked if she had any idea what things were like before TJ came to live with her. This simple question opened the door. "TJ's parents used to fight a lot," Rosa said. "They both drank. Things got so bad his mom had to leave. Travis Sr. wouldn't let her take TJ. He kept TJ. The doctors say that after she left, Travis Sr. hurt TJ. He said it was an accident; said TJ fell out of the crib. I don't know what happened. Child protective services took him away. At first, I didn't know about it. TJ was with a couple of other families." As the therapist listened, she heard that TJ had experienced domestic violence, parental substance abuse, possible child abuse, and separation. She also heard how badly his Aunt Rosa felt about this. "I knew things were bad," she said. "I just didn't know how bad things were until TJ's mom called me begging me to take him. I don't know why she didn't tell me sooner." Rosa agreed to go through the trauma screening questionnaire so that she could think about how to ask TJ's mom what had happened. His mom was going through substance abuse treatment and could not come to therapy, but she and Rosa were close. As they went through the questionnaire, the therapist told the aunt some of the details from the child protective services worker's report. The worker had given permission for the therapist to do this. As she heard some of the stories, Rosa repeatedly shook her head and sighed.

The trauma screening instrument facilitates dialogue about difficult topics and the construction of a joint trauma framework; it allows caregivers to begin connecting experience to functioning. Even if, at this stage, families choose not to share information with the therapist, they understand that the therapist is aware that these events happen within the lives of children and families, that therapists are willing to listen and work with them in addressing these challenges, and that events such as these can have negative consequences for children's development. As the therapist completes the questionnaire, opportunities for dialogue and psychoeducation often arise. The therapist keeps the following goals in mind and looks for ports of entry that might permit discussion related to these goals.

- Create a therapeutic climate where the caregiver feels supported in speaking about difficult circumstances, including traumatic experiences.
- Listen for and acknowledge caregiver and family strengths in terms of their response to the traumatic event(s).
- Understand both the caregiver's factual response (whether the caregiver acknowledges what happened) and emotional response (e.g., integrated, triggered, avoidant, mixed) to the child's trauma history.
- Help the caregiver make connections between the child's symptoms and the child's experience.
- Normalize the traumatic response in both the caregiver and the child.
- When the caregiver's affect is integrated, gather information regarding the child's moment-by-moment experience of the traumatic event(s).
- Provide psychoeducation around trauma reminders.
- Listen for potential ruptures in relationships that may have occurred during or as a result of the traumatic experience.

As part of this session, time permitting, the therapist also assesses for the child's trauma symptoms. Doing so within the same session allows the therapist and caregiver to make links between the experiences the caregiver identified the child as having and that child's symptoms.

Session 4

> **Session 4: Suggested Tasks and Procedures**
>
> ❏ Assessment of the caregiver trauma history, preferably using a structured instrument
> ❏ Assessment of caregiver trauma symptoms
> ❏ Assessment of caregiver depression symptoms

The primary goal of this session is to learn about traumatic and stressful events that the caregiver may have experienced, to explore possible links between these experiences and the caregiver's symptoms, and to reflect with the caregiver on how these experiences may influence the way he responds to or parents the child. The session takes place with the caregiver alone and typically involves a 1½- to 2-hour meeting. If more than one caregiver is involved in treatment, each caregiver is assessed separately to protect privacy because many caregivers have not disclosed aspects of their history to anyone before the assessment. Separate meetings give caregivers a chance to make a clear choice about what to tell about themselves to their partner, rather than having disclosures emerge simply as a consequence of the partner having been present during the screening.

The rationale for asking about the parent's personal history is given during this session if the therapist has not already done so in the initial meeting when describing what would happen during the Foundational Phase. Some caregivers come to treatment eager to think about and receive support for their own history so that they can change intergenerational patterns that include violence. Others may feel that treatment is for the child and may be confused about why the therapist is asking about their histories. The explanation offered is that although parents typically come to treatment looking for services for their children, what happened to the child often brings up for parents their own memories of things that happened to them when they were growing up, and the therapist wants to support the parents in managing those feelings so that they can feel better able to support their child.

As with Session 3, the therapist and caregiver must have a protected, reflective space to engage in this process. If there are multiple interruptions, it becomes challenging to help caregivers connect emotionally and make links between past experiences and current reactions. For parents who are mandated to treatment or may otherwise be reluctant to engage, it is in thinking about their own childhood experiences that they often come to understand how their child may be affected by current experiences of violence and danger.

When listening to the caregiver's traumatic past, the therapist often gains a new understanding and empathy for that caregiver's struggles. The therapist may learn that danger was part of the environment where the parent grew up and that, while not fully protective, the parent has actually managed to provide the child with a safer and more loving upbringing than she received. For families who continue to be at risk for exposure to violence, the information gleaned during this session gives the therapist an opening to help the parent reflect on her history of endangerment and to explain how these experiences may influence current expectations about danger and safety. This link between past experience and current traumatic expectations is also used to encourage an attitude that prioritizes safety as a core value for the parent, child, and family.

EXAMPLE.

In early conversations with Jaylen's father, the therapist had begun learning about James' trauma history and developing a framework where James readily saw that his history mattered in how he was responding to his child. As they spoke about his trauma history, using the Life Stressors Checklist—Revised (Wolfe, Kimerling, Brown, Chrestman, & Levin, 1996) to guide their discussion, the therapist learned that, in addition to having witnessed the bus accident when he was 11, losing his dad to a heart attack in the last year, and having recently witnessed the shooting of the young child about 2 months ago, James' life has been marked in numerous ways by community violence. When he was 7, his teenage cousin, who had been living in his home, was killed by rival gang members. James remembered coming back from school and seeing that the police had sectioned off his block. His cousin lay on the ground shot to death about four buildings from his home. James said that his parents' relationship changed significantly after this event. His mother became distant and depressed. She had helped raise her nephew, and she never fully recovered after his loss. James' parents separated and divorced when he was 9. The violence in the neighborhood declined for some time but picked up again, and when he was 16, his brother was targeted by gang members. His mother moved him and his brother out of state to stay with their grandparents, with whom they lived for 2 years. His sister stayed with his dad because she had started nursing school. James missed his father, who lived back in the old neighborhood, but he said it wasn't all bad because he enjoyed spending time with his grandparents. His grandfather took him fishing and, although they didn't catch much, he told James a lot of good stories about the family and about James and his brother when they were growing up. His grandmother made sure he knew how to cook because, she said, "He sure knew how to eat," and James thought he might want to be a chef some day. He returned to his old neighborhood when he was 18 and lived with his father. He met his wife, Tiana, during his first year of community college. Listening to James describe his life and himself gave the therapist a solid grounding to understand his responses to the shooting and to help him modulate his own responses and his responses to his child.

EXAMPLE.

The situation with TJ's Aunt Rosa was different because she was initially confused and reluctant when the therapist said that she wanted to ask Rosa about her history. She became more receptive when the therapist explained that things TJ did might remind her of things she had gone through while growing up. She said that her mother died when she was 9 and that her father was a "scary drunk" who beat her and her sister. She went to college and was able to get a good job, but both she and her sister ended up with violent men. She managed to leave her husband, but her sister became an alcoholic and was in a number of violent relationships. This was why her niece, TJ's mother, lived with Rosa off and on when she was growing up. As Rosa and the therapist completed the trauma screening instrument, Rosa could see that the family violence had passed from generation to generation. She mentioned that when she was an adult, she learned from another relative that her father had been sent to a Native American boarding school and was mistreated and physically abused while he was there. Rosa commented that perhaps this is where the family violence started. She wanted things to change. TJ's mother was in a substance abuse program, but Rosa was pretty sure that she wasn't talking about what had happened to her while growing up or with TJ's father. She told the therapist that it was hard to think about the past, but it helped her make sense of what was happening, and she wished that TJ's mom would have a chance to talk about things in this way.

Session 5

Session 5 is usually the feedback session, which marks the end of the Foundational Phase. In preparation for this session, therapists review what they learned during the assessment process and develop a clinical formulation that includes how the presenting symptoms in the child and the parent may be related to their life events as well as areas of strength and vulnerability in each of them. The therapist reviews the CPP objectives, noting whether positive changes were made in the course of the assessment, and outlines a treatment plan. Therapists in training have commented that it is useful to complete the *CPP Foundational Phase: Assessment and Engagement* forms to ensure that they have done the different elements listed on the Procedural Fidelity: Assessment and Engagement section of the form and to conceptualize their future work with the family using the CPP Case Conceptualization and Content Fidelity section (see Appendix A).

The therapist then meets alone with the caregiver to discuss what they both learned from the assessment, address any urgent concerns, talk about treatment (how it might help, the goals it might address, and what it might involve), and come to an agreement on what to tell the child about the reason for coming to therapy. This session typically lasts 1 hour and may include primary caregivers who may have been involved in some aspects of the Foundational Phase, even if they will not be regularly involved in treatment. For example, Jaylen's parents decided that Tiana, Jaylen's mother, could not typically attend treatment due to her work schedule. She did, however, meet with the therapist once during the assessment, and James and Tiana decided that it would be good for Tiana to be present at the feedback session and at the session where they introduced Jaylen to treatment.

The Foundational Phase does not always result in an offer of CPP. Other treatment configurations may be used when families have significant safety and stabilization needs that interfere with the parent's ability to form a therapeutic partnership with the therapist on behalf of the child. In these cases, the therapist makes recommendations to the parent that may involve individual treatment for the parent or the child, couples or family therapy, substance abuse treatment, or domestic violence interventions.

When CPP is the treatment of choice, the feedback session becomes an opportunity to cover or revisit relevant topics, as described here.

1. *The rationale for dyadic treatment.* The therapist explains that parents/caregivers are the most important people in children's lives, and this emotional importance makes them indispensable in helping the children recover from trauma because children's primary concern is to keep the love and approval of their parents. This premise serves to explain that the therapist will rely on the parent's active participation during

treatment, both as a playmate to the child and as the person who reassures the child that he was not the cause of what happened and that the parent loves him, is sorry for what happened, and wants to take protective care of him.

2. *The need for regular weekly sessions.* Parents do not always know the importance of consistency in coming to sessions regularly and may miss sessions without calling to let the therapist know. The Foundational Phase is a time when parents demonstrate whether or not they are punctual and regular. When this has been a problem, the therapist uses the feedback session to revisit the reasons for the parent's inconsistent attendance and to restate the importance of coming regularly and on time as a way of providing predictability and continuity to the child.

3. *Cultural beliefs about talking about trauma.* The therapist looks for opportunities to explore with the caregiver about how she feels about talking openly about trauma. The therapist may acknowledge that, in most countries and cultures, people are taught to be quiet about traumatic events, particularly interpersonal violence. When caregivers say that talking about trauma or violence within families may not be consistent with the beliefs of their cultural group, the discussion does not stop there. Instead, the therapist begins a dialogue that is respectful of the caregiver's cultural beliefs while explaining why it might be helpful to consider doing something different.

EXAMPLE.

In speaking with TJ's aunt, the therapist used a metaphor that has been helpful for many families. "Imagine," she said "that our bodies are like pots. When bad things happen, it's like the heat has been turned on really high, and it starts to boil inside. Most of us have learned to put a lid on our feelings. In most cultures, we are taught not to talk about bad things and instead to hold them in." She took a toy pot and put a lid on it. "This usually works, but what we are learning is that this can affect our bodies. It can cause changes in the pot. Sometimes we get headaches, our bodies hurt, like our backs and shoulders, we get high blood pressure, or diabetes." As she spoke about these health problems, the aunt nodded her head vigorously. "Well, with tiny bodies like TJ's, it's really hard to keep that pot covered, especially when the heat is turned on really high. Sometimes even though they try to cover it, they blow up." The therapist opened the lid wide. The aunt nodded her head and agreed that TJ often blew up. "One way we help kids is by turning down the heat. Another way is that we can sometimes let them open the lid. We don't want them to blow out, but if we let them talk about and play about what happened, they might release some steam. It may seem strange because talking and playing about things doesn't change what happened, but it helps because he knows he has your support, he's not alone, and you can help him learn that things can be different."

This metaphor opened a door for TJ's aunt. She said that when growing up, she and her sister never talked about how much they missed their mother. Their father used alcohol to numb the pain, and that is also how they learned to deal with sadness and anger. She was grateful that she was able to stop abusing alcohol, but she wished her father and her sister could have found a way to cope with the loss that would have spared them as well as TJ's generation.

Parents and caregivers from many different cultural groups negotiate successfully the process of remaining true to their cultural values while also shifting their attitudes regarding talking about traumatic events once they understand why this will help their child and family. Many of them also find ways of doing so in ways that are culturally compatible. For example, one caregiver from North Africa introduced her child to her therapist, saying, "I told her you are like auntie. We can talk to you about everything because you are like family."

4. *The role of play in CPP.* As part of the assessment, the therapist has an opportunity to observe how the child and caregiver typically play. During the feedback session, the therapist both respects the way the caregiver plays with the child and helps the caregiver understand how one might use play in CPP.

EXAMPLE.
Jaylen's therapist noticed that during the parent–child play assessment, his dad did a lot of teaching within the context of play. They found a doctor's kit in the toy box, and as Jaylen checked out his dad,

his dad continually asked him, "And what do you call this? . . . and how does the doctor use it?" During the feedback, the therapist mentioned how effectively he was teaching Jaylen about the doctor's tools. James noted that Tiana was a physician's assistant, and he wanted Jaylen to know he could grow up and be a doctor or anything he wanted to be. "Dr. Jaylen" his therapist joked. "That would be cool. Well, he knows how to use a stethoscope already." "That's all his mom" James responded. "Well, you're pretty good at teaching him, too" said the therapist. Then the therapist became more serious and said that he wanted to explain that sometimes, in treatment, kids used play to tell their stories. Jaylen might use the doctor's kit to show how he wished the doctors could have helped Victor or to check out his dad and make sure he was OK because they were both in danger. The therapist explained that, in other places or at other times, one might use toys to teach Jaylen vocabulary and how things work, but in therapy, the goal was to understand the story that Jaylen was telling through the toys. James agreed that this would be OK, even though it would be hard if Jaylen played out what happened.

EXAMPLE.

When TJ played with his aunt during the assessment, he made a big lion growl at the little baby lion, and TJ's aunt told him, "Play nice. That's not how you treat a baby." Over and over, TJ used toy animals in aggressive ways, and TJ's aunt responded by quickly asking him to play nice. During the feedback, TJ's therapist talked to the aunt about the way he played with the animals, noting that the aunt was teaching him how we should treat others and how to take care of toys. The aunt beamed and explained that he hadn't learned these things when he lived with his mother, and she wanted to make sure he knew right from wrong. The therapist wondered what they would do in treatment if TJ needed to play out themes related to anger. He had heard people yell and get scary, so maybe he needed to make the animals growl. The aunt said she would think about that, but she did not like it when he growled. In this case, the core phase of treatment involved extensive efforts to bring the aunt to understand the importance of giving TJ freedom to play.

5. *Choice of toys for the sessions.* Careful thought needs to be given to the toys provided for the session. The selection usually includes a family of dolls with the same racial composition and family members as the child's; toys representing objects that were salient in the traumatic event (e.g., a car if there was a car accident, a police car and police dolls if police were involved in the traumatic event) as well as toys that are usually associated with protection (e.g., an ambulance, a medical kit); toys associated with food and cooking; dinosaurs to represent danger and unmodulated feelings; and families of wild and domestic animals to represent threat and home life. During the feedback session, it is helpful to show the parent the toys that will be used in treatment and to explain the reasons for their selection so that they are prepared for what will happen during the first treatment session with the child.

EXAMPLE.

The therapist made sure to show Jaylen's father the ambulance because, during the assessment, the dad mentioned that they saw the ambulance arrive at the scene, and Jaylen now froze whenever he heard sirens. The father pressed the siren on the top of the toy ambulance and listened. He said that just hearing the sound brought back memories of that day. "Will it be OK to have the ambulance in treatment?" his therapist asked. The dad answered that it would probably help Jaylen. This response gave the therapist a clue that he would need to attend to the father's response to the sound of the siren when Jaylen played with the ambulance.

EXAMPLE.

TJ's therapist reminded the aunt of her comment that TJ gorged himself on food and took food anyway when his aunt told him he could not have another helping. The aunt thought that he might have been often hungry while in his parents' care. Food-related toys were used in the sessions to assess how he used them and to help him feel safe in the knowledge that at his aunt's house, she made sure that he had a healthy amount of food to eat.

6. *The child's need for emotion regulation while processing trauma.* The feedback session is an opportunity to offer or revisit anticipatory guidance

about how the child might act during the sessions. One theme is that joyful playing is as much a part of the treatment as talking or playing about difficult things. Another theme is describing how children may manage strong feelings by shifting rapidly between different activities. A metaphor that has been helpful with many parents is to liken adult and child bodies to cups, sometimes using the teacups in the play set as illustrations. The cups (i.e., the bodies) get full of feeling when talking about difficult things. Young children have smaller cups than adults, so their cups get full faster. Many young children have an intuitive knowledge of when they can't hold any more negative feelings in their bodies, and then they often shift activities. The sessions give children a place to grow in their capacity to talk and play about their difficult feelings without being overwhelmed, and children show us their own particular ways of regulating their emotions.

7. *The parent's perspective of the treatment.* Co-creating a treatment plan involves eliciting the parent's perspective, questions, and possible hesitations or concerns. In families where there are ongoing risks to safety, the therapist considers with the parent how safety will be addressed during treatment. Sometimes, it emerges that the other parent does not know about the treatment, although legal custody is shared by both parents. In these situations, we explain that the other parent needs to be notified about the child's treatment because keeping treatment secret would represent an undue emotional burden for the child. This often leads to a lengthy discussion of the parent's concerns about the other parent. In some situations, it is in fact not possible to legally provide treatment unless there is a court order—for example, when the other parent has legal custody but does not want treatment for the child. If these issues have not emerged during the assessment, the feedback session is the time to make sure that there are no legal obstacles to treatment.

EXAMPLE.

In the case of Susan Chan, the therapist raised her concern with the mother about the safety of providing treatment for Susan because the child continued to have regular contact with her father, who did not know that Susan and her mother would be participating in trauma treatment as the result of their domestic violence experience. Given the father's violence, the therapist was concerned about how the father would respond when he found out. The mother responded that Susan was only 2 years old and would not say anything. The therapist pointed out that Susan was a very verbal toddler, and her language was developing rapidly. What would happen if she asked her daddy why he hurt her mommy? The therapist and mother decided that, in the beginning, treatment might involve only meetings between the two of them to focus on how the mother could speak with Susan about what happened and help her feel safer. The mother and father were going back to court to discuss custody arrangements in 2 months, and she planned to bring up the issue of therapy with the father at that time. Two and a half months later, after the mother's lawyer talked in court about the therapy and the father agreed, the therapist and mother planned how they would introduce Susan to treatment.

Although therapists offer feedback throughout the assessment process, the feedback session represents a turning point in the consolidation of engagement and treatment planning because it allows the parent(s) and therapist to clarify their understanding of the connection between the child's and family's experience; the child's behavior, feeling, and developmental functioning; and the ways that treatment may help. This "triangle" of explanations is depicted in Figure 1. Throughout the course of the Foundational Phase, the therapist and caregiver have been jointly building bridges connecting experience and functioning. Experience includes what happened, such as the child's exposure to traumatic and stressful events, prenatal conditions (e.g., exposure to substance abuse or to maternal stress during pregnancy), and family circumstances. The role of constitutional characteristics and temperamental style is integrated into the formulation when these factors appear to play a significant role because children with extreme regulatory sensitivities may be overwhelmed by events that might be viewed as moderately stressful to other children. The parents of these children are often perplexed by their reactions, particularly if they do not share their child's sensitivity, and a framework that integrates both the specifics of the event and the way it was perceived (its threat value given a child's constitutional proclivities) often enables the parents to better understand the child's response.

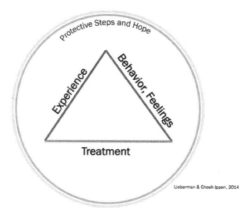

Figure 1. The Triangle of Explanations

The concluding task of the feedback session is to develop with the parent a working agreement about what and how the child will be told in the next session about why she is coming to treatment. Key phrases that guide the construction of the triangle include the following:

- Experience: You saw, you heard . . . (e.g., your mom and dad fight and hit each other).
- Behavior/Feelings: And now, you . . . (e.g., sometimes worry, hit when you get angry, get upset when you think people are going to leave).
- Treatment: This is a place where . . . .

In working with the parent on this formulation, the therapist also keeps in mind that hope is an essential component of treatment and makes sure to highlight and support the protective actions that were taken by the parent, including bringing the child to treatment and moving out of violent circumstances.

EXAMPLE.

When TJ's therapist and aunt thought about how they might introduce treatment to him, they acknowledged that there was much that they did not know about his early experience, and, at this point, Rosa was not able to speak to TJ's mother because his mother was in an inpatient substance abuse treatment program. They agreed that they would tell TJ that his mom and dad had problems, that there had been scary fighting, that TJ had been hurt, and that his mom had asked Aunt Rosa to take care of him and keep him safe. They also planned to tell him that his parents' fighting made him very scared and angry and that his aunt was bringing him to a place where he could learn not to hit or hurt others when he got mad. The aunt liked this last part. She said that TJ really needed to know how to calm down and stop hitting. She was concerned that TJ could not listen for long without becoming aggressive, and this led the therapist to propose the use of dolls to guide the telling of TJ's story—a suggestion that the aunt accepted readily.

As a final note, when parents have a trauma history that is affecting their functioning and perception of the child, it is often helpful to develop a triangle linking the parent's experience with the parent's feelings and behavior and how treatment may help. For example, TJ's aunt gained a new understanding of how her early experiences were linked to her fear that TJ would continue the family pattern of violence. Although she did not want individual treatment, she started to find TJ's treatment helpful for herself as well as for the child. Other caregivers respond to their new understanding of themselves by seeking individual treatment to complement the work that they are doing with their child.

PHASE 2
CORE INTERVENTION PHASE

The Core Intervention Phase typically begins with a 1-hour session where the child is introduced to the treatment and the dyadic treatment format begins. This first session is described next. An exception is made when the parent is not able to acknowledge the harm caused to the child by the traumatic event(s)—this stance jeopardizes the child's safety and well-being. In these situations, the therapist may choose to work with the parent individually for a limited period of time to determine whether therapeutic change in the parent makes dyadic CPP feasible.

Introducing the Child to CPP

Therapist: *Do you know who I am?*

Child: *Yes, you are office people.*

Many years ago, a trainee told this story in supervision. She had just begun working with a mother and her 4-year-old daughter and was in the process of introducing herself and explaining to the child why she and her mom would be coming to see her. When she asked the child if she knew who she was, the child's response made all of those who heard her story laugh: "You are office people." This was a perceptive observation. This particular child had met with numerous office people. There was the child welfare worker, her speech-language therapist who saw her at school, her occupational therapist, her former individual therapist who did nondirective play therapy, and, now, her new child–parent psychotherapist. As supervisor and supervisee thought about what the child might be conveying, they realized that all of the service providers dressed in the same semiprofessional garb and spoke in similar ways to children. It made sense that this child had classified all of them together as "office people," and yet each of them did different things. This child's perception underscores the importance of describing in clear, emotionally meaningful terms the reason that the child is coming for treatment. The goal is for the child to know that although the CPP therapist may look like an office person, the therapist is the kind of office person who knows how to help with difficult feelings and challenging experiences.

The first treatment session implements the agreement made with the parent during the feedback session. The parent or the therapist describes the experience–behavior/feeling–treatment triangle and gives the child permission to show and tell how he or she feels. Many parents report that "speaking about the unspeakable" with the child was easier than anticipated and brought them some relief.

> **EXAMPLE.**
> TJ's therapist used a baby doll and said that when TJ was little, he lived with his mother. She put the mom doll and the baby doll on top of a chair together to represent that home. She said that Aunt Rosa didn't know how things were over there. She put a doll for Aunt Rosa on another chair separate from the mom and TJ dolls. She knew his mommy loved him a lot, but she heard that his mommy and daddy had problems. Sometimes, grown-ups fought, and TJ got hurt really badly. TJ listened intently and then started hitting his leg. The therapist paused, and, remembering the details in the child protective services report, she said, "You got hurt real bad on your leg when you were very little." She looked at the aunt, and the aunt nodded. The therapist

picked up the TJ doll and pointed to his leg. "Poor little TJ had a lot of owies." She gave the doll to the aunt and said, "Aunt Rosa didn't know things were so scary, but when she found out, she worked hard to get you." Aunt Rosa held the doll, and TJ went over to his aunt and looked at the little doll. "He's gonna be OK now," Aunt Rosa said. "TJ is with me now." "Yeah," the therapist said. "He's with you, and you're keeping him safe, but we think that sometimes when TJ feels angry or sad, maybe he doesn't feel safe, and he hits people." TJ looked up. The therapist continued, "Well, Aunt Rosa knows you saw hitting, but she wants to show you there are other things you can do when you get mad. That's why she's bringing you here. When you come here, we can talk and play about what things were like when you lived with mom and dad." The therapist brought out a father doll and put the father doll near the mother doll. "And you can learn what to do when you get mad." TJ walked over to the father doll and, with one swipe of his hand, knocked him off the table. Then, he went to the other toys. He drove the cars into the cabinets, and when he found the police car with a siren, he kept pressing the siren over and over. "You see how he is?" his aunt said. She still found it difficult to remember in moments of heightened emotion how TJ's behavior expressed what he had experienced.

This introduction to treatment includes the essential elements of the triangle of explanations. TJ seemed to be listening, and, at times, his actions seemed to be contributing to the story the therapist and his aunt had begun to tell. His behavior as the session continued—and the aunt's response—illustrated clearly what the treatment should focus on. TJ's dysregulated behavior continued to worry his aunt, so much so that she had great difficulty looking past this behavior to the story and feelings he was trying to convey. During the Foundational Phase, the therapist and aunt had developed a solid relationship and had engaged in important dialogue that supported the treatment during the Core Intervention Phase. More aspects of this treatment are discussed in Section III.

Clinicians learning CPP report that introducing treatment to the child by naming the trauma is one of the most challenging aspects of the model because they are afraid of retraumatizing the child. Although neither children nor adults become retraumatized by the mention in a safe situation of an event they remember—although they certainly may become uncomfortable—the fear of hurting the child and the parent is a powerful obstacle to addressing the trauma directly. Avoidance of trauma reminders is one of the PTSD diagnostic clusters that is difficult to address, and therapists may themselves develop a vicarious avoidance because affect tends to be contagious, and therapists are trained to be empathic with the families they treat. This effort is misguided in the case of very young children, who have not yet developed rigid defenses against feeling and who are usually eager for adult explanations and support for their fears. The example in the box shows a new CPP therapist who uses the conventional introduction to treatment in his his first session with Jaylen, with the father and mother present.

Jaylen Fisher: Standard Introduction to Treatment, Not Trauma Informed[3]

Therapist: *Hi, Jaylen. My name is Martín. Your mom and dad have been telling me that you've been having trouble sleeping and also listening to them. This is a place where we can talk and play about how you are feeling. You can talk about if you are happy, mad, or scared. We have lots of toys* (shows toys). *We have puppets that we can use to talk about feelings, we have puzzles, and we have dinosaurs.*

Dad: *Jaylen really likes dinosaurs*

Therapist: *Great, shall we play with those?*

Jaylen spent most of the session playing with his mother, father, and the therapist. They made dinosaur families, and the baby dinosaur was lovingly cared for by the big dinosaurs. Jaylen said that they were going to have a baby dinosaur. His mom smiled and noted that they had told Jaylen that soon there would be a new baby in the family. Jaylen went and lay down on his mother. The therapist noted that if the parents wanted, they could read books to prepare Jaylen for the birth of the new sibling. Mom thought that might be helpful. Jaylen then wanted to play with the puzzles. The family spent the remainder of the session building puzzles.

---

[3] Reprinted with permission from Ghosh Ippen et al. (2014)

The parents and therapist agreed during the feedback session that the treatment would involve Jaylen and his father, and during the next two sessions, the child and father played again with the dinosaurs. The little dinosaurs got into fights and got mad and hit the big dinosaurs. The therapist said, "Oh, the dinosaurs are mad," and guided the father in showing Jaylen how to use words with the big dinosaurs instead of hitting them. The therapist thought the father was responsive and effective with Jaylen.

The therapist described these sessions in supervision, saying that the family was doing good work, but he was a little anxious because neither Jaylen nor the father had mentioned the shooting. As he described the introductory session, it became clear that Martín had not himself mentioned the shooting in describing the reason for treatment and as a result had not clearly connected experience, functioning, and treatment. As a new trauma-trained clinician, Martín had reverted back to the traditional way of introducing children to therapy and had not clearly named the experience that had brought the family to treatment. In clinical supervision, Martín asked, "Do you mean I should really tell him he's coming to therapy because he saw another little kid get shot? Shouldn't we just wait and see if he brings it up?" "It is so hard to think of saying something like that," his supervisor noted. "Let's think of what might make sense to you and to Jaylen's parents, but it is important that we have the courage to name what has happened because Jaylen already knows what has happened. He was there, and he has nightmares about it. He needs the adults to help him know it is safe to talk about it." As they talked, Martín remembered a story he had heard during the introductory CPP training. A therapist had just begun working with a child who had been seen in treatment for several years with another therapist. As they began talking about the child's experience of violence, he asked the child whether she had told her previous therapist about this. "No," she said. "She wasn't ready." Martín acknowledged that perhaps he, too, had not been ready, but he wanted to get ready, and with his supervisor's support, he did. Martín decided to meet separately with the father to plan how to tell Jaylen that it was OK to talk about the shooting and all that he had experienced. They then met with Jaylen.

Jaylen Fisher: Reintroduction to Treatment[4]

Therapist: *Jaylen, your dad told me that once you and he were going to the store.* Takes two dolls. *Here is Jaylen and here is Daddy, and they are going to the store.*

Jaylen: Gets up and wanders away.

Dad: *Jaylen, you need to listen to Martín.*

Therapist: *I wonder if Jaylen remembers the day that we are talking about and finds it hard to listen.*

Dad: Nods. *Jaylen doesn't like going to the store anymore. He also doesn't want me to go.*

Therapist: *Jaylen, your dad thinks that you remember that day when you were going to the store and something scary happened. Your friend Victor got hurt. The ambulance came to help, but Victor was hurt really badly, and he died. Lots of people are so sad and angry that he got hurt and died.*

Jaylen: *I gave him a bear.*

Dad: *Yes, Jaylen.* Dad turns to the therapist and explains. *We brought one of Jaylen's teddy bears to the spot. He saw that other people left toys, and he wanted to know why. His mom told him that people were giving them to Victor so that he would see them from Heaven and know how much we missed him. He wanted to give Victor one of his bears.*

Jaylen: *Victor is with Paw Paw.*

Therapist: *Yes, Jaylen. Daddy told me that Victor is with Paw Paw and Jesus.*

Jaylen: *I want to see Paw Paw.*

Dad: *Jaylen. I told you, we can't see people when they're in Heaven, but they can see us.*

Therapist: *You miss Paw Paw.*

Jaylen: Nods.

---

[4] Reprinted with permission from Ghosh Ippenet et al. (2014)

Therapist: *It was sad when Paw Paw died.*

Jaylen: *Daddy cried.*

Therapist: *Daddy misses Paw Paw just like you do.*

Dad: Nods.

Jaylen: Goes off and looks at the toys.

Therapist: *So, Jaylen, you're going to come here. Sometimes, it will just be you and Daddy, and sometimes, Mommy will come, too.*

Jaylen: *My mommy works.*

Therapist: *Yes she does, but sometimes, she will also come, like when we played with dinosaurs.*

Jaylen: *I want the dinosaurs.*

Dad: *Hey, J., you gotta ask nicely.*

Jaylen: *Please.*

Therapist: To dad. *That OK with you?*

Dad: Nods.

Therapist: To Jaylen. *Want to see them? You played with them before.*

Jaylen: Nods excitedly.

Therapist: Takes out the dinosaurs and identifies the family. Then, he takes another dinosaur. *This is me. Hi, Jaylen. Hi, James.*

Jaylen: *Hi . . . what's your name?*

Dad: *Martín.*

Therapist: Using the dinosaur. *Yes, my name is Martín. I'm here to help you and Daddy. Daddy said sometimes you have bad dreams, and you get really upset when Mommy or Daddy leave. He thinks sometimes you are scared because of what happened to Victor. It was very scary. When you come here, we can talk about that day, and Daddy can help you when you feel scared or angry.* Turns to dad. *Is that about right?*

Dad: *Yep.* Turns to Jaylen. *We can talk to Martín about Victor or about anything. He's gonna help us.*

Jaylen: Wanders around the room and sees the ambulance. *An ambulance.*

Therapist: *Yes. We have an ambulance.*

Jaylen: Tries really hard to take a boy doll and put it in the ambulance.

Dad: Dad is watching but does not move.

Therapist: *Here, I can help you.* Puts the doll in the ambulance.

Jaylen: Takes the ambulance and drives it around and around. It smashes into things.

Dad: *Be careful, Jaylen. You're going to break it.*

Jaylen drives around some more. The father starts texting on his phone. He says he wants Tiana to know what time they are coming home. Jaylen gets up and goes into the cabinets. He gets out a tool set and asks his dad to build with him. The father gets on the floor and plays at building a house with Jaylen. Later, Jaylen finds the doctor's kit in the cabinets. He pulls it out and begins checking his dad.

This session shows the increased comfort of the therapist in addressing the shooting and linking it with Jaylen's feelings. This trauma-informed introduction enabled Jaylen to bring up reparative steps (giving his bear to the child who was killed) as well as other adversities (his grandfather's death) and continuing efforts at repair (the ambulance, the medical kit). This session showed his clear engagement in trauma work once he was offered the opportunity to do so.

Children show a wide variety of responses to the introduction of the triangle as a condensed combination of trauma narrative (what happened, how the child is now showing how she is feeling about it) and protective narrative (what the parent tried to do to make things better, treatment as a place to learn to be and feel safe). The child's responses serve to inform the therapist's understanding of the child's temperamental style, strengths, and vulnerabilities in coping with trauma reminders. The therapist's evolving clinical formulation of the child's style, in turn, serves to inform treatment. The following examples illustrate some of the responses that children show to being told about the reason for treatment.

EXAMPLE.

José was a father who had entered treatment with his two children, Josesito (3 years old) and Valeria (5 years old). José had immigrated from Mexico as a child, crossing the border by himself when he was 11 years old. He was placed in foster care and was adopted by a loving family. He met the children's mother, Angelina, in high school and had a tempestuous relationship with her that involved physical fighting followed by passionate reconciliations. They both liked to go to parties and drink, but he hoped they would settle down after they had children. They did not. When Josesito was 2½ years old and Valeria was 4½ years old, their parents had a severe altercation with the children present, where José slammed Angelina against the car door, shoved her into the car, and later broke the car window. He later reported that he had been furious with her because she had had affairs with numerous men. He also reported that, on a prior occasion, he had smashed the TV and punched his fist through the wall. According to him, these were the only two times he had been violent. He said that Angelina had been consistently aggressive, throwing plates and lamps at him and attempting to scratch him when they argued. José sought treatment immediately after being released from jail for domestic violence, saying that he wanted help for himself and for his children. He wanted them to know that what he did was wrong and that he was very sorry. During the first CPP session with the children, he began the session by apologizing to them. He told them that hitting their mother was wrong and that he knew he had scared them. Before he could say much more, Valeria launched into a series of questions. "And, Daddy, why did you do it?" she said. "Why did you break the window and throw the TV?" Valeria was looking for answers for why her usually loving daddy could have become so scary, and her dad could acknowledge what had happened and begin to respond to her. As José and Valeria talked, Josesito was becoming more and more dysregulated by this direct conversation. At first, he played with the animals and growled, but then, after climbing around on his dad in an anxious way, he pulled him toward the door and said in an anxious tone of voice that he wanted to leave. The different responses of the two children became an integral focus of the treatment.

EXAMPLE.

Gina, a 4-year-old White girl, was referred for treatment for suspected sexual abuse by her father. The reports of what had happened and how Gina disclosed it came from her mother, who was in a heated custody battle with Gina's father, and the abuse had not been verified by the child sexual abuse interview that Gina had undergone at a child abuse center. The therapist and the mother had to negotiate what to tell Gina as the reason for treatment because the mother wanted to refer to it as "sexual abuse," but the therapist did not want to affirm an event that had not been confirmed. The compromise agreement between therapist and mother involved the therapist telling the child that when her mother and father lived together, they used to fight a lot, and her father did things that her mother thought were scary and confusing for Gina. With the mother's agreement, the therapist also said that her mother thought Gina was missing her father because she had not seen him for a long time (9 months) and that Gina seemed sad and had a hard time playing with other children at school. Treatment was to be a place where Mom and therapist could help Gina talk about her feelings and about what things were like in "the other house." Immediately after this introduction, Gina turned her back to the therapist and cooked. She continued to cook for over three sessions, offering food only to her mom. On the fourth session, she offered the therapist a plate with toast. For many more sessions, Gina played without any mention of her father. She drew pictures of princesses, she played about school and children who were mean to her, and she cooked nearly every session. Then, at one session, while in the waiting room, she found a doll; it was a cloth doll and had removable clothes. She pulled down his pants and exclaimed excitedly to her mom, "This is the 'bad man' of my dreams." "Shall we bring him in the room?" the therapist asked. "Yes," she said, and they did. Once the man was brought into the room, the therapist asked what should happen to the bad man. Should he get punished for doing bad things? Gina looked up excitedly and said, "Yes!" The therapist mentioned she had a jail. "Go and get it," Gina said. The therapist did, and for the remainder of this session and the next couple of sessions, she punished the bad man with the mother's and therapist's help, setting up an alligator and a lizard as his jailers and at one time remarking that they would eat his liver if he was bad again.

EXAMPLE.

Desheon, a 4-year-old African American boy, came to treatment with his grandmother 6 months after his mother was murdered. He was not present and had not been told what happened, but he had nightmares about her murder. He had recently been expelled from school and was in danger of being expelled from a second school due to his aggressive behavior, but the therapist observed that he was well mannered and obedient with his grandmother. Following his introduction to treatment, which included a statement about the fact that his mother had been killed (a fact he already knew), Desheon played out a violent and confusing scene. He took out the child dolls and put them in a circle, perhaps acting out a school scene, although he did not name it as such. Then, he took a Batman doll and had the Batmobile run repeatedly all over the dolls, including himself. The therapist said that "bad things were happening to the kids." The grandma shook her head and said, "I thought Batman was supposed to be one of the good guys." Then Desheon identified a doll as his grandma. "She has nice hair," he said, and the grandma agreed. Within 5 minutes, the Batmobile had run over the grandma doll and all the adult figures that Desheon had selected. The Batmobile continued its path of destruction, and the therapist watched as the grandma's body stiffened slightly.

These examples show that children respond very differently to the introduction to treatment. The therapist and parent need to adapt and transition from the Foundational Phase, where they were able to engage in adult conversation, to sessions with the child and multiple forms of communication, including play. Within this introductory session, the therapist attempts to keep three therapeutic strategies in mind.

1. *Track the child's response to the introduction to treatment.* The therapist makes note of the child's behavioral responses (e.g., becoming aggressive, needing soothing from the caregiver, moving away) and play themes that emerge, the sequencing of these themes, and the emotional tone of these responses. Therapists who are learning CPP find it helpful to write detailed narrative notes as a way of later reflecting on what transpired during the session. It is helpful to differentiate between the distressing content of what the child may narrate and the child's emotional reaction. Many children, like Jaylen and Valeria, play out or talk about distressing scenes in a remarkably integrated and focused manner, as if they had been waiting for the opportunity to describe and try to make sense of their experience. A therapist described a poignant story that captured this beautifully. She was working with a very aggressive young child who had been adopted as a toddler and was supposedly unaware that he was adopted. After much work, his parents agreed to tell him his story. Together with the therapist, they told him that when he was very little, he had another mommy, and she had problems and hurt him. The boy, now 5 years old, looked at them, sighed deeply, and answered, "I know."

2. *Remain aware and supportive of the parent.* Young children's play and behavior can be a kind of siren's song, pulling the therapist toward the child and away from the parent. The parent, who has been meeting individually with the therapist during the Foundational Phase, may feel this response as a loss of the therapist's attention and care. This response may be especially detrimental to the treatment when the child's behavior elicits negative emotional reactions in the parent. In addition, without the therapist's support, the parent may not understand what the child may be trying to convey if the child is using the vehicles of symbolic play or behavioral re-enactments. This may lead the parent to feel confused, unimportant, or disengaged, or to misunderstand what the child is saying. For these reasons, it is critical that during the introduction, the therapist take care to visually track the caregiver's response and provide emotional support and translation as needed.

3. *Provide a benevolent or developmentally informed explanation for negative reactions/behaviors.* Young children's responses to the introduction to treatment can take surprising forms. Similar to Desheon, who ran over

the grandmother doll with a car, they may enact violent scenes that would be disturbing for any parent. Children may use play to kill off their caregivers, make dinosaurs eat babies, have the houses they build destroyed by cars that plow into them and animals that batter them, and terrible fires where no one can be saved. Parents watching this play often feel helpless and disturbed. Without the therapist's support, they may question whether therapy is, in fact, therapeutic and helpful. A benevolent, developmentally informed explanation helps to keep development moving toward health. The therapist may explain to the parent that the play may be an expression of the child's deepest fears that something could happen to the caregiver, or it may be a re-enactment of what he witnessed or experienced. Their play, even when disturbing, contains the urgent message of a request for help.

Core Intervention Phase: Beyond the Child's Introduction to CPP

Sessions during the core intervention phase last usually 1 hour, although at times, a longer format (e.g., 1½ hours) may be warranted.

- On occasion, the therapist and caregiver may observe that the child begins processing difficult content only after an extended period, warming up by "simply playing." Although this may shift as sessions progress, the therapist and caregiver may decide that lengthening sessions to 1½ hours would allow the child the time that he needs.
- At times, it may make sense to extend and split the session so that the therapist can meet both with the caregiver alone and with the caregiver and child together.
- When there are urgent safety or stabilization concerns, extended sessions involving safety planning and case management may be required.
- In rural areas, where the family travels long distances to the clinic or the therapist makes home visits, it may be more cost effective to have longer sessions, provided that the child and parent seem to benefit from the extended time.

An intervention manual cannot address the thousands of individual circumstances that emerge in the course of treatment. The next section offers commonly emerging domains of intervention and specific therapeutic strategies that need to be tailored to individual situations. The clinical vignettes illustrate *ports of entry*, the term used by Daniel Stern (1995) to describe clinical moments where intervention is most likely to promote therapeutic progress. Ports of entry serve as the CPP unit of intervention, and what the therapist does or says in response to these clinical moments shapes interactions and the course of the intervention.

The behavioral/representational domains described here start with play because this is the universal language of childhood. Healthy children play in healthy ways, and children who need help to become healthy use play as an avenue of expression for their needs. The remaining domains of intervention are organized in terms of their developmental salience. Very young infants, who have not yet developed a coherent organization of the attachment system, tend to respond to stressful and traumatizing conditions with sensorimotor disorganization and disruption of biological rhythms. As the child develops and organizes responses to danger in relation to the attachment figure, interactional behaviors involving proximity and contact-seeking, avoidance, resistance, and aggression become increasingly salient, although sensorimotor disorganization and disruption of biological rhythms may persist. Among older toddlers and preschool children, who are increasingly capable of mental representation, language and symbolic play become vehicles for the expression of affective experience and their construction of reality. The domains described here should be seen as concurrent and overlapping, with some domains prevailing at different times, depending on the child's developmental stage, constitutional characteristics, and environmental supports and challenges.

Timing of Therapeutic Interventions

The timing of specific interventions is guided by two overarching principles.

1. *Try the simplest and most direct intervention first.* For example, if providing developmental guidance is sufficient to change inappropriate parental behavior, exploring the childhood origins of this behavior is unnecessary and might be intrusive and inappropriate.
2. *Encourage the parent to intervene on behalf of the child whenever possible.* Take direct action with the child only if this effort fails or if the circumstances demand it. For example, if a child is about to engage in risky

behavior, calling the parent's attention to it might be sufficient to mobilize protective action. If the parent does not respond or if the child is in immediate danger, the clinician needs to act quickly and decisively to protect the child. The intervention items specify forms of intervention that are the hallmarks of CPP.

In applying these two principles, clinicians must be aware of the context in which the intervention takes place. Timing, although difficult to define, is essential in clinical practice. The same intervention may be successful or it may backfire, depending on when and how it is implemented. In deciding on the timing of an intervention, parameters to consider are as follows:

- The culturally determined values and child-rearing mores of the family,
- The quality and sturdiness of the therapeutic alliance,
- The level and style of the parent's and child's psychological functioning, and
- The mood of the moment in the parent and the child.

These factors are described in greater detail throughout the manual.

Domains of Intervention

This section describes 12 clinical domains that are particularly salient as the focus of the intervention. The ports of entry constitute a brief abstract statement describing an intervention strategy and are followed by clinical vignettes from narrative notes from sessions. The vignettes reflect the work of different clinicians with different levels of training and who are working with a range of families of diverse backgrounds. The purpose of the vignettes is to illustrate ways of being and responding, not to model specific phrasing.

Domain I: Play

Play serves multiple functions in development. Through play, children experiment with different approaches to their relationship with other people and their mastery of the world. Erik Erikson (1964) proposed that play is the childhood version of a lifelong human propensity: setting up model situations to experiment with different ways of controlling reality. In this sense, play is a tool for learning to manage anxiety. It gives children a safe space where they can experiment at will, suspending the rules and constraints of physical and social reality. Play allows children to enter into the minds of other people and to give meaning to their own and to the other's actions, plans, and wishes.

The centrality of play in children's lives makes it a natural vehicle for therapeutic intervention. In his book, *Playing and Reality*, Winnicott (1971) went so far as to conceive of psychotherapy as a form of play when he wrote:

> Psychotherapy has to do with two people playing together. The corollary of this is that where playing is not possible then the work done by the therapist is directed towards bringing the patient from a state of not being able to play into a state of being able to play (p. 38).

This statement is particularly relevant to the treatment of young children, for whom play is often the preferred mode of emotional expression and social communication. Children use play to repeat an anxiety-provoking situation, to change its outcome, or to avoid it altogether by changing all the parameters of the situation or by choosing a different play theme. The long history of the psychodynamic understanding of play hinges on an effort to understand the symbolic meaning of its content and to then give it verbal interpretation. In this approach, the play content is seen as the symbolic expression of unconscious wishes, and the therapist's role is construed as the translator of these hidden wishes into words for the purpose of bringing them to consciousness (A. Freud, 1936/1966; Klein, 1932).

These approaches, which emphasize interpretation of the underlying measures of play, have in recent years been expanded to include an appreciation for the multiple and overlapping functions of play (Slade & Wolf, 1994). The importance of "simply playing," involving a noninterpretive, collaborative enterprise between child and therapist, has been persuasively described as a way of helping children to build psychological structures and to make meaning of their experience (Slade, 1994). "Simply playing" serves simultaneous functions, among them (a) developing a narrative that brings together fragmented, disorganized, and incomprehensible elements into a more or less coherent pattern; (b) integrating affect into the narrative in order to promote modulation and integration of affect; (c) promoting a therapeutic relationship in which the child is able to communicate a range of feelings and experiences to the therapist; and (d) developing self-reflection by stepping outside the play and finding meaning in it as a joint enterprise between child and therapist (Slade, 1994).

Overwhelming anxiety that cannot be contained in the play sequence leads to a disruption of play, and this disruption provides a useful clue to the child's inner experience (Erikson, 1964). When the child is traumatized, the character of play becomes driven, so that the child may repeat again and again the concrete representation of the traumatic scene without gaining relief from an increased mastery of it or from the ability to move from concrete to symbolic levels of representation (Gaensbauer, 1995; Terr, 1991). In these situations, "simply playing" is the first step toward helping the child contain overwhelming affect, tell the story, and convey the unspeakable horror of it to someone who understands and protects.

CPP builds on these functions of play by encouraging play between the parent and the child. This is particularly useful in the case of traumatized children. Because young children rely on their parents for safety and protection, it is of the utmost importance that the parent (and not just the therapist) understands the meaning and impact of the trauma on the child. For young children, the joint meaning created with the therapist in individual psychotherapy is incomplete because this meaning is not available to the child's most important organizer of psychological experience—the parent.

Play functions differently as a therapeutic modality in CPP than in individual psychotherapy. Both therapies rely on play to access the child's inner world, but in CPP, the clinician shares his or her knowledge of that world with the parent. This sharing enables the parent, alone or together with the therapist, to join in the child's play and to help the child construct different, more adaptive meanings of people and experiences.

There is no substitute for witnessing the child at play as a means to fully understanding how the child experiences the world and the important people in it. In joint parent–child sessions, the child–parent psychotherapist serves as a mediator between the child's play and the parent's understanding of it. The therapist's role, in this sense, is helping the parent and the child create joint meaning by playing together and, when timely, stepping out of the play and reflecting on it. This process involves helping the parent tolerate the painful affects and internal representations that the child conveys through play for the purpose of a more real, less dismissive, and less idealizing portrayal of the way things are for the child. Interpretation of play content is used when both the parent and the child are able to move from enacting to reflecting.

Often, the parent is unable to play or to join in the child's play. At other times, the child cannot play with the parent but uses the therapist as a partner in play. Some children engage in only solitary play for weeks at a time, rebuffing the parent's or the therapist's efforts to join in. Sometimes, the play is chaotic, vague, and disorganized; sometimes, it is excessively rigid and constricted, or limited to concrete activities such as cutting and pasting or board games. These variations need to be understood as stages in the development of the child's capacity to play rather than as definitive statements about the capacity of the child and the parent to play together.

When the clinician conveys a conviction that child and parent can find a way of playing together, they most likely will be able to do so. On the way to this goal, there may be detours and diversions, which may include periods of individual play between child and therapist, either alone or in the presence of the parent. The underlying intention, however, needs to be the involvement of the parent and child in joint play. A successful treatment outcome is when the child and the parent no longer need the therapist to be with each other in developmentally appropriate and rewarding ways.

Many parents do not know about the importance of play in children's development. They may consider that "just playing" is a waste of time that does not constitute "real therapy." It is advisable to use reflective and unstructured developmental guidance to help the parent understand that play is the vehicle through which children learn, experiment with their realities, and express their feelings.

PORTS OF ENTRY AND CLINICAL EXAMPLES

1. **The therapist uses the child's play as an opportunity to help the parent participate in the play in a variety of roles that promote protective narratives such as efforts to save the child from danger.**

   EXAMPLE.
   Sandra witnessed her mother being brutally attacked and severely injured when she was 3 years old. At 4 years old, she is brought to treatment because she is increasingly frightened and withdrawn at school and is not keeping pace with the classroom activities. Her ability to learn is severely affected, and her speech is much regressed. In

joint child–mother sessions, Sandra spends weeks creating again and again an impregnable fortress using the playroom furniture. She hides inside this fortress and does not allow anybody to come inside. The therapist helps the mother understand the protective meaning of the fortress while speaking to Sandra from outside the "walls." As the mother understands, she begins to speak to Sandra about the terrible attack they suffered. With the therapist's encouragement, the mother also stresses the steps she has taken to make sure she and Sandra are safe. Sandra responds by first opening a crack on the fortress wall and then progressively alternating between coming halfway out of the fortress and inviting the mother in. After several months, she says to her mother, "He came in because I did not close the door on time." The mother understands the daughter's sense of responsibility and self-blame, and she says, "You are a little girl. You could not close the door. It is not your fault that I got hurt." After this session, there is a noticeable change in the child's play, and the theme of the fortress is replaced by reciprocal play centered on the doll house, with the child telling the mother how to rearrange the furniture.

2. **When the parent resists or cannot tolerate the meaning of the child's play, the therapist creates a space in which the child can tell the story while supporting the parent in observing and participating in the play in as full a manner as is possible, given the parent's own emotional demands.**

EXAMPLE.

Angelo, 2 years old, is watching silently as his father speaks heatedly about his wife's betrayal, which led to a bitter divorce after a violent physical fight that Angelo witnessed. As the father speaks, Angelo approaches the doll house and begins putting every piece of furniture upside down. He throws the dolls out of the house. The therapist says to the father, "I know you are very angry right now, but I have to ask you to stop and watch what Angelo is doing. He is trying to tell you something." As the father watches, the therapist says, "Angelo, everything is upside down. The mommy and the daddy and the baby fell out of the house." Angelo says, "Baby hurt." The therapist repeats, "Baby hurt?" Angelo hurls the baby across the room. The father says, "Don't hurt the baby." Angelo responds by hurling the father figure across the room. The father says, "Don't do that." The therapist says, "Angelo is telling us how he feels. His whole world fell apart. You are angry, and he is angry and scared." The father says, "He's too little to understand what is happening." The therapist answers, "Too little? He seems pretty eloquent to me. How much more clearly can he show you what is happening?" The father is quiet for a long moment, looking at his son, who is looking at him. Then, the father says, "Come here, Angelo." As the child approaches him, the father holds him on his lap and says, "I love you, baby."

EXAMPLE.

Jamala, 3 years old, ties the therapist's wrists with rope and says, "You are going to jail! You are bad!" In session after session, this game is repeated with minor variations, and it always includes insults and curses. The therapist responds by saying that she is scared, that she is not so bad, asking for forgiveness, and in other ways expressing fear, sorrow, and remorse. Jamala is unmoved and continues by escalating the punishment yet never doing anything that can actually hurt the participants in the play. The mother watches uncomfortably at first but becomes increasingly fascinated by her young child's accurate portrayal of the scenes that the child saw between her mother and father. In this session, the mother's efforts to participate are answered by the child's refusal to let her play: "You stay out, Mommy. You are ugly." The therapist speaks to Jamala's anger at her mother because her father went away. Jamala asks the therapist to tie her wrists and to send her to jail. The therapist says, "I will be too sad if you go away. I don't want to do that." Jamala screams, "Do it!" The therapist tentatively does it, checking with Jamala in a stage whisper to see if she still wants this to happen at each step of the play. When Jamala "goes to jail," the therapist and the mother loudly call for her, telling each other how much they miss her. Jamala reenters, smiling, and is greeted with great joy. In one of the sessions, months later, Jamala says to the therapist, "Even when I am angry with you, I love you," and sighs as if realizing something very important.

3. In CPP, it is critical that the parent understand and be involved in the narrative that the child is telling through play. The therapist helps the child share this narrative with the parent, so that the parent can assume a rightful role as the child's guide and protector, even if the narrative emerges in sessions that the parent did not attend.

EXAMPLE.

Lidia, 4 years old, came for CPP with her aunt. She had suffered many losses in her short life. Her mother abandoned her to the care of her grandmother when Lidia was 2 years old. One month before Lidia turned 4, her grandmother died after a long illness. Lidia's aunt was herself in poor health, and she sometimes missed sessions. The family valued the therapy, however, and when Lidia's aunt was too ill to come to a session, she would ensure that a relative brought Lidia to see the therapist. Lidia's play, in sessions with her aunt as well as in sessions when she was alone with the therapist, was filled with themes of being overly busy, overly burdened, and needing to care for many children. In these play sessions, Lidia was always the caretaker, providing for her aunt, the therapist, and the many baby dolls in the playroom. Both the therapist and Lidia's aunt spoke to how hard Lidia was working, how busy she was, and how much responsibility she had. Lidia spoke of her wish to be "grown so I can buy the food and pay the bills."

In one session, when Lidia's aunt did not come and Lidia was alone with the therapist, Lidia began her play, as usual, busily taking care of the therapist and the baby dolls. As she played, she began to talk about getting ready to go to a party with her boyfriend. She told the therapist, "You will have to stay home with the babies while I'm gone." Then Lidia said, "My boyfriend is here, and we're fighting because he's late. He's mad, and I'm mad. He's banging my head on the wall, and I'm crying." Then, Lidia turned to the therapist and said, "That's what happened to my mommy when we lived in the big house. I was just a baby, and I was scared." The therapist asked Lidia if she told anyone. Lidia said, "They don't know. I can't tell them."

Lidia's aunt came to the next session. The therapist tried several times to introduce the story, but each time, Lidia shot her a threatening glance and said, "Don't talk." In supervision, the therapist talked about how burdened she felt by having a secret that Lidia's aunt did not know. With her supervisor, the therapist reflected on the fact that she was burdened by the secret just as Lidia had been. The supervisor noted that the difference was that the therapist was "grown" and that Lidia was just a little girl, too young to have the responsibility of deciding what to do with such an important secret. The supervisor encouraged the therapist to help Lidia share her secret with her aunt so that her aunt could be aware of the burden that Lidia carried and could help her with it.

In the next session, the therapist watched and listened as Lidia again played that she was caring for her aunt, the therapist, and the babies. The therapist, joined by the aunt, began to question Lidia's assumption of so much responsibility. They noted that she was only 4 years old, too little to have such big jobs. The therapist said that Lidia had some grown-up secrets that she had been keeping, too. Lidia looked at the therapist angrily and said, "Don't talk." The therapist acknowledged that Lidia didn't want her to tell the story of what happened with her mom but said that it was too big and too scary a secret for a little girl to keep to herself. She said, "Your auntie needs to know so she can help you and take care of you." Lidia turned her back on the therapist and her aunt and listened tearfully as the therapist told the aunt what had happened to Lidia's mother and about Lidia's reluctance to tell anyone. Lidia's aunt listened and then turned to Lidia and said, "Did you think I wouldn't believe you?" Lidia nodded silently. Her aunt said, "Did you think you would be in trouble?" Again, Lidia nodded. Her aunt said, "You aren't in trouble, baby. I believe you. I think it happened just the way you said. Of course you were scared." Lidia sat crying softly for a minute and then said that she wanted to play. She walked to a bin of toy food and picked up a plastic ice cream cone. She pretended to lick it, bringing it closer and closer to her mouth while she watched her aunt closely. Just before Lidia put the ice cream cone in her mouth, her aunt said, "Don't lick that, baby. It's dirty." Lidia put the cone down, smiling with relief at having been cared for, and then crawled into her aunt's lap.

Domain II: Child Sensorimotor Disorganization and Disruption of Biological Rhythms

This section focuses on sensorimotor disorganization as manifested in frequent, intense, and prolonged crying; inability to be soothed; motor rigidity, agitation, or restlessness; head banging; temper tantrums; and other behaviors that denote lack of bodily control. Disruption of biological rhythms are discussed in terms of problems with eating, sleeping, and elimination.

All of these behaviors are common in typically developing children and are not necessarily associated with traumatic experiences or with parental maltreatment. They are often outgrown as the result of neurophysiological maturation and the acquisition of increasingly effective coping skills. However, while they last, these behaviors can be very distressing to the parents and child care providers, and they can set the stage for adult misperceptions of the child as willfully annoying or noncompliant. As a result, these behaviors can trigger anger and withdrawal in the caregiver, generating a self-reinforcing aversive cycle of interaction between parent and child. When the behaviors are a direct response to trauma, they tend to last longer, are more difficult to alleviate, and tend to return after abating when stressful conditions reappear.

Regardless of the reasons for the child's behavior, it is helpful to use developmental guidance to explain the possible meanings of the behavior to the parent and to search together for ways of responding that are empathically responsive to the child, support development, and alleviate the problem behavior. If, in this process, it becomes apparent that the parent cannot collaborate in the search for a solution, then the clinician might need to explore the parental negative perceptions of the child and their possible links with the parent's individual experience before a developmentally appropriate intervention can become effective.

PORTS OF ENTRY AND CLINICAL EXAMPLES

1. **When the child's behavior does not respond to the parent's efforts to stop it, the clinician elicits the parent's view of the situation and engages the parent in searching for an effective strategy for calming the child.**

   ##### EXAMPLE.
   Carmen, 5 months old, cries frantically when she wakes up, when her diapers are changed, when she is given a bath, and when she sees

unfamiliar people. Her mother feels unable to console her. She has begun to change diapers less often, to give sponge baths, and to avoid going out to minimize situations that might trigger Carmen's crying. When the clinician arrives for this particular session, Carmen has been crying nonstop for about 15 minutes by the mother's report. Her face is red, and she is sweaty. The mother is holding the child over her shoulder, bouncing her rhythmically because she read that this is optimal for crying babies. The clinician speaks sympathetically to the mother, telling her that this is a very difficult situation, and offers to hold the child if she needs a break. The mother accepts the offer. Carmen's crying intensifies when her mother transfers her to the clinician's arms. The clinician comments, "You want to be with your mommy, don't you? You like your mom best of all even when you are crying." The mother says ruefully, "Much good it does me. I can't do anything right for her." The clinician says, "I wouldn't blame myself if I were you. Some babies don't do what one expects of them, and Carmen and you have gone through a lot when her father used to get violent with you in front of her." The mother's eyes fill with tears. Carmen continues crying. The clinician says, "What do you say if we try something different? Maybe Carmen gets too stimulated if we hold her up and bounce her. Maybe she needs a lot of quiet. What if we dim the lights and put her on her tummy and sing to her softly while we pat her back?" The mother answers, "Nothing to lose." The clinician asks, "Do you want to do it yourself, or do you want me to do it?" The mother says, "You do it. I'm too frazzled." The clinician says lightly that the mother will have to bear with her because she sings out of tune, and the mother gives a little smile while dimming the lights. The clinician starts humming a lullaby while patting Carmen rhythmically on the back as the child lies on her tummy on the couch. When the baby's crying begins to subside, the clinician motions to the mother to take over. The mother does so, singing with a trembling voice at first, then with more self-assurance. The clinician joins her softly. After a while, Carmen falls asleep. The mother says, "What a relief." The clinician says, "We learned something about Carmen. When she cries, one thing to try is cutting down on the light and on moving her. She is soothed by patting but not by bouncing, it seems."

The mother listens attentively.

The clinician then asks the mother how she is doing, and the mother speaks about her grief in losing her relationship with Carmen's father and her simultaneous fear that he'll resume his violence if they get back together. The clinician uses this sequence to note to herself that this mother's ability to soothe her baby breaks down when she is overcome by her concerns about her personal situation. She does not verbalize this realization because her relationship with the mother is not yet well enough established to make an interpretation of this type, but she tells herself that she needs to remember to inquire about the mother's personal experience on a regular basis as part of the intervention. Before leaving, the clinician makes use of the mother's improved emotional state to tell her about the new pediatric knowledge regarding the importance of having babies sleep on their backs to decrease the danger of SIDS and encourages the mother to turn the baby over for the night.

If this incident occurred later in the treatment, when the clinician's relationship with Carmen's mother was better established, the clinician might have gone farther after helping to calm Carmen. She might have noted that Carmen, like all babies, is sensitive to the states of mind of her mother. The clinician could then help the mother reflect on whether she is less effective in calming Carmen when she herself is upset. Together, the clinician and the mother could work to help the mother be more observant of her own internal states and to find ways to calm herself so that she can better help Carmen relax.

2. **When the parent seems at a loss to implement a routine, the clinician provides reflective developmental guidance while expressing support for the parent's concerns.**

   EXAMPLE.
   The mother of Camila, 8 months old, explains that she needs to go back to work after her pregnancy leave but is worried that Camila will "starve to death" because she does not accept a bottle and insists on breastfeeding only. When the clinician asks about the course of breastfeeding, the mother explains that she has always fed on demand

because she believes that breastfeeding is important for bonding, but now this is presenting a problem because of Camila's refusal to be fed by anybody other than her mother. On further inquiry, it emerges that the mother feeds Camila four or five times per hour and that they have never been apart. Camila also wakes up several times each night to breastfeed. Lately, the mother tried a couple of times to withhold breastfeeding during the night, and each time Camila "knocked herself out" crying until she fell asleep. The mother felt as if she was "torturing" Camila. The clinician sympathizes with the mother's struggle and suggests that it might be less stressful to introduce Camila to a bottle during the day, when both are more rested. She explains that the mother's milk will have more time to be replenished if there is a longer period of time between feedings and suggests stretching the length of time between feedings so that Camila gets fuller at each feeding. The mother and the clinician speak in detail about the mother's fears that this will displease Camila, and the clinician suggests ways of distracting Camila by introducing activities that the child enjoys. The clinician reassures the mother that even if Camila is displeased in the moment, she will learn that she can tolerate the change with her mother's support.

3. **When the parent seems unable to follow a routine to help the child acquire better biological regulation, the clinician asks the parent about the obstacles that stand in his or her way and offers alternatives based on the parent's concerns.**

    EXAMPLE.
    Bobby, 18 months old, screams when he is put to bed. His mother deals with this situation by lying next to him until he falls asleep. This can take between 1 and 2 hours each night because Bobby wakes up whenever the mother tries to get up unless he is in a very deep sleep. The clinician has suggested a nighttime ritual of telling Bobby that it is time to go to bed, dressing him in his pajamas, brushing his teeth, reading him a book, turning off the lights, and turning on a musical mobile above his bed while saying, "I'll see you in the morning." The mother has been unable to implement any of the components of this ritual. She sounds evasive and out of sorts when the clinician asks how

the nighttime preparations are working, but she continues to complain about Bobby's crying. The clinician says, "I have the feeling that the suggestions I made are not being helpful. Can we review them to see what is not working?" The mother says, "It's too much trouble to go through all those steps." The clinician says she agrees with the mother that there are a lot of steps and asks which ones are the most trouble. The mother says, "Just the whole bunch. It feels so artificial." Again, the clinician agrees that it doesn't seem to come naturally to have a nighttime ritual. She asks how the mother used to fall asleep when she was little. The mother says, "I used to stay awake for a long time because I was scared of ghosts. I kept being afraid I would see one, but I couldn't tell my mom because she would whoop me if I made noise." The clinician says that many children and even grown-ups are scared of ghosts, and she asks if the mother is still scared of them. The mother says that she is. The clinician says, "Does staying with Bobby makes you feel safer, instead of being all alone in the house with him asleep?" The mother mumbles, "Yes" in an embarrassed way. The clinician says, "That's nothing to be embarrassed about. A lot of people have those fears. Would listening to music help you?" The mother says she doesn't know but agrees it is worth a try.

4. **When the child's behavior becomes unmodulated and out of control, the clinician uses a combination of words and actions to help the child de-escalate to a more modulated state.**

   EXAMPLE.
   Robbie, 2 years old, screams when his mother takes his baby brother's milk bottle away from Robbie. His mother says dismissively, "He needs to learn not to take his brother's bottle. He's not a baby anymore." The clinician answers, "He doesn't know that. He would like to be a baby and be on your lap, like his little brother is." Robbie continues screaming. The clinician says to the mother, "Do you mind if I try something?" The mother agrees. The clinician kneels down very close to Robbie and says, "You really want that bottle. Let's look for something else you can have." Robbie looks at her for a moment as he stops crying, then resumes his screaming. The clinician says, "Give me your hand, and we will find something else that you want." She takes

Robbie's hand and purposefully takes him around the room, pointing at different things and naming them in a questioning tone, as if asking whether Robbie wants them. Robbie's crying diminishes. The clinician takes a stuffed animal and cradles it in her arms, saying, "Don't cry, baby. Don't cry." Robbie watches her with a sober expression. The clinician helps Robbie cradle the stuffed animal, singing softly. Robbie sits on the floor and starts exploring the animal. The clinician turns to the mother and says, "It is hard for him to share you with his brother. He is not a baby, but he is still little. And I know it's hard for you to take care of two little ones." The mother nods quietly.

Domain III: Child Fearful Behavior

Infants, toddlers, and preschool children routinely experience a bewildering variety of fears. Infants may react with excessive distress to unfamiliar sights or noises, to transitions in routines, and to regular caregiving activities such as bathing or changing diapers. For toddlers and preschoolers, seemingly irrational fears such as fear of the flushing toilet, of the moon falling down, of puppets and masks, and of a monster under the bed intermingle with fears that, from an adult point of view, appear more readily based in reality, such as fear of being alone, fear of the dark, and fear of loud noises. Much has been written about the relationship of these fears to the young child's rudimentary construction of the world and of his or her place in it, which led Selma Fraiberg (1959) to call this period "the magic years." These developmentally appropriate fears are connected with toddlers' and preschoolers' animistic conception of the world and with the child's struggles against forbidden impulses, "bad wishes," and the ever-present possibility of losing control either of bodily functions or of recently achieved coping skills.

For children whose parents are reliably protective, these normative fears are an essential rite of passage that enables them to test out their beliefs and to do battle with their most forbidden wishes and powerful impulses. Eventually, they will establish some kind of truce with them, using the safe and benevolent powers of their parents as allies in the process of learning about the world and about themselves. In contrast, children growing up in violent households cannot rely on their parents for reassurance. They do not know when the parent will protect them and when he or she will become dangerously similar to the monsters that they fear. Their construction of reality, to be accurate, needs to incorporate fear of the parents as an essential component of self-protection. Unconditional trust in the parents is foolhardy for children who have seen their parents hurt each other or who have been hurt by them. Vigilance and suspicion are more adaptive in the conditions in which they live.

In the treatment of children exposed to violence, the clinician needs to establish a delicate balance between two important objectives: (a) recognizing the legitimacy of the child's fear of the parent and (b) upholding the legitimacy of the parent's love and wish to protect the child. In CPP, the parent's presence during the session can bring awkwardness to the process of exploring the child's fear of the parent because parents may feel hurt, defensive, and offended by the realization that their child is afraid of them. Sometimes, the parents themselves, traumatized by violence, are too emotionally numb to actually feel love or to have an active wish to protect their children. Parents might also feel that they do not have the resources to protect their children even if they want to do so. In these cases, the therapeutic process must build the parents' confidence in their capacity to love and protect, realistically acknowledging at the same time that their children may wish for more love and protection than the parents are able to offer at the moment. It is of the utmost importance not to provide facile reassurance and not to minimize the child's fear. To protect and enhance the child's mental health, the clinician must support the child's right to feel, even if the feeling involved is pain, and even if the feeling produces pain in the parent.

Fear of the parent is superimposed on the two major developmentally expectable anxieties of the toddler and preschool child: (a) fear of separation and (b) fear of losing the parent's love. For children growing up in nonviolent, stable households, reassurance that the parent will return after a separation and that the parent continues to love the child even when angry are routine events that gradually build in the child an inner conviction that anger and love can (and do) coexist. In violent households, in contrast, the intensity of hatred too often obscures the reality of love. Watching one parent hurt the other, observing uncontrolled expressions of anger, and being physically and emotionally hurt cast doubt in the child's mind on the veracity of the parent's love and reliable presence, and exacerbate fears of being left and being unloved.

Many parents are unaware of that. Fears of separation and of losing the parent's love are developmentally appropriate in young children. Educating them about the emotional meaning of these fears—and their relevance to how their child feels about them—is very helpful in generating parental empathy and support for their children because parents have a greater feeling of self-worth when they realize how important they are to their children.

Sometimes, it is not realistic to assuage the child's fears. For children living in perpetually dangerous situations, it is untruthful to assure them that the adults in their lives will protect them. Empty promises, particularly from a trusted adult, are damaging to children because they fail to address legitimate emotional responses and teach the child that adults are deceptive. In these situations, the only honest intervention is to tell the child that it is right and proper to be afraid, that the adult is very sad about the frightening state of affairs, and that the adult will try very hard to change things for the better and to get help from others to make the situation as safe as it can be.

Ports of Entry and Clinical Examples

1. **When the parent is appropriately responsive to the child's fear, the clinician explicitly supports the parent's behavior.**

   Example.
   Antonio, 20 months old, screams when he sees his older brother, 8 years old, wearing a devil mask and gesticulating wildly in his direction. The mother picks him up and says to the brother, "Take off your mask so he can see that it is you." The brother does not obey and continues making loud noises and frightening gestures. The mother says to Antonio, "That is your brother; you are OK," and then, turning to the brother, says sharply, "Take off your mask right now." The child obeys. The mother says to Antonio, "See? It's your brother. He's just playing." Antonio calms down and stares at his brother with wild eyes. The clinician says quietly to the mother, "You sure know how to help him." The mother looks pleased.

2. **When the parent dismisses the child's fear, the clinician describes the reasons for the child's experience and tries to enlist a more supportive parental response.**

EXAMPLE.

Mabel, 12 months old, has been waking up at night screaming loudly for the past 2 months. The mother is exasperated and says that she lets Mabel cry herself to sleep. The clinician listens to the mother's description and then says, "I can understand how tired you are after working all day, but I think Mabel is worried that you won't be there when she wakes up. After all, her daddy left suddenly. Maybe she is worried that you will leave, too." The mother says, defensively, "Maybe she is, but what can I do? If I get up and take care of her, I'll just spoil her. Then she'll never go back to sleep." The clinician asks, "Is there anything in between, so she doesn't get spoiled but knows you are there?" The mother says, "I can talk to her from my bed." The clinician responds, "That sounds like a good idea to me." The mother says humorously, "I am already awake anyway; I might as well try something." Mother and clinician laugh; the clinician adds, "Well, if it works, you'll be able to go back to sleep faster than if she continued to cry."

3. **When the parent cannot come up with ideas to alleviate the child's fear, the clinician offers suggestions that are framed in the developmental meaning of the child's behavior.**

EXAMPLE.

Khalil, 3 years old, has become scared of monsters. He says, "The tiger and the monster will come and eat me." His mother says, "I keep telling him that monsters don't exist, but he is still scared of them. He doesn't believe me." The clinician says, "I think he wants to believe you, but his fear is so strong that he can't. Most children at this age believe in monsters. He wants you to believe that his monsters are real." The mother says, "But they are not real." The clinician says, "You know how some things can be real for us but not for others? That is how it is with children. They really believe in monsters and see them in their imagination. How about if you tell him that you will make sure the monsters don't ever come close to him because you will scare them away?" Amused, the mother says, "I can do that." The clinician encourages the mother to tell this to Khalil. The mother says to Khalil, "I will kick the tiger and the monster out so they can't eat you." Khalil asks, "How?" Hesitating, the mother says, "I will lock the door." Khalil asks again, "And what else?" The mother answers, "I will lock the windows." Khalil asks, "Will you say: 'Go away, bad monster, don't bother my little boy'?" The mother promises she will say that. Increasingly enjoying the exchange, Khalil and his mother continue in this way for a while before Khalil changes the topic, clearly satisfied that his mother will take effective action to protect him.

4. **When the parent does not notice the child's anxious or fearful behavior, the clinician brings it to the parent's attention and encourages the parent to reassure the child about the parent's willingness and ability to protect.**

   EXAMPLE.
   Angela, 7 months old, starts screaming when she sees a man wearing dark sunglasses and a hat in the hallway of their apartment building. Her mother pays no attention. The clinician asks, "What do you think is making her cry like that?" The mother shrugs and says, "I have no idea." Puzzled by the child's persistent crying, the clinician insists, "Does she know that man? She started crying when she saw him." The mother says, "Yeah, he's a neighbor, but he never dresses like that." The clinician says, "Maybe she doesn't recognize him." The mother replies, "Her daddy sometimes wears a hat and glasses like that, to look cool." After a period of silence, she says, "Matter of fact, he was looking like that when I threw him out." The clinician asks, "Do you think Angela is remembering the fight and that is why she is crying?" Surprised, the mother says, "Can they remember at this age?" The clinician says, "They sure can." The mother looks thoughtful. She then hugs Angela tightly and say, "It'll be OK, baby, shhh, shhh," as she rocks her.

5. **When the child expresses fear of the parent in a disguised form, the clinician clarifies for the parent the meaning of the child's behavior and supports the parent in relieving the child's fear.**

   EXAMPLE.
   Mario, 4 years old, is playing with the kitchen set and says to his mother, "Look, Mommy, here is the knife of my dream." He then tells the clinician that he had had a "very, very bad dream." She asks him

what the dream was about, and he says that the knife was in the dream. He adds, "There was this mommy, no, this monster, and he had this gray knife, just like this one, and it cut me right here; it cut out my heart." He dramatically enacts how the monster cut out his heart with a knife. The mother asks if she was in the dream, and Mario replies that she wasn't, that he wanted her to be there to help him, but she wasn't. The therapist says that it sounded like it was a very scary dream, and Mario agrees that it was. The mother explains that during the dream, he was screaming in his sleep, that she could not wake him up from it, that she had never seen him so upset, and that he slept in her bed for the rest of the night.

This episode needs to be put into context. Mario's mother was one of the women who, during the initial assessment, reported using physical aggression against her husband, and on one occasion, she actually threatened him with a knife in front of Mario. Mother and child had never talked about this before. Now the therapist asks the mother, "Are you a little mad at me that there is a knife among the toys here?" The mother replies, "At first I was mad, but then I thought that this is why we are in therapy, because he needs to talk about things, but it makes me feel guilty that I frightened him so much." The therapist says she understands the mother's mixed feelings and comments that all parents wish they could turn the clock back and do things differently at times. The therapist adds, "Unfortunately, one can't turn the clock back, but one can do what you are doing now, which is to try to help Mario make sense of what happened so that he is not so scared by it." The mother turns to Mario and says, "Mario, I think you are thinking of the time that I pulled the knife out at your daddy." Mario looks at her. She adds, "You are too little to understand this, and I will tell you again when you are older, but I was very mad at your daddy, and I am very sorry I scared you so much." Mario moves closer to her and says, "Sometimes you get really angry at me, Mommy." The mother is taken aback and looks helplessly at the therapist, who says, "I know that when your mommy gets very angry, it can be very scary. But your mommy loves you very much, and she will never take out a knife on you, no matter how angry she gets."

The mother has tears in her eyes. She says, "Mario, I love you so much that I am very sorry you saw me do that, and I promise I will never, ever do something like that to you." Mario smiles, turns to the new doctor's kit, and tries all the medical instruments on his mother, his baby brother, and the therapist. When the mother tries to continue talking about the knife episode, he says, "I'm finished with the knife right now, Mommy. You can put it away."

This sequence demonstrates the importance of viewing clinical material through two lenses: (a) the lens of trauma and (b) the lens of attachment and normative development. Mario and his mother, with the therapist's support, processed Mario's memories about the incident with the knife as fully as he could tolerate at this time. Mario heard and accepted his mother's reassurance that she would never frighten him again in that way or hurt him with a knife. Mario's play shows that he feels close to his mother and that he is now ready to move on and to play in a way that allows feelings of competence and helpfulness to coexist with feelings of fear. If Mario's mother and the therapist had insisted on staying with the trauma themes, they would have run the risk of overwhelming him.

6. **When the child expresses fear of a situation that is objectively frightening, the clinician encourages the parent to tell the child that those feelings are legitimate and that the parent and the clinician are trying hard to make things safer for the family.**

   EXAMPLE.
   Khalil, 3 years old, has supervised visits with his father, but he is scared to go. During one session, he says, "My daddy yells." The clinician repeats, "Your daddy yells?" and turns questioningly toward the mother. The mother tells that, a few days earlier, Khalil's father came by the house in a drunken state and yelled obscenities and threats at her. She called the police, but he was gone by the time they arrived. The mother's attorney has recommended that she ask for a review of the court order for visitation so that it includes mandated participation in an alcohol abuse treatment program, but she urged her to continue taking Khalil to the supervised visits in order to show good faith. The

clinician asks, "What can we do to help Khalil feel safer? Did you talk to him about what happened?" The mother says, "No, I thought he was asleep." The clinician says, "It seems like he heard what happened. Maybe his dad's yelling woke him up. I think it will help him if you talk to him." The mother says to Khalil, "Your daddy yells when he drinks too much. He was drinking when he came and yelled outside the window." The clinician adds, "It is very frightening, Khalil, when your daddy yells. It is not right that he scares you like that. Your mommy is trying very hard to make sure that he stops drinking. That is why there is always somebody who makes sure he is not drinking when you go to see him."

Domain IV: Child-Reckless, Self-Endangering, and Accident-Prone Behavior

Infants, toddlers, and preschool children who witnessed domestic violence or were themselves the victims of violence often engage in behavior that endangers their safety. Some children seem to lack age-appropriate skills for monitoring the environment for cues to danger, in spite of being at age level in other cognitive skills. Other children seem unable to control overwhelming impulses that lead them to hurt themselves or to put themselves in situations where they can easily get hurt. There is evidence that temperamental proclivities, such as emotional intensity and high activity level, may serve as a backdrop for the development of aggressive responses in response to stressful environmental conditions, although the research has focused on other-directed rather than self-directed aggression in young children.

In young children who have witnessed or experienced violence, self-endangering behaviors are best understood as the result of deprivation from protective caregiving and of premature exposure to danger and violence at an age when the fundamental building blocks of self-protection are established through relationships with caring adults. In this sense, excessive recklessness and self-endangering in the presence of the mother or other reliable caregiver constitute an attachment disorder. The primary function of the attachment system is to promote proximity and contact with the preferred caregiver in situations of uncertainty or danger in order to maximize survival (Bowlby, 1969/1982). Children with typical development use the mother figure as a secure base that helps them establish a balance between exploratory and attachment behaviors by serving as a haven to which they return when frightened or in need (Ainsworth et al., 1978). In contrast, self-endangering young children show a distortion of this secure base pattern because they fail to make age-appropriate use of the mother figure as a secure base for protection or as a resource for monitoring environmental cues about danger. Common manifestations involve darting away from the mother in unfamiliar settings, getting lost, and failing to heed the mother's calls by stopping or returning to her side. When hurt or needy, the children tend to ignore or rebuff the mother or strike out against her aggressively rather than to seek comfort from her. In more severe cases, the child may engage in self-biting, self-scratching, and self-hitting. Even very young children sometimes express a wish to not be alive or to want to die (Lieberman & Zeanah, 1995).

Self-endangering behaviors often co-occur with aggression toward others, presenting the most graphic manifestation of the frequently reported high correlations between internalizing and externalizing problems in young children. Less understood is the fact that self-endangering toddlers and preschool children invariably show concurrent manifestations of anxiety, which can manifest itself in fear of separation, clinging, hypervigilance about the parent's whereabouts (which contrasts with the episodes of suddenly bolting away), sleeping problems, intense and prolonged temper tantrums, low threshold for frustration, unpredictable crying, and multiple fears. These anxiety reactions are often overlooked because the accident-prone behaviors and aggression are so compelling that they galvanize the adults' perception of the child.

The seemingly paradoxical coexistence of anxious (fearful) and reckless (danger-encountering) behaviors suggests that self-endangering actions may be a counter-phobic defense against danger in children who do not show indications of biologically based conditions, such as hyperactivity, attention-deficit disorder, or mental retardation. In children traumatized by violence, the parental failure to anticipate danger and to provide protection and the parental infliction of pain through punitiveness and abuse create an ongoing insecurity about when danger will befall them. When the parent ignores dangerous situations, minimizes or ridicules the child's fears, entices the child to take risks, inflicts pain, and discounts the experience of pain when the child is hurt, the child's fear and attachment behaviors may be strongly aroused but are not responded to and terminated, thus causing severe distress.

A repetition of these frightening experiences may trigger in the child a defensive exclusion of the information that ordinarily mobilizes help-seeking or attachment behavior. Children make themselves not notice that they need help because they know that help will not be forthcoming. This defensive exclusion deactivates the attachment system, with the result that the child's impulse to explore is not counterbalanced by the ability to keep track of when it is safe to explore and when it is safe to seek the parent's protection. This disruption of secure base behavior leads to unchecked exploration, as if the child is attempting to mobilize protective parental response by testing the limits of what is permissible. The counterphobic nature of reckless behavior lies in the child's implicit search for an answer to the following questions, "Does my mother care enough for me that she will not let me get hurt? How much danger is so much that my mother will protect me? How far do I need to go before my mother will bring me back?"

Often, this behavior is labeled as "negative attention seeking" by parents and professionals who are not aware of young children's intense need to be loved and protected. An alternative explanation is that the child is attempting to gain mastery of overwhelming fear and helplessness by creating and re-creating a frightening scenario in hopes of bringing about a happier resolution than before. As pediatrician and child psychoanalyst Reginald Lourie put it, "Babies are very patient. They repeat something again and again until adults get it" (personal communication, February 12, 1978).

The goal of the intervention, in these cases, is to convey the message that the adults understand the urgency of the child's call for protection. Intervention strategies must show that the adults care about the child's safety and will not allow the child to be hurt. This message must establish, implicitly and explicitly, the adult's willingness and competence in taking care of the child. The adult must convey self-confidence in knowing better than the child which behaviors can be allowed and which behaviors are out of bounds for the sake of the child's well-being and the well-being of others. The hallmarks of interventions geared to containing and decreasing recklessness and self-endangerment are clear statements and actions that stop self-injurious behavior and speak to the importance of safety and protection. The clinician should consider an incremental approach in which the level of response is dictated by the degree and immediacy of danger and the appropriateness of the parent's response.

Ports of Entry and Clinical Examples

1. **When the child behaves in a self-endangering way, the clinician brings the parent's attention to the risk and engages in a conversation about the importance of recognizing danger and offering protection and safety.**

   Example.

   Rowena, 8 months old, bangs her head repeatedly on the floor and against the wall. Her mother looks on but does nothing. The clinician asks what the mother thinks of that behavior. The mother replies, "It doesn't seem to hurt her. She's not crying." The clinician says, "Yes, but it worries me that she is not crying. It's like she is teaching herself not to feel pain." The mother says, with a little smile, "Like me." The clinician asks, "Do you want her to be like you in that way?" The mother thinks for a minute, looking at Rowena, who is continuing to bang her head. Without saying a word, she goes over to the child and picks her up. The clinician says, "You are showing her that she doesn't need to stop feeling, that you will help her when she needs you."

   Example.

   Andrew, 3 years old, runs down the sidewalk ahead of his mother and the clinician. In alarm, the clinician asks the mother, "Will he stop before he gets to the corner?" The mother yells out, "Andrew, stop right now." Andrew continues to run. The mother runs after Andrew and retrieves him but says nothing to him. The clinician says, "Andrew, your mom and I were worried that a car could hit you. When she tells you to stop, you need to stop." She then says to the mother, "I guess he had no idea why you asked him to stop. He is so little that he does not yet know he can get hurt—he just likes to run."

   In this example, the essential first intervention was to ask the mother whether the child would stop when he got to the corner. In a different case, with another 3-year-old, the child ran ahead of his mother and the therapist on the sidewalk. Again, the therapist asked the mother, "Will he stop before he gets to the corner?" The mother replied, "He will. He always does." She continued walking calmly. The therapist held her breath waiting to see what would happen. The child stopped, as his mother had predicted. If the therapist had run after the child, it would have undermined his mother, implying that she could not read her child's responses or that she did not know to protect her child.

2. **When the parent seems at a loss about how to protect the child, the clinician actively guides the parent, using as specific and direct an approach as is required to elicit protective action.**

    Example.

    Tamara, 2 years old, lets go of her mother's hand as they are crossing a busy street and runs ahead. There are no cars coming at the moment, but the clinician anticipates the possible danger and says to the mother, "Grab her quickly!" The mother runs after Tamara and takes her arm. Tamara yells "No!" and lets herself collapse on the crosswalk, refusing to hold her weight and walk. The mother keeps trying to pull her up, with no success. The clinician says, "I think you need to pick her up and carry her." The mother complies as Tamara cries bitterly but lets herself be carried. The clinician says to Tamara, "You are too little to cross the street by yourself. You always need to hold your mom's hand." As the critical moment subsides, the clinician asks the mother how she felt about the clinician telling her what to do and asks whether it is all right to do so again in the future if the clinician realizes that the child is in danger.

3. **When the parent fails to take protective action that is urgently needed, the clinician models this behavior for the parent, enlisting the child's cooperation when feasible.**

    Example.

    Andres, 11 months old, climbs on a table by an open window. Fearing that the child will fall, the clinician responds instantly and takes him down. He then says to the father, "I am sorry if I took over; I was too scared that he would fall." The father replies, "He wasn't going to fall." The clinician says, "Maybe you and I see danger differently. At this age, they change so quickly that they can get hurt before you know it. What about if, just to be safe, we move the table away from the window?" The father agrees, and he and the clinician move the table to the side.

EXAMPLE.

Danny, 4 years old, opens the door of the clinician's car when they arrive at their destination and runs into the street. The clinician grabs him and says, "Damn it, Danny, you cannot do that. You can get hurt." Danny says, gleefully, "You said a bad word!" The clinician answers, "I did, and I'm sorry, but this is really serious. You scared me a lot. I don't want you to ever do that again." The child replies, "Yes, ma'am." The clinician continues. "Now, I want you to give your hand to your mom and to not let go until we tell you it is OK." The child says again, with utmost seriousness, "Yes, ma'am." The mother says, surprised, "He is really listening to you."

Domain V: Child Aggression Toward a Parent

Children who have witnessed their mother's battering often use physical or verbal aggression—or both—toward her in situations that elicit uncertainty, frustration, anger, or fear. This section focuses primarily on child aggression toward the mother because there are few clinical observations or empirical research involving children's aggression toward fathers, but the strategies are applicable to aggression toward fathers or other caregivers. Child aggression toward the mother is prevalent among the children whom child–parent psychotherapists treat. A variety of overlapping and mutually reinforcing mechanisms contribute to this aggressive response. Different theoretical approaches conceptualize these mechanisms differently, but the underlying theme is that children incorporate into their behavioral repertoire aggressive actions that were witnessed in the course of family life. Possible mechanisms are outlined as follows:

- Children blame their mothers for the pain and difficulty of their lives. This includes believing that the mother is responsible for the separation from the father when the parents are not living together. For young children, the mother is an all-powerful figure who, in their minds, can do anything she wishes. They generalize her role as their primary caregiver into a belief that she can make things happen or not happen if only she wanted to. It follows that when young children are faced with circumstances that sadden and anger them, they attribute the cause to the mother's power.

- The child might be re-enacting aggressive scenes witnessed at home. Children imitate what they see and are compelled to enact frightening and overwhelming experiences in an effort to understand what happened, elicit appropriate care from adults, and, in this process, master their feelings of helplessness and fear.

- The child might identify with the perpetrator of domestic violence against the mother and imitate his behavior, particularly if the perpetrator is also an attachment figure, such as the child's father or stepfather. Children strive to be like the people they love, and parents are particularly powerful role models who serve as a blueprint for children's behavior.

- Given that physical punishment is a socially prevalent form of discipline and that battered women tend to show increased harshness and punitiveness toward their children, the child might identify with and imitate the mother when engaging in aggression toward her.

- Children who have witnessed domestic violence tend to misperceive the intentions of others, over-attributing hostile intent. This is particularly likely to occur when a parent is not only aggressive toward the spouse but also harsh and punitive in relation to the child. The child might then construct a perception of the parent as dangerous, frightening, and someone to be fought off for the purpose of self-protection. In these situations, child aggression toward the mother may be a mirror image of maternal aggression toward the child.

- Paradoxically, battered women may fail to protect themselves or to use appropriate limit setting when their children are physically or verbally aggressive toward them. They may give in to the child's demands in order to forestall the child's aggression. This maternal helplessness has the effect of confirming the child's perception that "aggression works," reinforcing aggressive action toward the mother. It is also possible that maternal helplessness, in itself, triggers child aggression because children equate helplessness with ineffectiveness in providing adequate care.

- Aggressive action is a frequent defensive response to intense fear and a profound sense of vulnerability. Children who have not been reliably protected by their attachment figures have not had opportunities to learn age-appropriate coping skills for managing intense negative emotions. As a result, their self-protective actions tend to be immediate and primitive, along the lines of biologically based "fight-or-flight" survival responses. Psychologically, it can be argued that aggression gives the child an in-the-moment feeling of mastery over overwhelming fear, which tends to perpetuate this response in children who are in a continuous state of exposure to frightening situations.

The clinician's response to the child's aggression toward the mother needs to take into account this variety of underlying mechanisms. **The main rationale for the intervention is to help the child acquire more appropriate modulation of negative feelings, including greater impulse control.** The goal is to help the child and the parent to stop or reduce their reliance on destructive and hurtful behaviors and to replace these behaviors with socially appropriate actions, including verbalization, alternative behaviors, and play.

In considering how to respond, the clinician needs to be attuned to the parents' feelings and perceptions of the child's behavior and respectful of the family's cultural values and child-rearing mores. Parents may have strong reactions to the child's aggression, but they may not express these reactions in the presence of a nonfamily member, particularly someone whose opinion they value or who is perceived as having a position of power or authority, such as the clinician. The parent may feel humiliation, shame, anger, and a wish to retaliate, or may misperceive the child's aggression as humorous or loving. The therapist needs to be careful not to exacerbate the child–mother conflict or to embarrass the parents as a result of the intervention.

Witnessing aggression can generate a strong reaction in the clinician as well, setting the stage for a parallel process where unmodulated feelings in the family can lead to unmodulated feelings and impulsive action from the clinician. This is usually not helpful because the therapist's ability to contain intense negative reactions and to convey an attitude of calm and helpfulness are essential to the work. The clinician needs to keep a delicate balance between two polarities: impulsive action and passive observing. Impulsive action might come across as judgmental; doing nothing may indicate collusion with the aggression. Clinicians need to cultivate an inner stance where they train themselves to tolerate painful situations and give themselves permission to observe but without becoming complacent in condoning hurtful actions. The clinician needs to feel free to take educated risks by intervening promptly, yet not feel forced to act before having a sense of what the appropriate intervention might be.

The items listed here intend to reflect this breadth of approach. The items are not mutually exclusive, but they comprise a range of complementary actions that can be used in conjunction with one another. In general, a "minimalist" approach to intervention is preferable because the goal of the intervention is to facilitate adaptive exchanges between parent and child rather than to have the clinician take center stage as the "expert." If the parent responds appropriately to the child, the intervention might consist of a simple show of understanding and "joining forces" with the parent (an exchange of knowing glances between clinician and parent might suffice). Failing this, the clinician encourages the parent to respond to the child. The therapist takes action only if the parent is unable or unwilling to do so, trying whenever possible to enhance the parent's sense of personal competence in the course of the intervention.

The minimalist philosophy extends to how to intervene with the child. Prevention is best, and it consists of anticipating when the child is about to engage in an aggressive act. The clinician can then take action to distract the child and/or redirect the behavior.

The therapist can become the target of the child's aggression, as well. The following items are easily adapted to allow the therapist to help the child in modulating, redirecting, or transforming this form of aggression.

PORTS OF ENTRY AND CLINICAL EXAMPLES

1. **The clinician encourages the mother (and the child, when age-appropriate) to think of behaviors that will allow the child to express anger in nonhurtful ways.**

   #### EXAMPLE.
   Nadia, 8 months old, is teething. She constantly bites hard on anything that comes close, including her mother's face. The mother takes this personally, thinking that Nadia is hurting her on purpose. The clinician says, "I know it is hard not to take it personally, but let's observe Nadia together. She bites anything within reach, not just you." (The clinician shows the mother several examples.) After the mother

begins to realize the ubiquitousness of Nadia's biting, the clinician says, "Let's put together several things that Nadia can bite without hurting anybody. You can keep them at hand to give to her. But for the time being, be careful when you hold her close. She'll outgrow biting, but this is a time to be quicker than she is and to hold her at arm's length when you think she's ready to bite you." Mother and clinician assemble several cushiony objects that Nadia can chew on, and the mother decides to buy a teething ring for good measure.

EXAMPLE.

Sonny, 2 years old, hits his mother when she tells him he needs to put the toys away. The mother turns to the clinician and says, "He always does that." The clinician says, "I think he is trying to tell you that he does not want to put the toys away, but for sure that is not the way to do it. How can he do it better?" The mother turns to Sonny and says, "You can tell me you are mad, but you can't hit me." Sonny says, "Me mad, no hit," and then he refuses to put the toys away. The clinician suggests he might need help to get going and sets the example by putting one toy in the basket and saying, "See, Sonny? Your mommy wants you to do what I do." A game ensues where mother, clinician, and child take turns putting the toys in the basket.

2. **The therapist supports the mother's efforts to redirect the child's aggressive behavior and uses age-appropriate language to explain that the mother is doing her job in teaching the child about right and wrong behavior.**

EXAMPLE.

Tobias, 11 months old, pinches his mother hard. The mother says, "No pinching, Tobias. Here, play with some modeling clay. That will keep your fingers busy." The clinician says, "Pinching modeling clay is OK; pinching Mommy is not OK."

EXAMPLE.

Sylvia, 4 years old, throws a block at her mother, barely missing the mother's face. The mother says, "Sylvia, you need to go to your room as punishment for trying to hurt me." The child screams, "I won't go. You go to your room." The mother tries to physically take Sylvia to her room, but the child runs away and taunts her mother to get her.

The clinician says, "Sylvia, your mom is very serious. She really means it. She is your mommy, and she is doing her job. You need to do what she says." The child goes to her room and in a few minutes announces from behind her closed door, "I am ready to come out now." The mother gives her permission to do so and then says, "You need to apologize." The child says, "I am sorry." The clinician says, "Your mommy is teaching you not to do things that can hurt because that is scary for her and scary for you. I am here to help you with scary things like too much anger."

3. **The therapist asks questions of the child and the mother that are aimed at understanding the meaning of the child's behavior for each of them.**

   EXAMPLE.
   Sylvia, 4 years old, puts a pillow on her mother's face as the mother is reclining on the couch, holding it down tightly. The mother struggles to free herself. The clinician asks, "What just happened?" Sylvia answers, "My daddy did it." The mother explains that she and her husband used to have playful pillow fights that escalated into situations where he tried to suffocate her. The clinician says, "Sylvia, you are telling us that you remember what your daddy did when he lived with you." The child nods sadly. The clinician says, "It's hard to miss Daddy," and both mother and child nod their heads. (This exchange set the stage for further exchanges where the child's and the mother's conflicting feelings toward the father became recurrent themes, including their longing for the father, their fear of the father's unexpected swings from playfulness to anger, and their joint re-creation of overexciting scenes where play and aggression mingled as a way of bringing the father back into their everyday life.)

4. **When the child is verbally aggressive toward the parent (e.g., by insulting or threatening the parent), the therapist acknowledges the child's anger and states that this is not a good way of speaking to the mother.**

   EXAMPLE.
   Ruby, 5 years old, tells her mother: "You f— bitch." The clinician says, "I know you are angry, but that is not the way we do things around here."

5. The therapist creates an atmosphere where the meaning of behavior can be thought about and where different forms of behaving can be imagined and practiced. For this purpose, the clinician guides the mother and the child into a conversation about the child's aggression, the circumstances that triggered it, and the feelings that accompany it. This conversation might start with the clinician asking the parent what she thinks of the child's behavior. It is often useful to comment that the clinician finds it hard to see the child mistreating the mother in order to make clear that aggressive behavior need not be accepted as a regular part of relationships.

   EXAMPLE.
   In the previous example, the therapist follows up by saying to the mother, "How come Ruby is speaking that way to you?" The mother says she doesn't know. The therapist asks whether Ruby always does that, or whether anything happened that made her more upset than usual. The mother then reveals that Ruby had been with her father the day before, and soon afterward, he had been taken to jail. Ruby had overheard the mother telling a friend that the father was in jail, and Ruby had been so upset that she had cried nonstop at school and had to be sent home. The therapist speaks sympathetically about this incident and tells Ruby that maybe she is worried about her father. She then adds that sometimes, when we are too worried, we get angry more easily. At the end of the session, the therapist suggests to the mother that she might keep track of Ruby's behavior in the days that follow because the child may well be more irritable and aggressive as a result of her worries about her father.

6. When immediate protective action seems necessary because the mother passively accepts the child's physical aggression, the clinician stops and redirects the child's behavior, first asking the parent for permission to do so, if feasible.

   EXAMPLE.
   Angela, 15 months, starts having a tantrum where she hits her mother repeatedly and screams when her mother takes the scissors away from her. The mother does not respond. The therapist asks the mother whether it's OK if she steps in, and when the mother agrees, the

therapist tells Angela, "You can hit this cushion, but you can't hit your mommy." Angela lifts her arm to hit the mother again; the therapist takes Angela's arm and redirects it, helping her hit the cushion. She says, "Hit the cushion, not Mommy. Mommy can't give you the scissors because you can get hurt." She holds Angela's hand, helping her hit the cushion several times, saying, "Hit the cushion, not Mommy" again and again.

There is some risk in trying this kind of intervention, and the therapist should know the child well before she does so. In our experience, many children become more and more agitated if they are encouraged to hit anything, even a pillow. Containing and calming the child may work more effectively for most children than allowing them to hit an object.

EXAMPLE.
Samuel, 3 years old, kicks the door angrily. Just as he gets ready to kick it again, the therapist says, "I bet you can stop." Surprised, Samuel stops briefly and looks at the therapist, who quickly says, "You stopped, Samuel! Good for you! Give me five!" Samuel smiles broadly and "gives five" to the clinician, who says, enthusiastically, "I knew you could stop, Samuel!" Samuel says, "I am a good boy." The mother and the therapist agree.

EXAMPLE.
Sylvia, 4 years old, takes a sharp object and yells, "I will poke your eyes out, Mommy" while waving it very close to her mother's face. The mother says weakly, "Don't do that," but the child escalates her behavior. The clinician says to the mother, "Do you mind if I speak with Sylvia?" The mother nods her head helplessly. The clinician approaches Sylvia and says firmly, "Put that down, Sylvia. You have to listen to your mother." Sylvia obeys. The clinician then says, "I know you are angry with your mommy, but you can't hurt her. It is not good for her, and it is not good for you."

7. **If the mother misperceives the child's aggression as loving or playful behavior, the therapist expresses his or her point of view. If the mother insists**

that the child was being loving or playful, the therapist suggests that this can become a topic for further exchanges.

EXAMPLE.

Lorraine, 14 months old, alternates between kissing her mother, licking her face, and biting her. The mother grimaces in pain but lets the child continue doing it. The clinician asks, "How come you let her bite you?" The mother says, "She doesn't know she is hurting me." The clinician says, "You might be right, but I think she is experimenting to see if it hurts you or not, and she needs to learn that it does." The mother says, "I don't want her to feel guilty." The clinician replies, "But how will she learn not to hurt you unless you teach her?" The mother says, "She's too little right now. She'll learn in time." The clinician answers, "It's hard for me to watch when you are hurt, but I guess we can continue talking about it." The mother says, "Don't worry; it doesn't hurt that much." The clinician says, lightly, "You have to forgive me, but it's hard for me to believe that." The topic switches as the mother puts Lorraine down and gives her a toy.

EXAMPLE.

Reuben, 4 years old, responds to a maternal command by jumping up, pointing his finger at his mother as if his finger were a gun, and saying, "Don't make me have to shoot you, Mommy." The mother laughs. The therapist asks what she finds funny, and the mother responds that he looks just like a cowboy—very cute. The therapist says, "I find him very cute most of the time, but not when he wants to shoot you." The mother shrugs her shoulders and answers, "He is just playing. Children play." The clinician says, "You know, I think he was kind of serious about it. You and I are seeing it differently. Maybe we can think about it some more as we continue to meet." In a later session, the mother remarks that Reuben is having trouble at school because he hits, and again she laughs as she tells the story. Reuben laughs, too. The therapist comments on this, and the mother says, "He is so cute when he gets angry, but I know it can get him in trouble." The clinician says, "I think he likes it when you find him cute, and maybe that makes him hit more." Mother is silent. Turning to

Reuben, the clinician says, "Your mom and I are talking about hitting. We are trying to think of ways of helping you not to hit."

8. **When the child's aggression is a response to the mother's harshness, the clinician speaks to the anger between them and introduces the theme of finding nonhurtful ways of expressing anger.**

EXAMPLE.

Camilo, 4 years old, kicks his mother in the leg after she pulls his ear in punishment because he did not obey her harsh command to turn off the TV. The mother says, in exasperation, "You are bad! You are just like your father!" The clinician says, "Could we take a look at what just happened?" There is a silence. The clinician asks, "Camilo, can you tell us why you kicked your mother?" Camilo says, very clearly, looking at his mother, "You are mean." The mother lifts her eyes to the ceiling, as if asking the Heavens for mercy. The clinician says, "She's mean? How is she mean?" Camilo says, "She hurt my ear." The clinician says, "She hurt your ear, and then you kicked her because you were angry?" Camilo nods. The clinician turns to the mother and asks, "What do you think?" The mother says, "I need to teach him to obey. He never does what I tell him to do." The clinician says, "You get angry at Camilo and hurt him, and then Camilo gets angry at you and hurts you." There is a silence. The clinician asks, "Is there a way that you won't need to hurt each other?" Camilo says to his mother, "I want you to speak to me like this: 'My dear little Camilo, can you please turn off the TV?'" The mother bursts out laughing, joined by the clinician and, after a brief delay, by Camilo. The clinician says, "You want your mom to be very polite with you," and Camilo nods. The clinician says, "I know what you mean. It's nice when people speak nicely to us." The mother says to the clinician, "I don't know where he learns these things." The clinician replies, "I have seen you speak very nicely to him. I think he likes it so much he wishes you were always that way with him." The mother looks pensive. She then says to her son, "I am not a very polite person, Camilo. But I won't pull your ear, and I don't want you to kick me."

9. When the mother is so angry at the child's aggression that she is unable to perceive the child's appropriate remorse, the therapist calls her attention to it while supporting the legitimacy of her feelings.

   EXAMPLE.

   The mother of Ava, 4 years old, reports angrily that Ava punched her in the stomach earlier in the day and that it hurt very much. As she starts speaking, Ava leans against her and hides her face in the mother's chest. The clinician asks what happened, and the mother reports that while the movers were in the apartment, taking the belongings of a roommate who was moving out, Ava came "out of the blue" and punched her very hard. Ava's face was still buried in the mother's chest. The clinician says, "You know, I'm sure Ava's punch really did hurt because she is a strong girl. And, I think that, for Ava, having all these people here this morning, and knowing that your roommate that she likes is moving out, and everybody talking excitedly and things being moved out of the apartment—all that was sad and confusing. Sometimes, when you're small, you can feel lost and unseen and not be able to control how you get your mommy's attention, but I can see that Ava seems upset that she hurt you." The mother's tone of voice becomes much warmer as she comments, "Well, Mommy doesn't like it when Ava hits her, and we will have to try really hard not to let it happen again." Ava lifts her head from the mother's chest and motions that she wants to whisper something in her ear. Ava gently moves the mother's hair from her ear and whispers, "Can we play with the doll house now?" The mother responds, "Yes, now we can play with the doll house."

10. When the child's aggression indicates a misunderstanding of the parent's motives, the therapist explains what is happening in order to help the child achieve a more accurate perception of reality. This may involve bringing in other relevant themes in the child's life that fuel the child's distorted perception of the parent's intentions.

    EXAMPLE.

    The mother of Carina, 4 years old, reports in a very upset tone of voice that the child hit her and told her to "go away" at a party. The clinician turns to Carina and repeats what the mother said in a surprised tone of voice. The mother starts crying, and the child brings her some tissues. The clinician comments that the mother could probably use some because she seems very sad. The child goes back to playing with the doll house, with her back to the mother. The mother says that Carina had gotten very angry at her at the party because there was no pineapple pizza, which is her favorite kind of pizza. With much feeling, the therapist says to Carina, "Oooh, you must have been very angry." Carina nods. The therapist adds, "I bet you thought it was your mom's fault that there was no pineapple pizza." Carina nods but remains turned to the doll house. The mother's face brightens with a new understanding. The therapist continues, "Well, sometimes, when we are 4 years old, we think our mommies are so big and strong that they can get anything we want. Like they can make pineapple pizza come, and they can even make our daddy come when we want him. And the mommy really wants to help and even asks the aunt to order pineapple pizza or asks the daddy to come visit, and no matter how hard the mommy tries, things just don't happen. And then the mommy's feelings get hurt when she tries so hard and still the little girl is angry because she [the mommy] couldn't make it happen." Carina turns around and jumps on her mother's arms, hugging her tightly.

Domain VI: Child Aggression Toward Peers, Siblings, or Others

There is substantial research evidence that children exposed to marital conflict and violence have problems in peer relationships. These problems may be manifested in aggression toward peers or in being bullied by peers. Such findings are expected in light of the increased incidence of clinically significant problem behaviors in these children when compared with nonexposed peers. Many of the causal mechanisms implicated in aggression toward the mother are at work in triggering children's aggression to peers, as well. Common factors are anxious attachment; the lack of adaptive social skills and coping mechanisms to handle frustration; and the tendency to misinterpret neutral social cues, to overreact, and to strike back in response to peer rejection. Although research on sibling aggression in the first 5 years is limited, there is abundant clinical evidence indicating that siblings, particularly younger ones, are the most likely peers to become the brunt of children's aggression because of daily, moment-to-moment proximity and the competition for scarce resources, particularly the parent's attention and love.

The opportunities for direct intervention with peer aggression are necessarily limited in a therapeutic setting because peers are not present, but children and mothers often report on the child's difficulties in the child care or preschool setting, and these reports provide an entry point for intervention. More direct intervention is possible in sibling conflicts when treatment is conducted in the home. Although the primary focus of CPP is the attachment relationship, this focus is defined broadly because the attachment relationship is deeply affected by the child's perception of how he fits into the emotional landscape of the household. Sibling rivalry is fueled by the child's fear that the parent prefers one child over the others. The overall treatment goal of adaptive affect modulation and expression must include the child's ability to develop reciprocal and loving relationships with siblings and peers and to negotiate conflict with them in nonhurtful ways. Intervention strategies need to take into account that self-endangering behavior, aggression toward the mother, and aggression toward others (including the clinician) can occur in quick succession because the child's anger, when blocked, can turn from one target to another, becoming diffuse and uncontrolled.

PORTS OF ENTRY AND CLINICAL EXAMPLES

1. **When the child or the parent reports that the child used physical aggression against a peer, the clinician starts a calm discussion of the event, including an understanding of how it came about, the meaning of the child's behavior, and alternative ways of expressing anger.**

   EXAMPLE.
   The mother of Yael, 5 years old, reports that in preschool that morning, the child had pushed her friend Paula when Paula's father arrived to pick her up. The mother had witnessed the episode and called out to Yael, but the child did not respond. A teacher then told the mother that Yael always hits or pushes Paula when Paula's father comes to take his daughter home. The clinician now asks Yael what happened that made her push Paula when Paula's father arrived. Yael explains that she likes Paula's father and that she wanted to go home with him,

but she couldn't. The clinician asks, "Does that make you sad and also angry?" Yael responds, "I get sad." The clinician asks whether Yael wants a father like Paula's father. Yael says, "I have my grandpa, but he lives far away and I don't see him." The clinician comments that Yael is sad because she misses her grandfather. Yael says, "I was good in school today, and I will go to kindergarten." The clinician replies, "I know you want to be good, but you pushed Paula, and I think you are worried that the teacher will not let you go to kindergarten." Yael says, "The teacher says I can't hit if I want to go to kindergarten." The clinician says, "Let's think of what else you can do instead of pushing or hitting Paula . . . . Can you go to a quiet place and say to yourself, 'I am sad and angry because I am not going home with Paula and her father, but I can't push her and I can't hit her because I want to go to kindergarten'?" Yael says, "Yeah."

2. **When the child's aggression toward others seems related to parental physical aggression toward the child, the therapist helps the parent see the connection between the two and encourages a change in the parent's as well as the child's behavior.**

    EXAMPLE.
    The mother of Linda, 4 years old, and Sandy, 2 years old, reports that the children are hitting other children at school when they do not get their way. Sandy also hit a teacher that morning. The therapist asks whether anything happened in the family to make Sandy hit the teacher, and the mother shrugs her shoulders, saying that everything is the same and that she is baffled by this sudden aggression. The therapist asks whether it really was sudden, and the mother admits that Sandy's behavior has been slowly getting worse over time. The therapist asks the mother to describe a couple of recent times when she got upset with the children. The mother readily describes several incidents when she immediately yelled, "Stop it!" and slapped them. The mother adds, spontaneously, as an afterthought, "I guess they are doing what I do." The therapist asks how she feels about it, and the mother says, "I really don't know any other way of doing it; it's an automatic response." The therapist suggests that one way of making it less automatic is to start paying close attention to her feelings as they build

up, so she can do something before getting so angry that she snaps. The mother remembers an occasion when the therapist helped her talk about her feelings about a frustrating situation; she felt better afterward, even though the situation had not changed. The therapist says, "I remember that. Do you think it can also work if you use that with your children?" The mother says, "Well, when Linda looks at me with those 'Don't mess with me' eyes, I feel like clobbering her. Maybe I can stop myself if I try." The therapist turns to the children and says, "Your mommy and I are talking about how all of you are going to try not to hit." As mother and children are leaving the playroom at the end of the session, there is an opportunity to practice this because Linda grabs something from Sandy's hand and Sandy lifts her hand to hit her. Before she can do it, the mother grabs Sandy's hand and then turns uncertainly toward the therapist, who steps in to help, saying, "Linda and Sandy, your mommy really means it that she doesn't want to slap you any more, and she doesn't want you to slap each other. You need to tell each other in words what you want." A conversation ensues about what triggered the conflict and how to solve it, with the therapist guiding the mother in this effort.

3. **When the child engages in aggressive behavior, the clinician tries to set up a situation that de-escalates the behavior.**

   EXAMPLE.

   Paulo, 4 years old, is swinging a yo-yo in a way that can hit his older brother. The mother has gone momentarily out of the room. The clinician tells the older brother to move away from Paulo so that he will not get hit. The brother complies. The clinician then says to Paulo, "Paulo, we can't be close to you when you are doing something that can hurt us. You have to stop doing that." Paulo responds by making smaller circles as he continues to wave the yo-yo. The clinician says, "That is better, but it is still not good enough. Make the circles even smaller." Paulo complies. The circles are now so small that they pose no danger to a bystander. The clinician says, "Good job, Paulo. Now it is safe to be near you." Paulo looks visibly pleased. He stops swinging the yo-yo and tries to make it go up and down.

4. **When the child engages in escalating aggressive behavior, the therapist takes whatever steps are needed to ensure safety until the aggressive behavior subsides, assuring the child that the adults will take care of him and not let him hurt himself or others.**

EXAMPLE.

Danny, 4 years old, is pushing the swing in a way that is threatening to hit his sister Dottie, who is toddling about. The clinician suggests a game that Danny likes, but Danny looks at her defiantly and keeps moving the swing in his sister's direction. The mother tries to take his hand to bring him over, but he suddenly starts writhing and kicking at her. Seeing that she seems scared and helpless, the clinician goes over to help restrain him, but the child seems stronger than both adults. The clinician instructs the mother that they will divide their efforts, and both hold him to stop him from kicking. The mother holds Danny's legs, and the clinician holds his upper body. He flails and writhes very hard, and both have to struggle very hard to stop him from hitting and kicking them. He starts screaming, "I want to kill myself! Kill me, kill me! You don't love me!" looking at his mother. He then looks at the clinician and screams, "Don't touch me!" The clinician tells him that she and his mother are holding him because first he was trying to hurt his sister and then his mother and now he was saying that he wanted to hurt himself, and his mother and the clinician did not want that to happen. In all of this, as soon as he was able to free one arm, he would hit his mother or punch his own face. He also managed to bite his mother's hands. He also kept screaming that his mother did not love him. She would say, tentatively, "You know that I love you very much?" He would wail, "No, you don't love me!" The clinician tells him that both of his parents love him and want him to be safe, but sometimes they did not know how to show it. He wails that this is not true and screams to the mother, "You call me 'stupid'!" The mother freezes, and the clinician speaks for her, saying that his mother is sorry that she called him names, and then asks the mother to tell him the same thing. All along, the clinician has been talking to the mother, saying things like, "You are doing really well; it is hard to hold him" and "He is very scared and wants us to reassure him that we won't let him hurt himself, and that is why we have to keep him still." The clinician now says to the mother, "Tell him that you want to keep him safe." The mother hesitates, and the clinician says more firmly that he needs to hear her say it. She says it, half-heartedly. The clinician encourages the mother to tell him that she loves him and would try not to call him names. She says, in a questioning tone, "You know I love you?" Danny yells, "No!" The clinician tells the mother to keep it simple, saying only, "I love you. I will keep you safe." The mother repeats these words several times, with increasing conviction, and then she begins to hold Danny more effectively.

Danny then starts asking the clinician to let go of him. The clinician answers that she does not want to let go of him because earlier he hit his mom and himself when he had his arms free. She says that she will let go of one of his hands and see whether he is more calm, adding, "If I see that you won't hit yourself or your mom when I let go of one hand, then I will let go of you." She lets go of his hand, and the child does not hit. The clinician says to the mother, "Let's let go of him and see if he is calm." They both let go of him, and he cuddles up in his mother's lap very quietly, leaning against her. The mother puts her arms tightly around him, and he almost immediately falls asleep.

Domain VII: Parental Use of Physical Punishment

The use of physical punishment as a form of child discipline is a source of heated controversy. It is widely used in the United States, but it is met with almost uniform disapproval by child development professionals. Social class and cultural factors play an important role in how people perceive the use of physical punishment. When there is a social class difference between parent and clinician, the implicit power differential between both parties can become more acute when the clinician expresses disapproval of the parental actions. Similarly, when the clinician and the parent belong to different cultural (i.e., ethnic or national) backgrounds, it is easy for parents to feel that the clinician is expressing disapproval for their traditional patterns of child-rearing. Recent immigrants who are unfamiliar with the range of child-rearing mores in the United States might be particularly vulnerable to feelings of insecurity and defensiveness, whereas ethnic minorities with histories of discrimination may react with anger and resentment at perceived efforts to impose child-rearing patterns that feel alien to them.

Physical punishment takes a variety of forms, from a mild slap on the child's hand or bottom to slapping the child's face, pulling hair, pinching, biting, using an object to inflict pain, and leaving marks on the child's body. We take the position that, although an occasional mild slap on the hand or bottom is not likely to have a serious deleterious effect on the child, it is not an optimal form of discipline, and it should be discouraged. This is particularly the case for children who have witnessed violence and who, as a result, tend to be hypervigilant and hyper-responsive to threats and danger signals that would seem minor to other children. For this reason, we recommend that any form of physical punishment needs to be addressed with the parent at some point, not necessarily in the moment but at a time when there can be constructive discussion. The clinician should always make an explicit effort to understand and respect the cultural underpinnings of the parent's use of physical punishment, even when disagreeing with it.

Few situations arouse as strong a feeling of disapproval toward parents as watching them be harshly physically punitive to their children. The clinician must develop a deep conviction that, although parental physical punishment is inappropriate, it does not justify becoming judgmental or punitive toward the parent. One must avoid enacting a parallel process by which the clinician becomes harsh with the parent who is harsh with the child. The goal of the intervention is not to give the parent moral instruction but to enable to parent to have better impulse control and to modulate strong negative feelings, including anger and fear. For this goal to be met, clinicians must have the capacity to restrain their own punitive impulses toward the parent and to modulate their anger and disapproval of the way that the child is being treated. Remembering that punitiveness toward the child is rooted in the parents' own experiences of harsh and inappropriate punishment often helps the clinician to curb angry and critical feelings. It is also important to remember that, whenever possible, discipline needs to be discussed as an effort to help the child learn rather than as a form of punishment.

There is sometimes disagreement among professionals and even among child welfare workers about which kinds of physical punishment qualify as legally reportable physical abuse. When the clinician is in doubt, we recommend calling the child protective services emergency response unit to describe the incident and ask for advice. This section of the manual focuses on forms of physical punishment that do not qualify as child abuse. The next section focuses on procedures to follow for reporting possible child abuse.

PORTS OF ENTRY AND CLINICAL EXAMPLES

1. **When the parent uses socially accepted physical punishment (e.g., a mild slap on the child's hand or buttocks), the clinician finds an appropriate time, preferably after the heat of the moment has subsided, to ask the parent about her values and beliefs about how children should be disciplined. This opportunity is used to develop a dialogue about this topic, to offer developmental guidance if the parent seems receptive to it, or to discuss how the parent was brought up, if this seems appropriate.**

   EXAMPLE.

   Briana, 4 months old, kicks vigorously while her mother is changing her diapers. Mother slaps her on the bottom—not too hard, but firmly. Briana startles and stops moving, making a brief noise of distress. The clinician asks whether it bothers her when Briana is so active. The mother says, "Yes, she doesn't like to be changed, and she's making it hard for me to do it." The clinician asks, "What do you hope she'll learn when you slap her?" The mother answers, "To stop moving and cooperate." The clinician says, "I think she had no idea that is what you want. She looked so surprised. I think she was just so happy to be out of those soiled diapers and was letting you know how good it felt to be free." The mother looks skeptical but listens attentively.

   EXAMPLE.

   Peter, 2 years old, pulls his baby brother's hair. His mother slaps him on the hand. Both Peter and his brother cry. The mother picks up the wailing baby and consoles him, while Peter sobs loudly alone in a corner. The clinician looks at the mother sympathetically and says, "I guess everybody is having a hard time." The mother looks over- whelmed, and the clinician asks if she can talk to Peter while the mother consoles the baby. The mother agrees, and the clinician speaks softly to Peter, telling him that she knows it is very hard to be hit and to watch his mother hold his baby brother instead of him.

When things calm down, the clinician asks the mother whether she finds that slapping works as a way of teaching Peter how to behave. The mother says, ruefully, "It hasn't worked yet, but I hope someday it will." The clinician asks if that is the way she was disciplined while growing up, and the mother replies that it was. The clinician asks, "What was it like for you? Do you feel it was useful as you grew up?" The mother says, "It taught me respect. I was afraid of my parents, but I respected them." The clinician asks, "Is that how you want Peter to feel about you?" The mother says, "I want him to respect me, but I don't want him to be afraid of me." The clinician answers, "I can understand that, and there are ways of doing it. Children Peter's age really want to please their parents, even if sometimes it is hard to believe that they do. They love it when their parents approve of them, and they feel bad when the parents disapprove of what they do. If you tell Peter what you like and what you don't like, I think he will learn it very well. If you like, next time Peter does something wrong when I am here, we can try it together and see how it works."

2. **The clinician asks the parent for her motivation in using physical punishment, asks the child how she or he felt, and guides parent and child toward a dialogue about how each of them sees the situation that led to physical punishment.**

   EXAMPLE.
   Lisa's mother slaps her on the bottom when the child uses a dirty word to refer to her sister. Lisa, 4 years old, looks at her mother with angry eyes but says nothing. The mother tells her angrily, "I can hit you again just for giving me that look." Turning to the clinician, she says, "I hate that look. It is so hateful." The clinician asks the mother what she wanted to show Lisa when she slapped her. The mother says, "I want her to learn not to use dirty words." The clinician says to Lisa, "What do you think about that, Lisa?" Lisa replies, "She says the same word to me." The mother protests that Lisa is lying. The clinician says, "You want to use the same words that your mom uses, and you get angry when she punishes you for it?" Lisa says, "Yes." The mother says, "Maybe sometimes I use that word, but I'm a grown-up, and you are a child." The clinician says, "I see your point, but I bet Lisa doesn't.

She thinks you're cool, and she wants to be like you."

3. **The clinician finds an appropriate time to suggest an alternative to physical punishment that teaches the child about unwanted consequences for undesirable behavior.**

   EXAMPLE.

   Joe, 3 years old, is climbing on his mother's dresser and falls, banging his head on the floor and nearly pulling the dresser over on top of him. His mother runs to him and pulls him away. Mother and child are clearly frightened. The mother checks Joe's head and is able to calm him in a few minutes. After he stops crying, she says, "I have to get the paddle now." Joe jumps, runs away from her with a terrorized look, and stands mutely in the corner of the room, shaking. The clinician says to the mother, "Could we please talk about it for a minute? Joe looks so frightened. Can we see if there is anything else that can teach him without frightening him so much?" The mother stops but replies that he deserves the paddle. The clinician says, "Look at him. He just fell and hurt his head. Do you think maybe that is what he should learn, that if he climbs on the dresser something bad will happen? Isn't falling and hurting his head the lesson that he needs to learn?" The mother relents, and says to Joe, "OK, no paddling for today, but don't you ever climb on that dresser again." During this conversation, Joe continues to tremble and to stare at his mother with a frozen gaze. He gradually relaxes after she tells him that she will not paddle him.

4. **When the parent expresses a religious or cultural conviction that physical punishment is morally necessary, the clinician explains that children who witnessed violence, particularly involving loved ones, are emotionally overwhelmed by physical punishment and are unable to learn from it.**

   EXAMPLE.

   Samuel, 3 years old, drops a glass on the floor as he reaches across the table to retrieve a toy. The glass breaks. His mother yells at him and slaps him on the bottom. Samuel cries heartily while the mother berates him for the mess he made. The clinician listens and observes quietly. She then helps the mother to pick up the pieces of glass and mop up the spilled water. When the mood softens, the clinician asks, "Do you usually slap Samuel when he does something wrong?" The mother says she does. The clinician asks, "How did you decide to do that?" The mother says, "I am a Christian, and in the Bible, it says that if you spare the rod you spoil the child." The clinician comments, "I can see that your religion is very important to you." The mother replies, "It certainly is. I go to church three times a week, and my pastor is very helpful to me." The clinician asks in what ways her pastor is helpful. The mother answers, "I am a single mother; my child has no father. My pastor is like a father to him. He helps me when I don't know what to do with Sam." The clinician asks whether the pastor believes that sparing the rod spoils the child. The mother says with conviction, "He sure does. He taught me that." The clinician says, "You know, I respect how important it is for you to learn from your pastor what it says in the Bible. Let me tell you what I am thinking. Maybe you can ask your pastor about it. He certainly knows the Bible much better than I do, and I wouldn't want to tell you anything that goes against your religion. But one thing that we learned about children who saw a lot of violence between their mother and father is that hitting is not helpful in teaching them how to behave. It reminds them of how scared they got when their mom and dad fought, and they get so scared all over again that they can't learn what you are trying to teach them. What they actually learn is that hitting is OK, and they start hitting also because it makes them feel less scared, like they are strong and able to defend themselves. I worry that if you slap Samuel as a way of teaching him, then he will start slapping because he'll think that if you do it, then it means it's fine for him to do it, too." The mother says, "I never thought about it that way. I will tell my pastor what you are saying and ask him what he thinks about it." (In a subsequent session, the mother reported that her pastor agreed with the clinician's recommendation, and she decided to stop hitting the child.)

5. **When the clinician believes that discussing the parent's use of physical punishment in front of the child would be perceived as disrespectful by**

the parent, the clinician waits for a private moment to raise the topic or requests a telephone appointment or an individual session with the parent.

EXAMPLE.

The mother of Khalil, 4 years old, slaps him on the hand for wanting to drink from her glass. "It is my juice. Go get yourself some of your own," she says. Khalil complies. Knowing that the mother has strong feelings about being in charge of Khalil, the clinician takes advantage of his being in the kitchen to say, "You know, I think that Khalil's hitting at school might have something to do with what happened just now. Could I come a little earlier next time, so we can talk about it before Khalil is back from school?" The mother says, "I'm not too sure what you're getting at, but sure." The conversation stops when Khalil returns from the kitchen with a glass of juice and offers some to the clinician.

6. **If it becomes clear that the parent and clinician have widely divergent views and values about the use of physical punishment, the clinician acknowledges that this is the case and suggests an ongoing discussion of this topic to see whether areas of agreement could emerge.**

EXAMPLE.

Amelia, 15 months old, spills juice on the carpet, and her mother matter-of-factly slaps her on the hand. Amelia does not respond. The clinician comments that Amelia seems to take the slap in stride. The mother says, "She's used to it. She knows that I slap her when she does something wrong." The clinician asks if slapping helps Amelia not do things wrong. The mother says, "Of course. If I slap her, she knows she is not supposed to do it again." The clinician says, "I actually think that sometimes, children get confused. Maybe they know they did something wrong, but they don't know how to make it right." The mother says, forcefully, "Of course they know. Like now, Amelia knows she needs to be more careful with her juice. Don't you, Amelia?" Amelia nods soberly. The mother says to the clinician, "See? I told you. She knows." The clinician says, "I guess this is one place where we see things differently. I think Amelia is trying very hard to please you, but she doesn't know how to be more careful with the juice. Let's continue talking about it in the future and see whether we can understand where each of us is coming from." The mother says, "That's OK by me."

7. **When the clinician finds himself or herself flooded with strong feelings of anger and disapproval toward the parent, he or she refrains from taking immediate action and engages in an internal process of searching for emotional balance and modulation of feelings.**

    EXAMPLE.

    Charlie, 30 months old, does not respond fast enough when his mother asks him to bring her something from the kitchen, and she slaps him quite hard while telling him angrily that he never listens and he is trying to annoy her on purpose. While Charlie cries, the mother tells him that he is just pretending to be scared and that he is a manipulator. The clinician feels flooded by rage at the mother, with whom she has been working for many months to help her understand that toddlers do not always respond readily to commands. The clinician feels a strong desire to yell at the mother that she is mean and nasty and that the clinician is sick and tired of working with her. The clinician has a clear internal image of herself walking out the door while calling the mother names. As she is struggling with these feelings, the mother expresses regret for having hit Charlie and apologizes to the child. The clinician remains internally very angry and imagines herself telling the mother that her regret comes too late and that she is a terrible mother. At the same time, the clinician keeps telling herself, "You know that there is more here than meets the eye. Think. Think. Try to understand why she is acting this way in front of you." After about 2 minutes, the clinician remembers the mother's abysmal sense that she is no good and that she deserves nothing good, a theme the mother has often spoken about in previous sessions. She says to the mother, "There are times when it is hard to remember how patient you can be with Charlie because the anger is so hot and so real, and when that happens, you get really down on yourself. But it is important for us to remember that you can come back to the part of you that does not want to hurt Charlie, and to keep reminding Charlie of that so he does not forget." Turning to Charlie, she says, "Your mom is trying really hard to learn not to hit, but sometimes, it takes a long time to learn." Charlie nods his head sadly, as if saying he understood. The mother's eyes fill with tears, and she says softly, "I wish it did not take so long, honey."

8. **When the parent is unresponsive to other forms of intervention, the clinician urges the parent, politely but firmly, not to hit or use physical punishment because it is not good for the child's respect for the parent and healthy development.**

    EXAMPLE.
    The mother is describing in exacting detail, clearly quite satisfied with herself, how she "whooped" her child for being sassy. The clinician listens, fully aware that he has tried many tactful forms of intervention before, all to no avail. He feels that he has a good relationship with the mother, who trusts his good judgment without necessarily always following his advice. The child is outside of hearing range in the next room, and the clinician feels that he can disagree with the mother without humiliating her in front of the child. He says, "Adela, I know we have talked about this before, but I really need to tell you something. You need to find other ways of teaching Monique not to be sassy. Hitting her is no good. She will think that she is no good, and she will also lose respect for you." The mother laughs heartily, and says, "If I do what you say, will you come and keep her in line when she is a teenager?" The clinician says, also laughingly, "You will need me more if you keep hitting her. She will become a wild teenager, and then how will you stop her? She could even hit you back because she will be stronger and quicker than you! We need to find ways of teaching her that you can use even when she is a teenager."

Domain VIII: Parental Use of Derogatory Names, Threats, or Criticism of the Child

Parents can cause considerable emotional damage by calling their children by derogatory names, ridiculing them, being harshly critical, and threatening them. These parental behaviors present a difficult therapeutic challenge. Clinicians do not want to appear as if they are criticizing the parent or taking the child's side, yet continued failure to act can have the effect of colluding with the parent, confirming the supposed "truth" of the criticism or the rightness of the threat, and leaving the child emotionally alone.

Optimally, the clinician's response needs to simultaneously express interest and empathy for the parent's anger and frustration, and empathic support for the child's fear and worry in response to the parent. The overall attitude to be conveyed is a wish to create a more positive emotional climate between parent and child. For this to happen, the clinician's emotional position needs to be equidistant between parent and child. Compassion for the child's suffering must be balanced by awareness that the parent also suffers, although this pain is covered over by anger and bitterness.

It helps to remember that the focus of the intervention is neither the parent nor the child as individuals—but, rather, their relationship. When witnessing a difficult scene between parent and child, clinicians need to give themselves permission to do nothing if they find themselves in an internal state of turmoil and confusion. Although complacency should be discouraged, it is better to do nothing temporarily than to intervene out of anger, striking out blindly at the parent in a futile effort to protect the child.

Knowing about events that happened during the week prior to the session is often essential for constructive intervention. Behaviors that seem inexplicable or irrational suddenly acquire clear meaning when one knows about real-life events or about how a person has been feeling. Asking direct questions about what happened since the last session can provide a context that clarifies the reasons for the parent's anger or the child's defiant, sullen, aggressive, or recalcitrant behavior.

The items that follow involve interventions that often overlap with each other. In the flow of the session, clinicians often start with one strategy that is followed and complemented by another. Interventions are not "sound bites" but part of a concerted effort to enhance intimacy and communication between parent and child, help them express intense feelings in nonfrightening ways, and help them modulate and regulate overwhelming emotion. An overarching goal of all the intervention strategies suggested is to develop a joint plan for appropriate alternative behaviors. Clearly, this goal cannot be achieved in every session or as a result of every intervention. However, the clinician needs to take every opportunity to help the parent and the child develop and practice specific forms of behavior that feel safer as well as more comforting and pleasurable.

Ports of Entry and Clinical Examples

1. When the parent is harshly critical of the child, the clinician first empathizes with the anger and frustration whenever possible, and then explores why the child's behavior prompted this response. In this process, the clinician offers alternative explanations that give a different and more balanced meaning to the child's behavior. These suggestions may involve reframing the child's behavior or the parent's perception of it, suggesting possible motives for the child's behavior that the parent might be unaware of, and/or describing the developmental appropriateness of the child's reaction.

   Example.

   Lisa and her mother are talking about the mother's boyfriend leaving without saying good-bye. The mother is saying that she has been depressed all week—barely able to make herself go to work, and grouchy and exhausted when she gets home. Lisa, 4 years old, is looking very sad. The mother notices it and starts rubbing Lisa's back. Lisa comes closer to the mother, falling back so that the mother can do it more easily. The mother then starts playing with the toy dishes, trying to engage Lisa. She tickles Lisa and hands her a plate of pretend food, but the child refuses to take it. Lisa starts to whine and sort of "commands" her mother to continue rubbing her back. The mother's empathic mood changes abruptly, and she yells, "Don't whine. Use your words. I don't want to rub you any more. Let's play." Lisa starts crying loudly. The mother turns to the clinician and says angrily, "You see? She never gets enough. She always wants more." Turning back to Lisa, she says, "I rubbed your back for a long time, and I am tired of it." The clinician says that it seemed as if the problem wasn't about rubbing Lisa's back; it was about something else—that Lisa looked sad and disappointed, but it did not seem to be about her back. The mother's anger leaves her, and she says tenderly, "I know you are sad, Lisa. It's about his leaving, I know. Come sit on my lap." Lisa sits on the mother's lap, and the mother cuddles her. Lisa kisses her, and the mother kisses Lisa back. Lisa sits quietly, clearly comforted by her mother. When the therapist leaves, mother and daughter walk her to the door holding hands.

2. **The clinician points out to the parent, in a serious and interested way and without anger, how the child feels when criticized or called by derogatory names.**

    EXAMPLE.
    Gabriel, 5 years old, and his mother had a difficult day. Gabriel chased his 2-year-old sister with a shopping cart, and the little girl ran into the parking lot just as a car was coming by, barely missing her. As she recounts the event, the mother says, "He is just like his father. Do you remember the film *The Evil Seed*? Sometimes, I think I gave birth to a child like that." As she speaks, Gabriel approaches his sister and hits her. The mother screams, "Stop hitting your sister! I won't let you murder us!" Gabriel walks away and starts pulling a baby doll apart. The clinician says, "Gabriel, you are showing us how you feel when your mom speaks like that about you." There is a silence. The clinician adds, "I see that it upsets you very much when your mom speaks of you that way." The mother says, "I said he would murder us, didn't I?" The clinician answers, "That is what I heard, and that is what Gabriel also heard. Children really believe what their mothers say." The mother says, "Sometimes, I forget he is just a little boy; he reminds me of his father so much." The clinician says, "Gabriel, your mom is telling us that she forgets that you are only a little boy. She is angry at your dad, and then she gets angry at you, but you are just a little boy who needs to learn how not to hurt your sister. I am here to help your mom remember that you are only a little boy and to help you learn what to do with your angry and scary feelings."

3. **The clinician puts into words how the child is responding nonverbally to the parent's criticism, speaking to both parent and child in a supportive and sympathetic manner.**

    EXAMPLE.
    The clinician has to cut the home visit short because the family has acquired a new cat that triggers a severe allergic reaction. When the clinician explains to Joshua, 3 years old, that she needs to go home because the cat is making her sick, he starts crying loudly. Between sobs, he says he wants the clinician to stay and play. The mother yells

at him, "You are a crybaby! Don't do this to me! She has to go home, and that's all." The clinician comes close to Joshua and says, "Joshua, I know you are very sad that I have to leave and take the toys with me. I know you thought I would stay longer, and I am very sorry that I am sick and have to go." Joshua stops crying. The clinician adds that she will talk to his mother to figure out a place where they can all meet so the cat won't make her sick. She says, "I'll see you next week and bring the toys again, and then we'll play some more." Joshua bends down and quietly helps to put the toys away. The mother tells the clinician, "I see what you did. You acknowledged his feelings, and then you let him feel them." The clinician asks, "Do you think it is OK for him to feel his feelings? I mean, not stop crying right away?" The mother laughs and says, "Of course it is. He has to feel what he is going to feel, and I can't stop it—nor maybe should I. OK, I see what I am doing. This is good, this is good." The clinician says lightly, "You think maybe Joshua would like to hear it directly from you?" The mother says to Joshua, "I am sorry I yelled at you, Joshua. Of course you are sad that [clinician's name] is leaving. But we will make sure that we find another place to play so the cat won't make her sick. Then we can all play together again."

4. **The clinician includes the child in the conversation, speaking to the child's experience, rephrasing the parent's criticism in child-appropriate terms, and/or encouraging the parent and child to talk about what happened between them.**

   EXAMPLE.
   Linda's mother begins the session by saying that she is furious at the child. She glares at her daughter, and Linda, 5 years old, looks down at her lap with no expression on her face. The mother tells Linda to say what happened. Linda is silent. The clinician says to the mother that because she is so very mad at Linda, it might be better if she (the mother) were the one who tells what happened. The mother explains that Linda's teacher told her that Linda was playing with a boy in the "pretend house" and wanted a boy to get on top of her. The boy did not want to, and Linda tried to force him until he started to cry and the teacher intervened. The mother now says angrily to Linda, "Look

at me while I speak, Linda," but Linda continues to stare at her lap. The clinician says, "Linda, do you know what your mom is talking about?" Linda comes over to her, buries her head in the clinician's chest, and nods her head yes. The clinician says that her mother gets very upset when she hears that Linda makes boys lie on top of her. Linda says, "I know, but I can't help it. I try to, but I can't."

The mother continues to look angrily at Linda. The clinician says to Linda, "I know you feel you can't help it." Linda says, "And everyone gets so mad at me." The clinician nods her head, and they all sit in silence for a moment. Then the clinician says that it is hard for grown-ups when they see children do things that are for grown-ups, not for children. Linda nods and remains silent. She then looks down at her lap and says, "Mom and K. (the mother's former boyfriend) were in bed, they were naked, and they were fighting really, really loud, and Mommy had a knife and the police came and Mommy told me to stay in bed and she went outside."

The mother's eyes open wide, but she says nothing. The clinician comments that it must have been very, very scary. Linda says, "I was scared that he would hurt my mommy. And now, we see him every morning before school, and it scares me." The mother says, "That's a lie, Linda. We haven't seen him in a long time." Linda looks down at her lap again, her eyes filling with tears. The clinician says softly that she could not imagine Linda would lie about something that upset her so much, and the clinician asks the mother what she thought Linda was thinking about. The mother explains that, a while back, they used to see K. on the street on the way to school, and she would stop and talk to him because he is the father of her younger child and she thought he should see his daughter. Linda interrupts the mother's description to say she was scared K. would hurt the mother. The mother says sharply, "He won't, Linda." The clinician says, "But Linda can't be sure of that. She has seen him hurt you before, and she is very, very worried. Why would she think that he is any different now?" Linda starts to sob loudly.

The mother says that she did not realize it upset Linda so much, that it had not happened in a long time. Speaking to both mother and daughter, the clinician says that it is clearly very much in Linda's mind, and it upsets her very much. Looking at the child, she adds that Linda thinks about it at school because she worries about it so much on the way there, and then at school she plays the things she remembers. Linda's sobbing subsides, and there is a silence. The clinician asks the mother whether there is a way she could help Linda not worry so much. The mother says that she easily could: If she sees K. on the street, she will not stop. The clinician asks Linda if that would help, and Linda nods, "Yes." The clinician says that it is very important for Linda to really be able to count on that. The mother tells Linda she promises that she will never stop, that she did not know it scared Linda so much, and that now she understands. The clinician asks Linda how that sounded. Linda nods her head. The mother asks her if she feels better, and Linda nods again.

5. **The clinician helps the parent and the child search for alternative behaviors that will allow the child and/or the parent to express emotion without engaging in hurtful or socially inappropriate behavior.**

   EXAMPLE.
   In the example just described, Linda says to the clinician, when the mother goes to the bathroom, "But Mommy is still mad at me for playing with that boy."

   The clinician answers that she is probably right and adds that it is good to talk about that. The clinician adds that she is worried because she knows that Linda's play scares other children and scares her too because it gets her into trouble. Linda nods. The clinician suggests that Linda could try to not make boys lie on top of her at school or anywhere else, but she could play that game with the dolls or the toy animals, and she could do that also during their time together. Linda asks, "It's OK with my mommy?" The clinician says they could ask her mommy when she comes back. She asks Linda how she feels about trying to play the way she suggested, and the child says softly that she would try. When the mother comes back, the clinician describes the previous conversation and the plan, and the mother agrees.

Then Linda goes to the bathroom, and while she is gone, the mother says that both Linda and her younger daughter cry very hard when she drops them off at school. This reminds the clinician of a recent conversation with the children's teacher, who complained that the mother drops them off at school abruptly and without saying good-bye. The clinician now tells the mother that the school transition is very hard on kids, that they just learned how much Linda worries on her way to school, and that probably the mother's younger daughter worries, too. The clinician suggests that being around for a few minutes, saying good-bye, and telling the children that she'll pick them up at the end of the day would be very reassuring for them. It would help them feel less worried about letting the mother out of their sight. The mother says that she will think about it and maybe she will try.

6. **The clinician encourages the child to put his feelings into words in response to the parent's behavior.**

EXAMPLE.

Yael, 4 years old, says, "My mommy told me she will cut my fingers off." The clinician expresses surprise and interest in knowing what happened. The mother explains that she had been talking to her nephew about how, in her home country, in years past, they punished people who stole by cutting their fingers off. She stresses that she had not told Yael anything about cutting her fingers off. The clinician asks Yael about her fear of having her fingers cut off. Yael says, "My mommy will cut my fingers off if I'm bad." She goes to hide under a table as she speaks. The clinician remembers that Yael has been having problems at the day care center for taking things out of the other children's cubbies. She leans under the table and says, "Were you thinking that your mom will cut your fingers off because she gets angry when you take things from the children's cubbies at school?" Yael nods in agreement. The clinician tells the mother that Yael seems so scared that she is hiding under the table. The mother laughs nervously and says that she would never do something like that to Yael. She reaches under the table and asks Yael to come sit on her lap. As she hugs Yael, the mother tells her that she will never tell that old story again because she can see that it frightens Yael. The clinician approves of the idea and tells the mother that, at Yael's age, children can't always tell the difference between reality and a story, and they often believe that stories are real and could happen to them.

7. **When the parent seems unresponsive to all other intervention strategies, the clinician urges the parent, politely but with conviction, not to speak in those critical terms because it has a negative effect on the child.**

   EXAMPLE.

   Sandy, 2 years old, is rather clumsy. She bumps into things, drops the objects that she is holding, and is slow at mastering age-appropriate gross motor skills. Her mother, who is quite athletic, feels embarrassed by her clumsy daughter and has taken to calling her "klutz." The clinician has tried to address this topic, but the mother seems oblivious to it. In one session, Sandy trips over a toy and falls down, hitting her head on the coffee table. She cries briefly but gets up and keeps moving. The mother says, "That happened to you because you are a klutz." The clinician says, "I know you'd like her to be more agile, but children develop at different rates. I strongly recommend that you not call her a klutz any more. She takes what you say very seriously, and your giving her a label will only make her self-conscious. She'll think this is the way she'll stay forever." The mother says, "Well, isn't it? Do you think she can possibly grow out of it?" The clinician says, "I certainly think she can grow out of it, but even if she doesn't, she can either feel terrible for who she is or she can take it in stride and take pleasure in all the other things she knows how to do." The mother says nothing but looks thoughtful.

Domain IX: Relationship With the Perpetrator/Absent Parent

Children who have witnessed domestic violence between their parents and who then experience the father's departure from the home are subjected to the dual stresses of exposure to violence between their attachment figures and subsequent separation or loss of one of them—most frequently, the father. From the perspective of attachment theory, witnessing the mother being attacked and injured involves a profound assault on the child's capacity to trust the mother as a reliable protector. When the child most needs her proximity, contact, and reassurance, the mother cannot be available because she herself is in physical and emotional need and, perhaps, danger. When the attacker is also an attachment figure (as in the case of a father or stepfather, or when the mother is also violent), the child's mental representations of the parent are split between love and terror. Young children exposed to domestic violence cannot form or sustain internal representations of violent parents as a secure base that provides safety and protection. On the contrary, it is the parents who engender fear while simultaneously eliciting a strong wish by the child to rely on the parents' protection. For infants in the first year of life, who are in the process of forming and consolidating attachments, one parent's departure from the home presents the additional challenge of maintaining the memory of that parent across gaps of days or even weeks between visits. They need to reconnect emotionally and cognitively with that parent at sporadic intervals, which in turn taxes the child's emotional and cognitive resources.

The need to retain an image of their parents as loving and protective forces children into costly coping strategies that must be changed as the situations that they face change. For example, if they are spending time with their father, they may suppress memories of his violence and adopt a view of the mother as the guilty party. When they spend time with the mother, the reverse may hold true. As a result, the child who has witnessed domestic violence experiences different emotions that serve a defensive function in relation to one another. These include longing for the absent father, fear of him, and imitation of him through identification with the aggressor. With regard to the mother, the child may experience fear, anger, and blame, which coexist with fear of losing her and protectiveness of her. These conflicting feelings are exacerbated by the actual behavior of the mother and the father when they vie with each other for the child's love, loyalty, and approval by blaming the partner and asking the young child to join them in their perception of the family drama.

The goal of the intervention is to facilitate the formation of realistic ambivalence as a psychological achievement in the child's relationship toward the abusive parent. In other words, the clinician strives to enable the child to form a more balanced and integrated internal representation of the abusive parent, involving a conscious acknowledgment that the violent parent engenders love, fear, and anger simultaneously. This goal is applicable to the child's relationship with violent mothers as well as fathers because a significant subset of battered women report that they are themselves violent toward the partner and physically punitive toward the child.

This section focuses on the child's conflicting feelings toward the absent violent parent—most commonly, the father—because of the importance of facilitating an ongoing father–child relationship whenever this goal does not interfere with the child's and the mother's safety. This goal necessarily requires working with the mother's feelings toward her estranged partner and the way in which she expresses these feelings to the child. Mothers going through difficult divorces often need help in remembering that the child's relationship with the father is separate from the marital relationship and should be respected in its own right. Mothers who are traumatized, anxious, or depressed because of domestic violence may be even more likely to blur the differences between the spousal and the parental relationships.

At the same time, the reality of the mother's experience of violence needs to be acknowledged and legitimized. Many battered women are reluctant to allow their children to spend time with their violent fathers for fear that the father will endanger the child or paint a distorted and negative picture of the mother that will make the child angry and suspicious toward her. These fears are well founded in the context of the violence that the mothers suffered from their partners, and these fears should be neither minimized nor attributed to manipulative efforts by the mother to alienate the child from the father. Maternal reports about worrisome paternal behavior toward the child should be given serious consideration and should be referred to the appropriate legal channels for further evaluation and action. The clinician should keep in mind that domestic violence often co-occurs with child abuse and that abusive partners can well be abusive fathers and/or engage in domestic violence with their new partners in front of the child. The child's and mother's physical safety takes precedence over all other considerations, and the clinician must take prompt action to help the mother protect herself and the child when there is evidence of ongoing violence or inappropriate behavior by the child's father.

Some battered women continue to have loving feelings toward their abusive partners and harbor hopes that he will change and that the family can be reunified. These wishes can alternate abruptly with rage and fear as memories of the assaults become salient. This alternation of feelings reflects the mother's lingering traumatization. It is of utmost importance that the clinician not take a position in favor of or against reconciliation. The clinician's role is not to tell the mother what life decisions she should make but, rather, to explore with her the different facets of her feelings as she describes them to the clinician and to consistently bring the mother's attention to the implications of her experiences for her child, always supporting decisions that are consistent with safety.

When the father or perpetrator becomes involved in assessment or treatment, this therapeutic attitude must also be maintained. In order to do this work, the challenge for the clinician is to—at one and the same time—remember clearly the details of the violence and the hurt that were inflicted without losing sight of the more positive attributes that the violent partner might also have. To enable the child and the mother to develop a realistic ambivalence about the father, the clinicians must first achieve it themselves.

PORTS OF ENTRY AND CLINICAL EXAMPLES

1. **When the child refers to frightening scenes of violence and anger, the clinician encourages the child to speak about what happened and elicits the feelings experienced by the child, encouraging a dialogue between mother and child.**

   EXAMPLE.
   Prior to the session, the clinician received a message from Dahlia's mother that her estranged husband had hit her the day before because she refused to resume their relationship. The mother wanted to inform the clinician so that it would not take her by surprise during the session. At the beginning of the session, the clinician tells Dahlia, 5 years old, that her mom said something scary had happened. Dahlia nods in agreement. The clinician asks what happened. Dahlia says, "My dad came to the house and said he wanted my mom to cook him something. She was tired and in bed. I wanted to go up to her bedroom, but he told me to stay in the kitchen and went upstairs. When I went to Mom's room, her piggy bank was broken and all over the floor. My dad slapped my mom." The clinician asks what happened then. The child says, "I was crying and telling my mom not to call the police." The clinician asks about this, and Dahlia answers, "I don't

want my daddy to go to jail." The clinician asks what happened next. Dahlia says, "My daddy told my mom to get out and started throwing her clothes down the stairs. I was scared my mommy was going to leave." The clinician asks the mother what she thinks about what Dahlia is saying, and the mother replies, "I will never leave you, Dahlia. I made your dad leave because he hurts me, but if I go anywhere, I will always take you with me." Dahlia nods, and the clinician asks her to tell her more. Dahlia says, "I went to the bathroom to get a towel so my mom could dry her eyes. She was crying so hard." The clinician asks, "You were trying to help your mom feel better. What about you? Were you crying?" Dahlia says, "When I went to the bathroom to get a towel for my mom, I wiped my eyes also. My brain was going like this" (the child moves her finger around her forehead). The clinician asks what that was like, and the child says she does not know. The clinician asks, "Were you having a lot of thoughts?" Dahlia says, "Yes" but adds that she cannot remember any of the thoughts. "I don't remember how it was." After some more talk, the clinician suggests that the mother tell Dahlia what will happen next. The mother tells Dahlia that her dad is not in jail, but he will stay away from the house and not come there to pick her up anymore, and they will find a way for Dahlia to continue seeing her daddy. Dahlia looks sad. The clinician says that her mom had tried a lot of things, but they haven't worked, and her mom does not want to be scared anymore. Dahlia says, "I don't want my mom to be scared, and she was scared yesterday." The adults agree. Dahlia adds, "My daddy is causing trouble. I love him, but he drinks too much, and he causes a lot of trouble."

2. **When the child speaks about the absent father in a way that indicates a misunderstanding of the situation, the clinician invites the mother to elicit the child's thinking and to correct faulty perceptions—or, does so when the mother is unable to.**

EXAMPLE.
When she arrives for the home visit, the clinician finds Sylvia, 4 years old, playing ball in the backyard. They start throwing the ball back and forth for a few minutes. Suddenly, the child says, "My daddy's dead." The clinician replies that she did not think her daddy was dead,

but she could understand why Sylvia thought so because he had not called her for a long time. As they get to the apartment, Sylvia asks her mother for some paper and a pencil and announces, "I am going to write a letter for my daddy." As she makes random letters across the page, she says aloud, "Daddy, where are you? Why aren't you picking me up?" She stops abruptly, puts her skates on, and skates out of the room. While the child is out of the room, the clinician tells the mother about Sylvia's idea that her father is dead, and the mother expresses sadness that he has not seen the child in a long time. When Sylvia skates back into the room, the clinician says, "I think you went looking for your daddy. Your mommy just told me that he is not dead, but he is not coming to see you anymore, and it is very sad." Sylvia says, "I am now going to dictate a letter. You write: 'Daddy, where are you? You used to call me your princess. Daddy, why did you go to the moon?'"

3. **When the child says or does things that express divided loyalties between the parents, the clinician speaks for the different feelings of the child, enlisting the mother's help, when possible, in giving the child permission to love both parents.**

   EXAMPLE.
   Carina's mother seems unusually strained and upset with her child as the session begins. The clinician comments on it, and the mother replies that it had been a very tiring week and that, earlier in the day, when she picked up Carina from school, the child had thrown sand at her. The clinician asks Carina, 4 years old, what was happening to make her throw sand at her mother.

   Carina smiles coyly, and the mother says Carina had several tantrums that week, and it all began with the Sunday visit to her father. She adds that Carina had a very hard time saying good-bye to her dad. The clinician says to Carina, "You really miss your dad." Carina nods. The clinician continues. "You really love him, and it's hard to say good-bye to him." The mother interjects that Carina was not able to go to the jungle gym with her dad because they ran out of time and adds that when he brought her back, he yelled at the mother for 10 minutes for presumably keeping Carina away from him, even though he misses half of his visits and Carina is disappointed when she does not see him. Carina says, "I love my daddy best, and I want to spend more time with him." The mother looks visibly pained. The clinician says, "Right now, you love your daddy best, and you are angry at your mom because you think that she is keeping you away from him." Carina looks intently at the clinician. The clinician says, "Maybe your mom can talk to you about it." The mother says, "I know you love your dad and you miss him, and it would be great if you could see him as much as you want, but he lives far away, and he does not come to all his visits. That is not my fault." Carina says, "I went to the park with my dad." The clinician says it was good that she and her dad could do something she wanted, and it was hard that her mom and dad did not agree about the visits when she wanted so much to be with her dad and it was so hard to say good-bye to him. Carina says, "Someday, I am going to go on a plane and visit my dad, and Dad said I could call him anytime." Under her breath, the mother comments that it is up to the court to decide whether Carina can go on a plane to visit him, and that he makes promises that he does not keep. To Carina, she says that someday, Carina would get to travel on a plane but that it would be with her mom, and that right now, Carina is too little to go on a plane by herself, and her dad is not ready to come and get her on a plane. The clinician says, "Your mom and dad are thinking hard about what they want for you, because both of them love you a lot, but they don't agree, and your mom wants to make sure that when they tell you that something will happen, it will really happen, so you won't be disappointed." The child looks very attentive. The conversation continues in this vein for some time. As they leave, mother and child are visibly relaxed and affectionate with each other.

[handwritten margin note: Good to use when promises get broken.]

4. **When the child expresses anger at the father, the clinician empathizes with the child's feelings but leaves open the possibility of change for the better.**

   EXAMPLE.
   Jamal, 4 years old, says that he wants to cut his father up and bake him in the oven. The clinician says, "How come?" Jamal says, "He

threw a cup at my mother, and it hit her knee." The clinician says, "That's a very scary thing to do. No wonder you are angry at him." Jamal says, "My dad doesn't know the rules." The clinician says, "No, he doesn't. It takes some people a long time to know the rules. Maybe, one day, your dad can learn if he really tries."

5. **When the child engages in inappropriate behavior learned from the father, the clinician makes the connection between the father's and the child's behavior, explains that even fathers can make mistakes, and tries to enlist the mother's cooperation in this effort.**

EXAMPLE.
Samuel, 3 years old, says to his mother, "I will kill you. I will shoot you."

The mother does not answer. Samuel adds, "You whore." The mother's face reddens.

The clinician says, "Samuel, your mom told me that your daddy talked to her that way. I know you love your daddy, but you can't talk that way. Your dad makes a mistake when he does that, and we don't want you to make the same mistake. Your mommy is not a whore, and nobody should kill or shoot her." The mother looks relieved. The clinician tells the mother that she can help Samuel by standing up firmly for herself when he says things like that because he does not know any better and needs to learn from her what is right and what is wrong.

EXAMPLE.
Andy, 4 years old, kicks his mother soon after hearing her tell the clinician that she left Andy's father because he kicked her.

The clinician says, "Andy, you are remembering how your daddy kicked your mom, and then she decided the two of you could not live with him anymore." Andy puts his hands over his ears. The clinician keeps quiet, and when Andy uncovers his ears, she says quietly, "It hurts to remember that." Andy looks at her sadly. The clinician says, "Your mommy will not leave you, even if you kick her. You are her little boy, and she will never leave you. But your dad kicked her because he forgot how to use his words. I come to see you so that you remember how to use your words even when you are angry."

6. **When the child's behavior suggests guilt about the father's leaving, the clinician encourages the mother to explain that this is not the child's fault, or takes the initiative in doing so.**

   EXAMPLE.

   The mother of Saul, 5 years old, expresses regret that her behavior drove her husband away. She states that she got used to the hitting but could not stand it when he had an affair. She says that she should have known better and should not have confronted and talked back to her husband, and she adds that her older daughter knew about the affair but did not tell her in order to protect her. The clinician comments that children often feel responsible for their father's leaving. The mother's face lights up, and she says, "That's it! Saul and her sister are always saying that if they had not been so bad, their father would not have left." The clinician suggests that this might be a good thing to talk about as a family, how each of them thinks that if they did things differently, the father would not have left.

7. **When the child expresses longing or sadness about the absent father, the clinician empathizes with these feelings and encourages the mother to do the same.**

   EXAMPLE.

   The mother of Lidia, 4 years old, reports that her father will be living with his grandmother in another town and came over to say good-bye but was absent-minded and preoccupied during his brief visit and left abruptly. For hours afterward, Lidia kept asking, "Where is my daddy?" The clinician now asks whether Lidia knows that her dad left, and the mother says she doesn't know. Lidia looks up from her play and says, very upset, "My dad is gone?!" The mother looks helplessly at the clinician and asks whether she (the clinician) can tell Lidia what happened, adding, "I know I should, but I don't know how. Help me tell her." The clinician asks what she would like Lidia to know, and the mother, after hesitating briefly, says to Lidia, "Your dad is very sad and needs to go stay with his grandmother because it helps him feel better." Lidia asks, "Is he coming back today?" The mother answers that his grandmother's house is far away, and he will be gone for a long time. Lidia's affect becomes very subdued, and her eyes fill with tears. The mother looks at the clinician as if asking for help. The clinician says, "I know you are very sad that your dad had to leave and he did not spend much time with you during his visit." Lidia says, "He didn't even say good-bye." The clinician says she knows that made her sad. She nods sadly. There is a silence. The clinician says, "You know, Lidia, you are right that people should say good-bye. Saying good-bye is very important. But many grown-ups don't know that. They don't know that saying good-bye is very important. I think your dad doesn't know how to say good-bye because it is a hard thing to do. I know that hurt you very much, but your dad loves you even though he did not say good-bye."

8. **When the child expresses identification with the aggressive aspects of the father, the clinician speaks to the child's underlying confusion and fear.**

   EXAMPLE.

   Paulo's mother is speaking about being at the end of her rope and feeling unable to cope with Paulo, who has just been expelled from child care because he hit a child. Paulo, 4 years old, hits his mother and quickly bites the clinician on the arm when she tries to intervene. The clinician says, "You can't do that, Paulo. You can't hit your mom, and you can't bite me." Paulo replies, "I want to grow up to be bad like my daddy." The clinician says, "You are missing your dad, but you are also scared of him. He hurt you and your mommy." Paulo moves away and starts playing by himself. Later in the session, the clinician says, "Your mom had to leave your dad because he hurt her, but she doesn't want to leave you. She loves you and wants to help you, and that is why I come here." Paulo says, "Is Daddy bad? I want to be a good boy."

   The clinician says, "Your daddy hurt you and your mommy. Your mommy is teaching you not to hurt anybody, and I am here to help her."

9. **When the mother criticizes the father or brings up his faults in front of the child, the clinician finds a way of reframing the negative picture of the father so that the seriousness of the situation is acknowledged but the child's loving feelings for the father are supported and legitimized.**

EXAMPLE.

The mother of Mandy, 4 years old, has filed a child protective services report stating that Mandy's father sexually abused the child. She also has a restraining order against the father. Child protective services doubts the veracity of the report. In the session, the mother bursts into tears and says, "I told the child welfare worker how enraged Mandy's father became when I asked him to be more careful when Mandy climbed out of the sunroof of his car. And you know what the worker said? He said that it is a two-way street. Mandy's father has molested my little boy and has physically attacked me. It is not a two-way street!" The clinician speaks supportively to the mother, who calms down. Mandy is playing with a toy cannon, pretends that he has been shot by one of the cannons, and covers his face with a cloth as he is sprawled on the floor. The clinician tells the mother that Mandy looks "seriously hurt" and suggests that they drag him over to the pillows to see how badly he was injured. The mother joins in the play and says, "Mandy looks seriously injured indeed!" Mother and clinician check the child's limbs and find the "injury." The clinician says that some good medicine and some magic words will help Mandy get better, and she and the mother minister to Mandy. They agree that the magic word is "Abracadabra" and pronounce it over Mandy, who then takes the kerchief off his face with a big smile and announces, "I am all better." Later in the session, the clinician says to Mandy, "Your mommy is afraid that your daddy is hurting you, and she is trying very hard to make sure you are safe." Mandy says, "My daddy scares me sometimes, but he's nice." The clinician says, "It's confusing when your daddy scares you but he's also nice."

Domain X: Ghosts in the Nursery: The Intergenerational Transmission of Psychopathology

The image of "ghosts in the nursery" was created by Selma Fraiberg nearly 30 years ago to describe the parents' enactment with their child of their repressed experiences of helplessness and fear (Fraiberg, Adelson, & Shapiro, 1975). The ghosts represent the unconscious repetition of the past in the present through punitive or neglectful caregiving practices, which the now-parent internalized as a child in an effort at self-protection by becoming like the abusive parent. Parents who are haunted by the ghosts of their early experiences routinely fail to recognize, empathize with, and respond to their child's signals of need for care and protection. Instead, they perceive the child through the lens of negative attributions that mimic the perceived characteristics of the punitive or neglectful caregivers from their past. In essence, the child becomes a transference object, losing her own developmental and individual features while standing for a figure from the past. Children subjected to this kind of parental distortion progressively internalize a sense of self as unworthy and undeserving of love that can derail the course of healthy development (Bowlby, 1980; Lieberman, 1997, 1999; Silverman & Lieberman, 1999). This process involves the transmission from parent to child of the defense mechanism described by Anna Freud (1936/1966) as identification with the aggressor. This communication from parent to child comprises the psychologically damaging role of the intergenerational transmission of psychological patterns that, in more benevolent family circumstances, can be represented as the influence on development of "angels in the nursery."

In their pioneering work with mental health disorders in infancy, Fraiberg and her colleagues attributed the havoc caused by the ghosts of the parental past not to the actual events but to the repression of the affects associated with frightening early memories. These parental affects are often freely expressed toward the child in the context of CPP. The parent may behave during the sessions as if she were transformed back into a young child, helpless and terrified but endeavoring to master these feelings through harsh criticism, emotional withdrawal, and other behaviors that signal an identification with the abusive parental figures from the past.

The initial assessment sessions are geared at gaining an understanding of the childhood roots of the parent's current difficulties in caregiving. The clinician can use this information to develop tentative hypotheses linking the parent's early experiences of stress or trauma with current maladaptive caregiving practices. When the parent has been the victim of domestic violence, the emotional impact of this assault or series of assaults compounds the enduring effect of early adversities. The child who witnesses the violence often becomes associated with it in the parent's mind. Victimized mothers often engage in an unconscious equation of their children with their perpetrators, attributing to the child the characteristics of danger and brutality that properly belong to their partners (Silverman & Lieberman, 1999).

The preliminary hypotheses developed during the assessment period are not necessarily discussed with the parent, but they can be kept in mind for confirmation or disconfirmation from the material that emerges during treatment. When the interventions described in earlier sections of the manual are not effective in promoting parental attitudes and behaviors that are more developmentally appropriate, the clinician should consider switching to an exploration of how the parent's past is influencing current perceptions and behaviors toward the child. Time-limited individual collateral sessions are the format of choice in these circumstances. If a few individual sessions indicate that the parent needs more in-depth psychotherapy, the clinician may choose to expand the scope of the treatment to include ongoing individual sessions with the parent in addition to CPP or may refer the parent to another practitioner.

The capacity to integrate the good and bad parts of a loved person into a sturdy sense of object constancy has long been considered the hallmark of the adult capacity to love (Fairbairn, 1954; S. Freud, 1923/1966; Kernberg, 1976; Klein, 1932; Mahler, Pine, & Bergman, 1975; Winnicott, 1962). Helping the parent become more conscious of the pain associated with early experiences should not be an end in itself. Whenever possible, the clinician should endeavor to help the parent remember and hold in mind the multifaceted nature of his early relationships. Compassion and forgiveness for the imperfect parents of the past cannot be decreed by clinical caveat, but the parent–child relationship in the present will be immeasurably helped by the current parent's ability to reconnect with the angels while making peace with the ghosts in the nursery.

Timing is a crucial element in increasing the likelihood that an intervention will be effective in promoting inner growth and behavioral change. This is particularly the case when the clinician addresses aspects of the parent's life that are laden with pain, anger, shame, or helplessness, and when the parent has been engaged in protracted efforts at fending off these negative feelings through the use of displacement, projection, and denial. For this reason, it is difficult to itemize specific clinical strategies for linking early conflicts with current parenting problems. The following section provides a beginning approach through clinical examples, but case-centered supervision is needed to acquire or enhance clinical skill in this area.

Ports of Entry and Clinical Examples

1. **The clinician inquires explicitly about caregiving adults or specific experiences that made the parent feel frightened or in danger while growing up.**

   ### Example.

   Lenny, 2 years old, has been expelled from day care because he bit another child for the fourth time, and the school's parents have complained that he is a danger for their children. During the assessment, Lenny's mother, Mrs. O'Brian, describes extensive domestic violence perpetrated by Lenny's father, who is now out of the home and has an unpredictable pattern of visits with Lenny on approximately a monthly basis. Mrs. O'Brian is worried about these visits because she believes that her husband is using them to turn Lenny against her. She says that Lenny has prolonged tantrums when he returns from visits with his father, refuses to be comforted by her, and hits her and kicks her when she tries to hold him. After eliciting a detailed account of present circumstances, the clinician asks, "What were things like for you when you were growing up?" Mrs. O'Brian says that her parents divorced when she was a baby, and she never knew her father. She adds, "I have been thinking of going back with my husband because I don't want Lenny to grow up without a father, like I did." The clinician replies, "Given what you told me about how frightened you are of him, you must feel very strongly that you want Lenny to have a father to consider getting back with him." The mother agrees. The clinician asks, "What do you remember about growing up without a father?" The mother answers, "I felt humiliated when the other children talked about their fathers and I had nothing to say." The clinician asks, "Humiliated? How come? Did you think it was your fault that he left?" Mrs. O'Brian answers, "Maybe not my fault, but I thought that if he loved me, he would have stayed." The clinician asks, "Do you have any ideas about why he did not love you?" The mother says sadly, "I was not good enough." She has tears in her eyes. The clinician makes the link with Lenny by asking, "Do you want to make sure Lenny does not feel like he is not good enough to have his father stay, like you did?" The mother nods in silent agreement.

This exchange illustrates the clinician's efforts to uncover the aspects of the mother's early experience that are associated with her child's current difficulties. The preliminary hypotheses, which are based on the mother's report of her self-blame for her father's abandonment, involved the following set of related premises: (a) the mother's romantic involvement with a man who abused her was based on her conviction that she deserved no better because she was not good enough to keep her father's love; (b) she deserved to be punished for not being good enough; and (c) she wanted to protect her child from the self-blame and suffering of growing up without a father. Reuniting with Lenny's father would confirm and perpetuate her self-concept as undeserving of love while ostensibly protecting her child from the same fate. The clinician believed that Lenny was adopting the mother's distorted perception of herself by blaming her for his father's absence and punishing her by hitting and kicking her in much the same ways that he had witnessed his father doing to his mother. Mrs. O'Brian's failure to set limits on Lenny's aggression simultaneously confirmed the child's perception that she was "bad" and left him unable to regulate his intense traumatic stress responses from witnessing the violence, grief at his father's absence, and anger at his mother as the perceived culprit for what befell him. Having a "bad" mother is, in children's minds, inevitably linked to being "bad" oneself because one deserves no better. These hypotheses informed the clinician's pursuit of intervention strategies designed to help the mother realize that her father had left her not because she was unlovable but because he could not love; that witnessing violence frightened Lenny and made him feel that he could not trust his parents to love and protect him; and that, in stopping Lenny firmly but calmly from expressing anger through aggression, she was helping him to feel loved and protected by showing him that she would not leave him alone with his unmanageable feelings. In intervening calmly but firmly to contain Lenny's aggression, his mother was also able to disconfirm, in Lenny's mind and her own, the belief that she was not lovable and that she deserved punishment.

2. **When the parent engages with the child in an exchange that evokes early experiences of feeling unloved, frightened, or unprotected, the clinician links the present situation to those memories in an effort to make the parent aware of the early roots of the present situation.**

EXAMPLE.

In a joint child–parent session 2 months into the treatment, Mrs. O'Brian (see previous example) is telling the clinician that Lenny's father did not show up for a visit with the child. She says, "All he cares about is himself. He doesn't give a damn about Lenny. I prepared Lenny for the visit, had him all dressed up, and we were waiting and waiting. He did not even call. He simply did not show up." Lenny is playing with some blocks, making a tower. Listening to his mother, he kicks the tower and makes the tower fall down. The clinician says to Lenny, "Your mommy is telling me that your daddy did not come to see you. She is upset because she knows you wanted to see him." Lenny goes to the window and tries to reach it by stepping on the armchair that is next to it. The mother retrieves him, saying, "Don't do that! You are going to fall!" Lenny shrieks, flails at her to help him get down, and hits her after she puts him on the floor. The mother sits back down on her chair without reacting. The clinician says to Lenny, "No hitting Mommy. Mommy was trying to help you. She knows that you want your daddy." Lenny goes back to the blocks and continues playing. The clinician says to the mother, "I can't help but think of what you told me about growing up without your father and how sad that made you." The mother nods silently. The therapist continues, "When you were waiting for his father to come, do you think you were having the old feelings of waiting for your father all over again?"

The clinician used the mother's intense reaction to Lenny's father's missed visit as a port of entry to link her feelings in the present to her early unfulfilled longing for her father. The mother's unconscious equation of Lenny's father with her own father prevented her from remaining emotionally available to Lenny while they were waiting for his father and during the days that followed. Her feelings of abandonment, self-blame, and anger interfered with her ability to protect the child from the failed expectation of seeing his father. By introducing a bridge between the present and the past, the clinician was suggesting that the mother's response could be understood in a broader context than the concrete circumstances of the missed visit.

The chains of associations linking the present with the past need not be fully elucidated for therapeutic gains to take place. By its very nature, CPP involves a constant balance between (a) attention to the child–parent relationship and (b) the child's and the parent's individual experience. Emotional growth accrues from the accumulation of different interventions within a context of consistent emotional support. When skillfully timed, interventions linking the present with the past can be transformative—even when brief—because parents continue to reflect on them after the session and use them to increase their understanding of themselves and of the child.

Domain XI: Angels in the Nursery: Benevolent Influences in the Parent's Past

Parents are able to support their children's development even amidst adverse conditions when their sense of self-worth informs their commitment to the child's well-being. This sense of personal worth is rooted in early exchanges with important adults that were suffused with a sense of heightened intimacy because the child felt thoroughly understood, accepted, and protected. The often silent presence of benevolent influences in the parent's past has been likened to "angels in the nursery" (W. Harris, personal communication, April 23, 2003) because loving experiences are transmitted from one generation to the next in the form of caregiving practices that affirm the child's sense of being cherished and instill trust in the value of human relationships.

Traumatic experiences often block parental access to early experiences that nourished their self-esteem by making them feel loved and deserving of care and protection. Although the ultimate goal of CPP is to enhance the child's mental health, a simultaneous focus on the parent's subjective experience is necessary to enlist parental motivation and therapeutic collaboration on behalf of the child. Enabling the parents to remember experiences of nurturing and protection in their early life is a powerful therapeutic tool because it enriches the parent's sense of self, instills optimism, and promotes hope in the future by holding up a supportive model of the past.

The initial assessment sessions offer a prime opportunity to search for benevolent experiences in the parent's past because the assessment is explicitly devoted to learning about salient aspects of the parent's and the child's life. By asking about caregivers or interpersonal exchanges that made the parent feel loved, the clinician conveys the message that experiences of safety, trust, intimacy, and joy are fundamentally important and worthy of sustained attention. The parent's positive early experiences can then be used as building blocks to support parallel experiences with the child.

Loving early experiences may not be remembered during the assessment sessions when the parent is overwhelmed by the experience of trauma. The clinician may then remain alert for the emergence of this information in the course of the sessions. When the parent remembers moments of intimacy and joy with a caregiver, the clinician may join with the parent's affective experience by highlighting its value in the parent's life. The parent's experience may then be harnessed to the child's emotional needs by drawing parallels that increase parental empathy for the child.

PORTS OF ENTRY AND CLINICAL EXAMPLES

1. **The clinician inquires explicitly about caregiving adults or specific experiences that made the parent feel loved and cared for while growing up.**

   ### EXAMPLE.
   During the initial assessment interview, Mrs. Gowan speaks with intense anger about her husband and her child, 3-year-old Simon, both of whom she describes as "bullies" who are aggressive and impossible to control. In the course of learning about the family's circumstances, the clinician asks the mother about her childhood. Mrs. Gowan describes an abusive mother and an aloof, withdrawn father. The clinician asks, "Was there anybody that you could rely on as a little girl?" The mother remains silent for a long time. Then her face softens, and she says, "I had an aunt who was single and lived with us for a few years. She taught me to read. I used to love sitting next to her on the sofa, holding a book between us. Sometimes, she put her arm around me while reading out loud to me. I loved it. She smelled

so good." In telling the story, Mrs. Gowan's anger dissipates, and she has tears in her eyes. The clinician says gently, "What a beautiful memory to hold on to with all the pain that you are going through." The mother replies, "I had forgotten it until now. My aunt married and left our house when I was 9. I remember crying when she left. She left me a box of the books that we used to read together. I still have them." The clinician asks, "Do you ever read them to Simon?" The mother says, "No. He wouldn't appreciate them." The clinician replies, "Really? Maybe we can help him appreciate them during our work together."

This scene offers a glimmer of hope in the mother's troubled emotional landscape and her angry relationship with her child. By identifying a nurturing figure in Mrs. Gowan's bleak childhood, the clinician facilitated a temporary transformation in the mother's affect, reconnecting her with an early experience of loving intimacy. The clinician also opened the possibility that the mother's pleasurable memories associated with reading with her aunt could be extended to reading with her son, and upheld the hope that this could be a benefit of treatment in the face of the mother's skepticism that her son could appreciate the books that were so meaningful to her while she was growing up.

2. **When the parent remembers an early experience of being loved and cared for, the clinician links this memory with the possibility of making the feeling happen again through exchanges with the child.**

   EXAMPLE.
   Mr. Gomez, the father of Ronnie, 4 years old, recalls a scene from his adolescence where his father put a hand on his shoulder and said, "It's OK" after he made a mistake playing football that made his team lose the game. Clearly moved, the father says, "It made me feel that he loved me in spite of my mistake." The clinician asks, "That is such an important feeling. Did he usually behave like that?" Mr. Gomez answers, "Not really. He had a terrible temper and yelled at me a lot. But every once in a while, he could make me feel really good. Once

he told a kid who was threatening me that he would send him packing if he did that again. I felt so safe. He made me feel important—like he was really busy but he noticed what was happening and took the time to defend me. The kid never bothered me again." After a silence, the clinician asks, "Is that something you want Ronnie to feel with you?"

In this intervention, the clinician helped Mr. Gomez connect the visceral feeling of being accepted and protected by his father with the possibility of offering a similar experience to his son. Mr. Gomez often screamed in anger when Ronnie did something wrong, and he felt deeply ashamed of his son's visible fear when this happened. Mr. Gomez associated the memory of his father's acceptance of his mistake playing football with the feeling of being cared for and protected. By introducing Ronnie into this scene, the clinician worked toward an updating of Mr. Gomez's experience of himself from (sometimes) protected son to protective father and helped to establish a counterweight to the prevailing memories of disapproval and anger.

Domain XII: Separation and Loss Reminders

Separating from a person one loves ranks among the most difficult of human experiences. Losing a loved person is the most painful one. Both experiences, each in their distinct fashion, challenge the emotional foundations of the sense of self and evoke powerful feelings of sadness, anxiety, grief, and anger. When separation and loss occur early in life, or when the person is left without the support of other affectional bonds, the typical course of development can be seriously derailed, and adult mental health may be severely compromised (Bowlby, 1973, 1980).

For young children and parents exposed to traumatic events, everyday experiences of separation may evoke a profound sense of danger and anticipation of loss because fear for the integrity of the self and of the loved ones is already heightened. In situations where abuse or domestic violence resulted in separation from the abusive parent, the abusive parent's often abrupt and conflict-ridden departure from the home triggers a mixture of relief and guilt about the relief, feelings that compound and complicate the more normative responses of anger and grief.

Young children are particularly vulnerable to the pathogenic potential of traumatic separation or loss because their worldview is shaped by the age-appropriate egocentric conviction that their thoughts and actions can make things happen (Piaget, 1959). As a result, they are likely to blame themselves when adversities take place. This self-blame occurs with the backdrop of fear of separation and fear of losing the parent's love as the normative anxieties in the first 5 years of life (Fraiberg, 1959). These anxieties become indelibly internalized by the child when real-life events seem to confirm those fears.

These processes set the stage for the child's response to separation from the clinician at the end of each session and the child's response to loss of the clinician when treatment ends. The clinician acquires the role of surrogate attachment figure in the course of the treatment through the consistent focus on providing a haven of safety. The clinician also becomes a transference object that evokes the child's often suppressed feelings and unconscious fantasies about separation and loss.

For these reasons, the good-byes at the end of the session and at the end of treatment, difficult as they are, also represent valuable opportunities for providing the child with corrective emotional experiences of separation and loss. The primary lessons that need to be conveyed are (a) that separations can be followed by reunions and (b) that separation and loss do not always mean a loss of love. Through the clinician's responses, the child learns that the image of the loved person can be kept safe inside oneself even when that person is no longer present, and that this image and the memories associated with it can be brought back to mind at times of emotional need and can be used for comfort and support.

It is important not to downplay the importance of separations and to announce that "time is up" with enough anticipation that the clinician will not be rushed into a hasty good-bye. The child needs to be given time to prepare inwardly for this important transition and needs unhurried adult support in doing so.

Transitional objects, games that evoke separation and reunion such as "peek-a-boo" and "hide-and-seek," and the parent's support are good strategies in helping preverbal children weather the sadness of a good-bye. For older children, speaking about how they can think of each other and evoking what will happen until they see each other again build continuity of emotional experience between the sessions. Just as good-night rituals help children allay their anxieties before going to sleep, good-bye rituals are very helpful in reassuring the child that the clinician is not leaving out of anger or loss of love for the child.

PORTS OF ENTRY AND CLINICAL EXAMPLES

1. **The clinician helps the caregivers identify potential loss reminders, link them to the child's experience, and help the child learn new ways of coping.**

   ### EXAMPLE.
   Robert and Clay have been foster parents to Layla, 3¹/₂ years old, for 1 year. They meet alone with the clinician to discuss ways to help Layla when they go on summer vacation. Clay travels for work, and Robert says that every time he packs a suitcase, Layla starts to chew on her fingers and scratch her arms. "I wonder what it means to her when you pack your suitcase?" the clinician asks. Clay responds, "We know that she doesn't like separations. I always tell her that Papa is going on a business trip. I tell her when I'll be back, and I Skype while I am away." "Yeah," Robert says, "you're really good at preparing her, but it's more than that. Remember how she flipped out when we took that weekend trip to Palm Springs." "Yeah," says Clay, "and we were all going together." "What do you think made her flip out?" asks the clinician. "Wow," says Robert. "Now that you ask, I think it was the suitcase. I was cleaning the closet the other day, and she saw the suitcases and started acting really strange and biting her hands again. Layla doesn't like it when anyone packs." The clinician and fathers recognize that although Layla was 2½ years old when she became a part of their family, she had already experienced five moves in the course of her life (three of these occurred in the 4 months before she came to reside with them). "Suitcases may evoke fear in her body that she cannot put words to," says the therapist. "They may remind her of leaving, of losing people, and of ending up in a strange place with new people. Great people," the clinician adds, "but it still might have been scary for her." "What should we do?" asks Robert. "Well," says the clinician, "maybe you could let her know that Papa and Daddy

know that she had lots of moves before. We could let her play about moving and use toy suitcases, and we could help her to learn that, now, when you pack, you either go together or people come back."

2. **The clinician helps the child cope with the separation at the end of the session by announcing that she will be leaving soon and by giving the child choices about how to say good-bye. Rituals surrounding separation are very effective in helping children cope with the anxiety of saying good-bye because they create a sense of predictability and control.**

    EXAMPLE.

    Reesa, 3 years old, is playing happily with the clinician and the mother. The clinician says, "You know what? I have to say good-bye in a few more minutes." The child's face becomes somber. The clinician says, "So, when I say good-bye, do you want to open the door, or should I?" Reesa says, "I will." The clinician says, "Then, what will happen after that? Will we wave good-bye at the door or . . . " Reesa interrupts, saying, "Go to the bottom of the stairs, and look up and say good-bye." The clinician says, "OK, and then what?" Reesa answers, "Then you come back next time," and smiles. As the clinician walks down the stairs, Reesa says, "Wait, I have to go pee!" She turns to the mother, says "I have to go pee!" and races inside, yelling, "Wait for me, don't go yet! I have to pee!" The clinician yells back, "I am here; I am waiting!" Reesa comes back from the bathroom and says, "Wait, I have to give you a sticker." She gives the clinician a sticker of a dinosaur and then says, "I will give five more stickers." The clinician says, "How come I get so many stickers?" Reesa says, "Because you did a good job."

3. **When the child is having a difficult time at the end of the session (crying, complaining, or being angry), the clinician speaks about the difficulty of saying good-bye and makes available a symbolic transitional object, such as a sticker or a drawing made during the session, as a tangible reminder of the clinician.**

    EXAMPLE.

    Sandy, 2 years old, cries bitterly when the clinician gets ready to leave the home at the end of the session. She follows the clinician into the front yard and clutches the clinician's skirt to hold her back. The clinician kneels down, looks closely at Sandy, and says, "It is hard to say good-bye. You want me to stay and play with you and your mommy. Let's look for something that will make you feel better." She asks the mother for help, and together they find a colorful pebble lying on the grass. Very ceremoniously, the clinician puts the pebble in Sandy's hand and says, "This pebble will be with you until I come back." She repeats this twice as Sandy looks closely, first at the pebble and then at the clinician. She stops crying and is able to wave good-bye with her mother's help.

4. **When the child shows distress at the clinician's impending departure, the clinician plays a game of peek-a-boo or hide-and-seek to help the child learn that reunion follows a separation, involving the parent whenever possible.**

   EXAMPLE.
   Amelia, 15 months old, throws herself on the floor and flails while screaming when the clinician says it is time to say good-bye. The clinician says, with much drama, "I have an idea for a game! Can you find me if I hide?" She crouches behind a chair, in plain view, and Amelia, with tears still streaming down her face but a smile on her face, goes to find her. The clinician then asks whether Amelia can hide. Amelia hides, and the clinician finds her. They play in this way for a few minutes, and then the clinician asks the mother whether she can continue this game. The mother agrees, and the clinician says to Amelia, "Your mommy will do it now, because I have to go." Amelia gets very serious, but she quickly turns to her mother to continue the game, and the clinician says a quick good-bye as she leaves.

5. **When the child shows anger without linking it to the separation, the clinician makes this link by interpreting the child's behavior and reassures the child.**

   EXAMPLE.
   Khalil, 4 years old, throws a small toy car at the clinician when it is time to end the session. The clinician says, "You are telling me that

you are angry at me for leaving. We were having such a good time playing that it is hard to stop. I will think about you when I am away, and I promise that we will play again when I come back."

6. **When the child shows distress about the separation, the clinician speaks about the separation and tells the child that they will think of each other until it is time to see each other again.**

   EXAMPLE.
   Linda, 4 years old, says, "I want to go with you" when the clinician gets ready to go. The clinician says, "That would be nice. I know you want to come with me because it's nice to be together. You know what, I will think of you when I am away, and you can think about me too and what a good time we had together."

7. **When the child shows anger at the clinician in the weeks preceding the termination of treatment, the clinician makes direct links between the child's anger and the termination.**

   EXAMPLE.
   Hillary, 5 years old, says to the clinician, "I don't like you anymore," and throws a toy in her direction when the clinician says it is time to end the session. The clinician says, "You are remembering that soon, you and your mom will not be coming to see me anymore. We will miss each other, and it makes you angry that it has to be that way."

8. **When the child shows anger or distress at the clinician in the weeks preceding the termination of treatment, the clinician makes direct links between the child's feelings at termination and the child's feelings about the father's absence.**

   EXAMPLE.
   Timothy, 3 years old, sobs inconsolably when he cannot find a little car that he was playing with. He screams at the therapist, "You lost it!" The therapist says, "Timothy, I am so sorry. Your car is lost, and your daddy is lost, and soon I'll be lost and will stop coming to see you." Timothy continues crying, but in a more subdued way. The therapist continues speaking softly, saying, "It is hard when you can't

find the things you want. I am sorry." Timothy's mother opens up her arms to him, and he cuddles up against her. She says, "I will be with you, Timothy. I will help you."

PHASE 3
RECAPITULATION AND TERMINATION: PROMOTING SUSTAINABILITY OF GAINS

The third and final phase involves a gradually decreasing focus on areas of difficulty interspersed with an increasing focus on the positive changes that were made, reminiscing about specific experiences together, comparing how things were at the beginning of the intervention and how things are now, and acknowledging that the intervention is approaching its end. Feelings associated with loss as the result of termination (anger, sadness, regret over unfinished business, gratefulness for improvements) are addressed and reflected on.

Loss is a critical issue for adults and children who have experienced traumas. Trauma itself can be considered a loss: In the moment of trauma, one loses the assumption that the world is a safe place and that one is worthy of protection when threatened. Termination of treatment is, therefore, a critical milestone. It is important to allow both parent and child to express the many complex feelings that may arise and to manage termination in a careful and planful way.

For dyads that have achieved their treatment goals, termination may feel like a positive accomplishment, and their feelings of sadness at saying good-bye may be mingled with real feelings of pride and eagerness to move forward on their own. For these dyads, the last session may take on an air of celebration, with refreshments and, if appropriate, photographs taken on the spot to mark the occasion as a special event. Other terminations might have a less optimistic feel. The treatment may terminate because, for example, the therapist has reached the end of the training year and must move on or because the agency at which the parent and child are being seen offers time-limited treatment. In these cases, it might be a mistake to force an air of celebration at the end of the treatment. In any case, termination must be managed with utmost care. How the last session will be marked is something to be discussed collaboratively among the clinician, the parent, and the child.

Although the therapist and parent will have discussed the treatment process and planned for termination from the beginning of treatment, especially when an end date is determined by the end of the training year, the formal termination process ideally begins approximately 2 months before the end date. The therapist and parent meet alone to discuss treatment progress and to consider the possibility of ending. As part of this process, the therapist conducts a posttest evaluation. This evaluation may include structured tools to measure change in symptoms or an unstructured interview with the parent. In either case, the goal is to reflect with the parent on areas of improvement, factors that may have led to positive change, challenges that may remain, and ways the parent may address challenges now and in the future.

Psychoeducation with the parent about termination should include the information that trauma-related symptoms may fluctuate and that the process of meaning-making continues throughout the course of development. This theme is elaborated on below.

1. *The story grows as the child grows.* As children's capacity to talk about and process events develops, they may bring up new aspects of their story, ask new questions, and come to understand what has happened and its impact in ways that match their emerging developmental capacities. For example, young children who witnessed domestic violence may re-experience earlier difficulties when they reach an age when they begin dating or when their parent starts a new relationship. For children who have experienced sexual abuse, the onset of puberty and curiosity about sex and dating may result in renewed questions regarding what they experienced and what this means to them. Parents who are able to retain a trauma-informed framework to understand their child's behavior at these times of transition will be better able to provide assistance and to promote a healthy resolution of these re-emerging conflicts.

2. *"Trauma is like asthma: It may remit, but symptoms may return."* This simple metaphor is helpful to many parents. In the field of medicine, there are conditions that are cured and conditions that are managed. Asthma may remit with proper care, but the symptoms may return in a heavy pollen season. Similarly, traumatic stress symptoms may return when children are exposed to trauma and loss reminders, or when new stressors occur. The task for parents is to identify and acknowledge when

reminders are present in the environment, to try (without inviting avoidance) to reduce children's exposure to reminders, and to enhance children's capacity to cope with reminders while accepting that the expression of some symptoms may be unavoidable.

It is important to give children advance notice that treatment will be ending. This usually involves telling the child about termination approximately 6 weeks prior to the end date so that the child has sufficient time to process reactions to this news. From the point of view of the child (and, often, also of the parent), the end of treatment is an arbitrary event that does not take into account the good feelings among the participants. Verbal children invariably ask, "Why?" when the clinician announces that she will stop coming in a few weeks. There is no easy answer. It is often helpful to answer the child with a story that gives a brief recapitulation of how things were at the beginning of treatment and how things are now. Such a narrative can emphasize the progress that the child and the parents have made in grappling with difficult feelings, in moving toward safety and protection, and in making meaning of their experience.

One frequent but unintended by-product of beginning the termination process is that the child (and/or the parent) becomes symptomatic again in an unconscious effort to show the therapist that not all is well and that treatment is still needed. However, if the termination of treatment is addressed with enough time and care, this is usually a short-lived reaction that abates when the feelings of sadness and worry about saying good-bye are given the attention they deserve.

EXAMPLE.

Teresa and Jacob were a mother and child who had been in treatment for 1½ years. When treatment began, Jacob (3 years old) was in his grandmother's custody, and reunification seemed unlikely due to the mother's substance abuse history and her inability to separate from Jacob's father, Charles, who had been violent toward her. The therapist initially worked with the grandmother and Jacob, but she reached out to the mother and began conducting the CPP assessment with her to determine whether treatment was feasible. Teresa was straightforward and honest. She admitted to her substance abuse. She was in a residential treatment program. She also noted that she had taken Jacob to see his father, and she wasn't sorry about it. "A boy should know his father," she said, and she wasn't scared of him; she could "give as good as she got." Over time, Teresa and the therapist thought about the role of violence in Teresa's life and what she wanted for her son. She reunified with her son. She apologized to him and joined him in play sessions where he repeatedly played scenes of a baby in jeopardy being taken from its mommy by a large red dinosaur. "Save me, Mommy, save me," he would cry, to which she would reply, "I am coming, my son. I am coming." His play helped her to see how violence had affected him. They moved into a new Section 8 apartment together, and her son's father later joined her. Together, she and her partner talked with Jacob about how they had been violent and scary. Prior to termination, she shared with the therapist that she told Jacob that his parents are kind of crazy. "He's got to know that we get loud and we fight, but now we're not going to hit each other or try to kill each other anymore."

Termination was challenging. The therapist had been there for so many important changes and had advocated for them to be together. As the process began, Jacob began having challenges in school. "He doesn't want you to go," his mom said. "He needs you." "I don't really want to go" the therapist said, "but he has you, and you know how to help him." Mom gave the therapist a funny look. "Hey, Teresa, I know you don't like good-byes, either," said the therapist. "Yep," said Teresa. "You know I'm a runner." "I know," said the therapist. "You got your track shoes on?" "You know I do," said Teresa. "Well," said the therapist, "I hope you let me come and say good-bye." "I don't know," said Teresa.

As they neared the end of treatment, there was a session when the therapist arrived at the home visit, rang the bell, and no one answered. She waited and rang again, but no one came. She called and left a message. "Hey, Teresa, I know good-byes are hard, and I know you might not want to let me in, but I want to let you know that I will come back next week, and I would love to see you and Jacob and Charles." Teresa called her back. "OK," she said. "You can come." It was a difficult good-bye. During termination, they talked about how Jacob used to live with his grandmother. She and Mom didn't get along back then, but now they did. They talked about how they weren't together because things weren't safe, but Mom had changed, and dad was trying. There had been many positive changes, and yet there was still risk, given their previous level of violence and the father's ongoing difficulties. It was hard to say good-bye after such a bond had been forged. A year later, the therapist received a phone message from Teresa. She did not leave a phone number, but she said, "I wanted to let you know that we're doing real good. I joined the PTA, and Jacob is doing good in school."

As the ending nears, preschoolers are helped by concrete reminders of how much time is left before the final session. This can be done by marking each passing week on a special calendar and counting how many weeks are left. Parents also often appreciate this structure. Doing something out of the ordinary to mark the last session gives it particular significance, and the clinician works collaboratively with the parent and child to decide whether the last session should be a genuine celebration or whether a more reflective activity would better capture the complex feelings involved in ending an important relationship.

Some good-bye rituals include the following activities:

- Make a book using pictures or stickers that tells the family's story.
- Spend the last session writing cards to each other. The therapist writes separate cards for the child and caregiver. The caregiver and child typically make cards for the therapist. Prior to leaving, they exchange cards and read them aloud.
- Make picture frames and write key messages on the frame.
- Take pictures that the family can keep of each other and, sometimes, of the toys that the child used to tell his story.
- Draw pictures of what things were like when they started treatment and what things are like now.
- Make a memory pillow. The therapist brings in a small pillow, with three sides sewn together. During the session, the therapist, child, and caregiver write memories and messages, put them in the pillow, and then sew it up as a keepsake for the family. Sometimes, two separate pillows are made—one for the caregiver and one for the child.

These rituals allow the therapist and family member to share what treatment has meant to them, to create a concrete reminder of the experience, and to say good-bye in a way that is mindful and that holds emotional meaning to all involved.

SECTION III

MONITORING FIDELITY TO CHILD–PARENT PSYCHOTHERAPY

To the tune (very roughly) of "How Do You Solve a Problem Like Maria" from The Sound of Music

> How do you solve a problem like fidelity?
> How do you take CPP and write it down?
> How can you write a measure that is faithful?
> To history, authenticity,
> the evolving needs of each child and family?
> How do you solve a problem like fidelity?
> How do you take CPP and write it down?

CREATING INSTRUMENTS THAT MEASURE FIDELITY confronts treatment developers with the need to transmit to others in a structured and systematic manner the essential elements of the treatment, and as our team met to think about Child–Parent Psychotherapy (CPP) fidelity, some of us would hum bars of this song as a way of giving voice to the challenge that we faced. We knew how to conduct, supervise, and write about CPP, but we found it difficult to capture this multifaceted intervention within a single fidelity instrument. This challenge was magnified by the need to monitor a therapist's use of CPP with a variety of families facing a range of circumstances. For some families, the trauma had ended, whereas for others, safety remained a primary consideration. Some families actively sought out trauma-informed services, whereas others sought help mainly due to the child's behavior problems; still others were unsure as to whether they even wanted treatment. Some families approached us of their own volition; others were mandated for treatment by child protective services or the judicial system. These factors—along with numerous others, such as the child's age, the caregivers' psychological functioning, the severity and chronicity of the traumas experienced by caregiver and child, and the family's socioeconomic background and cultural values—could affect the course of treatment in ways that need to be accommodated by the fidelity tools.

How does one ensure fidelity to CPP while addressing such disparate clinical presentations? Over the years, we employed different methods for supporting therapists in doing CPP and assessing fidelity to the model. We began with in-depth reflective supervision by experts in the model. The next step was to increase systematization by developing a coding system, which—while useful—was too costly in terms of time and expertise for widespread use. During early dissemination efforts, we used a brief questionnaire where therapists rated their attention to core CPP goals and their ability to intervene in ways that focused on both parent and child. Although this questionnaire had merit, we found that treatment needed to be tailored to each family in ways that were challenging to capture using a brief checklist. Moreover, as our team began conducting large-scale dissemination efforts across the United States and in Israel, we discovered that there were core aspects of CPP that we taught during training and supervision but that were not included in this checklist.

As it often happens in clinical endeavors, we learned a great deal by asking the participants in CPP trainings what this treatment meant to them. They often responded by repeating to us phrases that we had used during the trainings—phrases that encapsulated for them core aspects of the treatment and that they used as beacons to guide their work. Some of these recurring phrases, which many practitioners termed "CPP mantras," are included here:

- When emotions are strong, the first affect to regulate is your own.
- Try not to be a better parent than the parent.
- Support the parent, so the parent can support the child.
- To differentiate between then and now, one has to remember that there was a "then."
- Try to understand a situation before you try to change it.
- When you address one partner, remember that you are also addressing the other.
- Do not let the "perfect" be the enemy of the "good enough."
- Ports of entry are like buses: If you miss one, another one will come by in due time.

- Remember that small changes can make a big difference.
- Do not be discouraged by the enormity of a family's pain.
- Hope is the most indispensable ingredient of treatment.

Hearing these phrases echoed back to us helped us recognize that fidelity in CPP is multidimensional and involves not only fidelity to content (the goals of CPP) but also fidelity to emotional, intrapsychic, and interpersonal processes. These sayings are expressions of the pillars of a therapeutic attitude, which can be summarized as the following ways of being:

- Notice feelings in the moment.
- Find emotional links between experiences.
- Uphold the legitimacy of the parent's and child's different motives and needs.
- Become a translator: Explain the parent's and child's conflicting agendas to each other.
- Seek out the benevolence in the conflict.
- Name the trauma: Dare to speak about what hurts.
- Remember the suffering under the rage.
- Take care of yourself.
- Offer kindness.
- Encourage hope.

This view allowed us to think about fidelity in a multidimensional way and to develop a CPP fidelity framework that consists of these six interconnected strands of fidelity:

1. Reflective Practice Fidelity
2. Emotional Process Fidelity
3. Dyadic Relational Fidelity
4. Trauma Framework Fidelity
5. Procedural Fidelity
6. Content Fidelity

These strands reflect the multifaceted nature of CPP, rooted in the rich tradition of infant/early childhood mental health and supported by research demonstrating the restorative power of safe relationships and emotional attunement in repairing momentum toward healthy development.

SIX STRANDS OF FIDELITY

Strand 1: Reflective Practice Fidelity

"How you are is important as what you do" (Pawl & St. John, 1988)

"It is not possible to work on behalf of human beings to try to help them without having powerful feelings aroused in yourself . . . In working with families who are in great difficulty, rage can become the most familiar affect, — at the system, at a world with too much violence that creates too much helplessness and also at a family who will not be better or even seem to try." (Pawl, 1995, p. 24)

These two quotes, read back to back, highlight a common therapeutic challenge: the inevitability of countertransference reactions that may interfere with the clinician's emotional availability and clarity of thinking.

Working with people traumatized by violence evokes strong emotional reactions in the treatment provider. This is particularly the case in work with young children, who, whether or not they have experienced traumas, are relatively unmodulated in their expression of affect. In addition, young children are unable to protect themselves and must rely on their parents and other adults to be safe and to thrive. Faced with this combination of circumstances, the clinician is likely to experience a range of intense emotions, including rage at the parent, wishes to adopt the child (or other rescue fantasies), emotional numbness, physiological responses, and feelings of incompetence and helplessness. Many of these responses mirror the typical symptoms of posttraumatic stress disorder (PTSD) and may be considered a vicarious traumatization of the clinician through exposure to narratives or visual images of the violence. Many clinicians have gone through experiences similar to those experienced by the individuals who they are now treating. Bearing witness to the trauma narratives of young children and their parents and helping to contain children's strong feelings may re-evoke earlier traumatic responses. Clinicians may also become enmeshed in the expectations of victims of traumatic violence by a process of *projective identification*. It is not unusual for those who have been victimized to see others, including the clinician, as potential sources of danger. Clinicians may find themselves acting out the aggressive motivations that have been projected onto them by the setting of overly rigid limits in the treatment or by aggressive interpretation or confrontation.

Countertransference experiences are valuable guides to understanding the clinical process. It is not uncommon for a clinician to actively dislike the parent, the child, or both of them. The clinician may dread the next session, feel relief when the parent cancels or does not show up, and wait impatiently for a session to end. If these clinician responses do not change in the course of treatment, it is safe to conclude that no improvement is taking place in the child and parent functioning. The move from disliking to liking the parent and the child is a valuable indicator of therapeutic change.

The clinician's reactions need to be carefully attended to in order to protect the clinician's personal well-being and professional effectiveness. Reflective supervision is an integral component of best practice in providing services to families exposed to violence and other traumatic experiences and should include sufficient time for exploring the clinician's experience as well as for didactic teaching of clinical principles and CPP strategies. This process needs to be safe and confidential to enable the clinician to disclose negative feelings and experiences of incompetence without fear of criticism or punitive responses on the part of the administration.

Reading through the brief descriptions of Jaylen, Susan, TJ, Marianna, and siblings Anthony and Alyssa in Section II leads to a reflection on the emotions that can be aroused in the clinician. Each family may present specific challenges to the clinician as the work unfolds. The clinician working with Jaylen and his parents struggled with his own rage at the social injustice experienced by families of color trapped in dangerous neighborhoods and had to remind himself to provide treatment to the family rather than focus primarily on the need for political change. He also had an 18-month-old child and, at times, felt overwhelmed as he thought about Jaylen's pain and the suffering of the parents who had lost their child. The clinician working with Susan and her mother, Nancy, felt alternatively frustrated, angry, critical, and scared when she learned that the mother had decided to return to Susan's abusive father. These emotions initially interfered with her capacity to (a) enter into dialogue with the mother, (b) listen to her perspective and make an effort to understand her motives and lend credence to her argument that the father regretted his violence and was seeking treatment for his alcohol abuse, and (c) help the mother integrate a focus on safety into her hopeful plans for reconciliation with her husband. In the case of TJ, the severity of TJ's aggressive behaviors and the aunt's increasing threats to give him up were such prominent features of the session that the clinician found it difficult to attend to the clear messages that TJ was giving them of his need for love and active assistance with emotion regulation. The case of Marianna and her mother made the clinician feel an intense need to protect the injured baby and help restore her healthy development. This protective stance often led her to focus primarily on the infant's needs, overlooking the cumulative burden on Marianna's young mother of poverty, immigration-related stress, threat of job loss, grief at her abandonment by Marianna's father, and helplessness at managing Marianna's medical needs. Anthony and Alyssa's situation evoked in their clinician strong anger at the child protective services system for allowing repeated foster care placements and reunifications and for failing to give proper weight to the damage that the children had suffered in their mother's care. The clinician felt enormous pressure to secure adoption for the children, and she at times transmitted this pressure to the foster mothers by trying to persuade them that Anthony's problems were temporary and that adopting Alyssa but not Anthony would be harmful for both children. The foster mothers, in turn, responded defensively to this message, leading to frequent impasses where communication between the foster mothers and the therapist became strained, although it remained always polite.

The complexity and urgency of these cases can affect even very experienced clinicians. As part of Reflective Practice Fidelity, clinicians, supervisors, and systems acknowledge the challenges inherent in the work and the importance of providing a supportive space where therapists are helped to recognize and regulate strong emotions prior to intervening, to reflect on their personal and/or cultural biases, and to consider alternate perspectives and the multiple factors that may contribute to different viewpoints (e.g., ecological and cultural context, trauma history). Challenges to Reflective Practice Fidelity can come from a variety of sources, including the family's lack of engagement; a child's exposure to extremely violent experiences, especially when safety has yet to be established; and pressures from systems that are involved in complicated and/or conflictual ways with the family or with treatment. For these reasons, reflective supervision should not be limited to beginning practitioners; it must be built in as an integral component of the clinician's practice, with peers providing supervision and support for each other and serving as sounding boards in situations of uncertainty and stress. It is important to remember that the process of supervision may parallel, in many ways, the process that is taking place in the intervention. A clinician who feels helpless in the intervention might, for example, evoke feelings of helplessness in the supervisor. Careful attention to the supervisory process can often give accurate clues as to how effectively the treatment is progressing.

Strand 2: Emotional Process Fidelity

> "What is it . . . that determines whether the conflicted past
> of the parent will be repeated with his child?" (Fraiberg et
> al., 1975, p. 419)

The answer, as Fraiberg and colleagues suggested, lies in the individual's capacity to connect affect to experience. Emotions play a central role in the therapeutic endeavor to help parents and children explore their reactions to the adversities and traumas that they have endured and to find meaning in their responses as a necessary step toward healthy adaptation.

Common emotional reactions to traumatic events include fear, guilt, shame, anger, sadness, numbing, and tuning out. Reflective Practice Fidelity addresses these reactions in the therapist. Emotional Process Fidelity highlights the importance of therapist attention to these processes in caregiver and child. The components of Emotional Process Fidelity are being aware of family members' emotional states, accepting and supporting strong emotional reactions, helping family members connect emotional reactions to their experiences, and promoting regulation of strong emotional reactions.

As an example, during early sessions with TJ, the therapist noted that his play was chaotic and violent. He often took a large dinosaur and had it stomp around the doll house. Everywhere the dinosaur went, destruction followed. The furniture was swept around the house, adult figures went flying out of the house, and then TJ made the dinosaur stomp on all of the children. This play sequence happened very quickly, followed by a quick shift of TJ's attention to other activities that included, in rapid succession, asking for the cooking toys, wanting to throw the ball back and forth with the therapist, and going to the toy cabinet, continually asking for new toys. TJ's aunt responded by remarking that TJ was aggressive and had trouble focusing. The therapist worried that perhaps TJ was becoming over-stimulated by all of the toys in the room. She began putting out fewer toys in the sessions, but the pattern of aggressive, chaotic play and inability to focus continued. The aunt continuously commented that TJ was like this all of the time. She said she was tired. The therapist was tired, too. Sessions with TJ were draining and seemed to make no sense. In an attempt to have a calmer session, one week the therapist decided to hide the dinosaur, but TJ was upset when he saw it wasn't there and refused to engage in any of the other activities that the therapist offered in an effort to help him interact in more regulated ways with his aunt. He only wanted the dinosaur.

The therapist brought this situation to supervision, and as she and the supervisor reviewed the sequence of the session as described in the narrative notes, they noticed that TJ was indeed unable to settle down, but, rather than just being unable to focus, he seemed to be asking for something that was missing. As she reflected on the session, the therapist noted that her own discomfort and the aunt's reaction to TJ dominated her perception of what was happening and kept her from seeing that TJ was asking for something beyond toys. He needed the adults to understand the anger and fear expressed in this play and to help him feel safe. He had played out a distressing scene—a scene where homes were destroyed by angry monsters, where caregivers left, and where children were hurt. As they witnessed his play and his inability to settle down, TJ's dysregulation became contagious to the therapist and the aunt, who felt worried, helpless, and tense. The aunt wondered aloud what she could do with him, the therapist felt confused and incompetent, and TJ was alone, stranded with the powerful feelings evoked by his enactment of his experiences of violence and neglect. Strong emotions that were unconnected to meaning served to separate the three of them.

In supervision, the therapist recognized that she was looking for a solution for TJ's behavior when perhaps a good starting point would be to become attuned to his affect. Consistent with the strand of Reflective Practice Fidelity, the therapist began by acknowledging, normalizing, and accepting her own emotional reactions. This enabled her to think more clearly about both the aunt's and TJ's perspectives. In the following sessions, she responded to TJ's aggressive play by asking him to describe what was happening, making narrative comments about what the dinosaur was doing and what the child dolls might be feeling, and suggesting ways of keeping the children safe. She used a tone of voice that reflected, in a modulated way, the intense affects played out in the scene and repeatedly articulated the themes of danger, fear in response to aggression, and the urgent need for protection. This therapeutic stance had a regulating effect on TJ, the aunt, and the therapist herself because (a) the modulated and empathic acknowledgment of emotion legitimizes the experience and (b) the trauma narrative that TJ was enacting was framed and contained by the protective narrative that the therapist was able to provide as a developmentally appropriate response.

The theme of the "short sadness span" was evident in the therapist's work with TJ and his aunt. TJ was initially unable to tolerate negative emotions that emerged as he enacted aspects of his history. He could not find comfort in the arms of a caregiver or within his own body, so he turned to toys and activities as possible sources of soothing and distraction, but these were not sufficient. As the therapist helped the aunt understand that TJ's chaotic play was a communication about his chaotic past, his aunt's arms and lap opened to him, and she was able to speak soothingly to him instead of comparing him to his father. After this happened, TJ's play, behavior, and storytelling of what had happened to him slowly become more organized as he grew in his capacity to play symbolically for longer periods, to use words to describe feelings, and to tolerate the difficult emotions associated with his past.

Susan also had difficulty tolerating negative emotions and shifted rapidly between activities whenever her mother or the therapist brought up the topic of her father. Susan's mother, Nancy, was able to connect the child's symptoms to her experience and was eager to help Susan understand and process what had happened. Nancy's sister was studying child development and suggested that Susan might be affected by what she had experienced. The two sisters talked about how no one in their family spoke about the horrors they had experienced in Cambodia, but they grew up under the weight of their grief and despair. Nancy wanted something different for Susan. Given her young age, the therapist and the mother used toys to introduce Susan to treatment. They showed how there had been a fight between Mom and Dad, and then Mom and Susan left and went to stay with Aunt Grace. Mom also said that Susan might miss Dad because she loved him very much, but he became scary when he was angry, and they could not stay with him. Susan listened intently, looking at her mother with a facial expression of serious concentration, but after this introduction, she walked away and went to play with the food toys for the remainder of the session. In later sessions, Susan continued to avoid both the doll house and the dolls. She spent sessions cooking food and drawing with her mother, asking the mother to draw flowers, butterflies, and smiling suns and coloring them with little scribbles. The therapist initially wondered whether Susan was perhaps too young to talk or play about what happened, but she then began to consider that Susan was avoiding difficult topics. This hypothesis was supported when she brought in a book about feelings. Susan sat in her mother's lap comfortably looking at the book, but when they came to a page where the character showed mild expressions of anger, she jumped off her mom's lap and began asking for other toys. Another time, when they were coloring, Nancy began drawing different feeling faces. "No," said Susan, and she scribbled all over the faces. Over and over, mother and therapist saw that Susan had great difficulty tolerating any kind of negative emotion and refused to talk about her father in any way. Susan's mother noted that the child had always been temperamentally sensitive, and she and the therapist agreed that her sensitivity might make strong feelings difficult for her.

Strand 3: Dyadic Relational Fidelity

"There is no such thing as a baby." (Winnicott, 1965)

Winnicott's statement captures the critical importance of early relationships in supporting normal development. His words prove equally true in helping young children recover from traumatic experiences. Although we wish they were too little to remember or resilient enough to overcome these challenges by themselves, traumatic experiences create expectations of danger and hurt and have the potential to teach young children key lessons about themselves, others, and relationships that may negatively affect their developmental trajectory. They need the help of adults, particularly those they love, to give them new experiences that counter traumatic expectations with new expectations of safety and protection.

The Dyadic Relational Fidelity strand addresses how the therapist supports the child's core relationships by simultaneously supporting the child and the parent. Components of Dyadic Relational Fidelity include balancing attention between caregiver and child and tracking both of their reactions during interactions, considering and supporting the child's and the caregiver's perspectives, serving as a translator between caregiver and child to enable them to better understand each other, intervening in ways that strengthen the caregiver–child relationship, and thinking about and supporting the child's relationships with other important caregivers, such as the child's noncustodial parent figure.

Although most CPP treatment involves dyadic parent–child sessions, other important caregivers may be asked to join in the treatment if this is safe and clinically indicated, moving the therapeutic focus and the format of the sessions from a dyadic to a triadic intervention or to an intervention involving more than three participants (e.g., the child, both biological parents, and the foster parent). The clinical motivation for this expanded configuration of participants is to show the child that the adults who are important in her life are collaborating with each other on her behalf. This expanded format often starts with the therapist meeting alone with the caregivers to work out conflicts and create a unified message of support for the child.

Even when the other parent or important second caregiver is not actively involved in treatment, the child has a formative relationship with that person, and treatment needs to include how the relationship with that person affects the child's life. If the person harmed the child or is in conflict with the primary caregiver on issues that are directly relevant to the child—for example, when parents who are separated argue over the schedule of visits or what happens with the child during the time with the other parent—the child may respond with self-blaming expectations that may remain unnoticed unless there is explicit attention to the child's web of primary relationships. The child may assume that he was placed in foster care because he was bad, or that the parents fought because she made one of them angry, or that one parent left because of something that the child did. Correcting these psychogenic expectations requires attention to the role that the all primary caregivers play in the child's outer and inner life. The child and the family benefit when all caregivers are able to acknowledge the impact of their actions on the child, say they are sorry, and show in words and actions that they are changing from perpetrators into protectors. As the child grows, the story is also likely to grow, and the child may turn to the caregivers to ask existential questions that may include, "Why did you hurt me?" and "Why did you leave?" The therapist's role is in part to support the parents in feeling capable of opening themselves to give an answer to these questions when the child turns to them. This includes not only an effort to imagine the experience of each parent, including the perpetrator, in ways that acknowledge the harm done to the child but also, whenever possible, the parents' struggles to do better and the "angel moments" that they might have provided to the child.

TJ and Susan had both learned that their parents could hurt them, leave them, and be unable to protect them. TJ responded aggressively and had difficulty connecting with his caregivers. He wanted desperately to be close, but he also feared that people would hurt him or send him away. In Susan's case, protection returned quickly, but Susan still became quickly anxious and avoidant of negative feelings. Both children needed their caregivers' help to learn new ways of being. As their caregivers acknowledged what had happened, responded in ways that were sensitive to the children's emotions, and acted to ensure the children's safety through repeated interactions, they taught TJ and Susan that relationships could be different and that they could depend on their caregivers to find safety, love, and joy.

The therapist's work with TJ and his aunt illustrated many aspects of Dyadic Relational Fidelity. As TJ played, he expressed his story through the language of symbolic play. His aunt responded to his aggressive play with socialization. She wanted him to play nicely and to be careful with the toys and became particularly upset when TJ played aggressively with the baby dolls. Given his father's history of aggression and TJ's extreme behavior problems, she wanted to ensure that she taught TJ that it was not acceptable to be aggressive. As the treatment continued, consistent with the strands of Emotional Process Fidelity and Dyadic Relational Fidelity, the therapist realized that it was important not only to attend to TJ but to support and give voice to the aunt's strong emotional reactions. The aunt was worried about TJ, and until the therapist understood the origins and depths of her concerns, it was difficult for the aunt to reflect about the possible meaning of TJ's behavior. She wanted desperately for TJ's mother to come back and take care of him. She told the therapist that she never thought her approaching retirement years would include taking care of a young child. She had long planned to go on a cruise to see the world. As she said this, she smiled with some sadness and noted that perhaps her next cruise would be a Disney cruise; TJ would like that. She was also realistic, and with time and support, she was able to acknowledge with deep regret that TJ's mother was not ready to take care of him. The therapist raised the question of how to help TJ understand why he was not living with his mother. The aunt decided to speak with TJ's mother, and during a difficult but constructive conversation that the aunt described to the therapist in a collateral session, the two women decided to let him know that his mommy loved him but had some problems, so she could not raise him right now. They also agreed that the mother would tell this to TJ during her irregular visits with him instead of continuing to use these visits to raise false hopes by assuring him that, very soon, they would live together again. The aunt also said this to TJ in therapy. With deep emotion and with her voice often shaking, she told him that his mom drank (something TJ already knew), and when she drank, she could not take good care of TJ and could not keep him safe from his dad. The aunt added that TJ's mom needed to get help so she could be a better mom, and she knew that Aunt Rosa was someone who had helped her when she was growing up and now would keep TJ safe. Saying this aloud to TJ seemed to change the aunt's own attitude. She claimed a role as his protector and began talking about how even if TJ's mom came back, she would be there for him. With these changes, the aunt became even more open to TJ's perspective.

The therapist acted as a translator to help the aunt reflect more fully on the communication behind TJ's symbolic play. "You know TJ," she said to the aunt, "and I speak play. Together, we will figure out what he needs." She told the aunt a core CPP belief that "the rightful place of aggression is in the play," and she suggested to the aunt that TJ might be using symbolic play to show them the aggression that he endured. When TJ had his character behave aggressively—hitting the dinosaur and other bad guys—and his aunt involuntarily sighed indicating her displeasure, the therapist made herself breathe and remember that she needed to craft an intervention that encompassed both the aunt's goals and TJ's needs. "I think your aunt really wishes that you felt safer, and you did not have to run around fighting and hitting." The aunt smiled and looked up as the therapist continued. "I know you want him to leave all this aggression behind. You are doing so much to keep TJ safe, but I wonder if TJ needs to feel strong and that beating up the bad guys in play is one of the ways that he does this. Maybe, in time, he'll see that we are there to help him, and he doesn't need to beat up the bad guys all by himself." This intervention was an example of what we refer to as a "double scoop," an intervention where the therapist symbolically scoops and holds the perspective of one partner (in this case, the aunt), then symbolically scoops and holds the perspective of the other partner (in this case, TJ), and then puts both perspectives together so that both partners can see each other's views. By legitimizing each perspective, the therapist helps child and caregiver feel united, knowing that although they may have different agendas, both are valid and do not need to divide them.

In a later session, when TJ played that the dinosaur ate and violently stomped on a male figure, the aunt seemed perplexed and disturbed by what she saw. The therapist recognized the importance of supporting the aunt and helping her to make meaning of what she was seeing, and again offered a possible translation. The therapist wondered whether perhaps the male doll was his father and TJ needed to punish him symbolically through play. This translation resonated with the aunt and allowed her to remain present when TJ played out these scenes. She gave voice to his anger and told him that she was also angry with the bad man. Over the course of time, they jailed the bad man. They told him that he was unsafe and that he could not be around the babies. Then, one day, TJ asked, "Why he bad?" TJ's aunt was unprepared, but she rose to the task. She looked at the male doll and said she had heard he was not always bad but that he had problems, and he did not get help. It was not a full answer, but it was the start to a discussion that would continue as TJ developed.

In Jaylen's case, the therapist needed to remember that the trauma witnessed by the child had also been experienced by his father. As committed as his father was to helping Jaylen process what he had seen, he pulled away when Jaylen played in ways that enacted their story, bringing in an ambulance, showing a young child getting hurt, and making shooting noises. At first, the therapist was irritated because at key moments in Jaylen's play, the father pulled out his cell phone and began texting, but Martín then realized that Jaylen's play evoked visceral reactions in Jaylen's father because he too was remembering the shooting and the body-based feelings associated with being under fire with his child. His reactions were also magnified because Jaylen's play served as a potent reminder to James of his cousin's murder, which he had witnessed as a young child but previously never talked about. Although he did not speak about it initially, recent news stories about young Black boys who had been shot were ever present in James' mind, and he worried about how he would ever keep Jaylen safe in a world that was predisposed to view and treat him as dangerous. James was thinking about and responding to not only the one shooting but to waves of violence and danger that had affected him and his community for generations.

Although the therapist came to understand the complexity of James' trauma history, he was still faced with the challenge of how to help Jaylen. The therapist noted that Jaylen readily told the story, but James had difficulty being present. He asked himself whether Jaylen might benefit from individual therapy but concluded that the father very much wanted to support his child, although he was not able to fully do so at the moment. Moreover, it would be more helpful to Jaylen in the long run to have his father be able to respond to him. Whenever they went to any store, even if they avoided the one near where the boy had been shot, Jaylen always brought up what had happened, and his dad needed to know how to respond in those moments. This realization enabled the therapist to be more patient and understanding with James. The therapist practiced focusing not only on Jaylen's narrative and play during the sessions but also on the father's responses; the therapist did this to help James remember the difference between the danger that they had experienced and the safety of the present moment and to use this differentiation to help regulate James' stress. These efforts bore fruit: At posttest, James showed lower symptoms of PTSD and depression. James and Jaylen were able to both talk and play about the shooting and to also engage joyfully in other activities. James commented that before the treatment, he felt overwhelmed and did not know what to do when Jaylen brought up the shooting, and he added that he now knew how to help his son.

Caregiver reactions were also the focus of treatment during the early phase of the therapist's work with 9-month-old Marianna and her mother, Aurelia. As they began treatment, the therapist learned that it was unclear whether Marianna's injury was inflicted or the result of an accident. Although the accident was not her mother's fault, Marianna had experienced intense body pain and separation from her mother during hospitalization. At a developmental stage where separation anxiety and fear of strangers are on the ascendancy, Marianna had gone through an intense traumatic moment followed by intrusive medical procedures and an extended stay in the unfamiliar, unpredictable setting of a hospital, with only intermittent access to her mother, who needed to continue to work. These experiences had a direct effect on Marianna's functioning. Whereas before the injury and its sequelae, she had been a calm and responsive baby, she now cried inconsolably, arched away when held in her mother's arms, and woke up screaming several times during the night. When the therapist met mother and child, she realized that Marianna's behaviors were at least in part exacerbated by her mother's response. Aurelia froze when Marianna cried and held her at some distance from her body, talking with her soothingly but somewhat detachedly. In response to the therapist's sympathetic questions about how it felt when Marianna cried, Aurelia responded that she felt guilty, helpless, and afraid to hold the baby too tightly for fear of re-injuring her. The therapist realized that Aurelia was hearing Marianna's crying not as a message saying, "Mommy, I need you" but rather as a question asking, "Mommy, where were you? How could you let this happen?" Aurelia's feelings of guilt led her to withdraw physically and emotionally, and Marianna remained inconsolable while waiting for her mother to respond.

The therapist understood from Aurelia's ready acknowledgment of her strong emotions that the intervention needed to include a very specific effort to address the mother's experience as a vehicle to help Aurelia connect with her baby—a "double scoop" intervention. Although at first hesitant to focus on herself, Aurelia readily opened up when her therapist explained to her—in response to her acknowledgment of guilt and helplessness—that the mother is also dealt a blow when her child has been injured. The therapist added that a trauma like what Marianna and Aurelia experienced can shake parents' confidence, and this is why it is so important to support parents in their efforts to help their child. The therapist then asked, "Is there a way that I can support you?" As she heard these words that normalized her experience, Aurelia said that she felt alone and isolated. The church had been a source of support, but she did not feel comfortable attending church now because the woman who harmed her child was a church member. Encouraged by the therapist's sympathetic requests to describe her life, Aurelia disclosed that she had been quite depressed during her pregnancy because her partner had left her and that after Marianna was born she found it hard to connect with the baby. Aurelia's own mother had been very abusive and had blamed Aurelia and thrown her out of the house at 15 years old after discovering that the mother's boyfriend was sexually abusing her. Aurelia went to live with an aunt who had six children of her own and who gave Aurelia food and shelter but little love. As Aurelia described her story, the therapist asked her how she thought these experiences had affected her relationship with Marianna. Aurelia responded that she did not know how to give love because she had received so little of it. She added that now she felt Marianna had been taken from her. She turned away. Marianna did not mold to her mother's arms as before, and she arched away from her. She seemed to interact very little. The mother thought that Marianna blamed her for getting hurt.

Aurelia's description of her personal experience and its effect on her relationship with her baby confirmed the therapist's impression that it was critical to support Aurelia in processing her experience to help her connect with her baby, who was becoming avoidant and resistant to her. Both mother and baby had experiences of fear and pain, and this pain blocked them from establishing the connection that they both longed for. As she worked with this dyad, the therapist helped Aurelia accept and tolerate the realization that Marianna's body had been in intense pain. While difficult to hear, this information helped Aurelia entertain the possibility that Marianna might be turning away from her not because she did not want to be close to her mother but because, immediately following the injury and the medical procedures, any contact with Marianna's body made her anticipate that she would again feel pain. Freed from her framework of rejection, Aurelia increased her efforts to woo Marianna. As she was changing her, for example, she reminded herself that Marianna's crying and recoiling were not her fault, and she continued to speak gently and caress the baby's legs and tummy. This new attitude enabled Aurelia to become a soothing presence to Marianna. *"Ay, te duele, te duele"* ("Oh, it hurts, it hurts") she would say when the baby cried. *"Lo siento, mi amor. Lo siento. Mamá está aquí. Te voy a cuidar amor. Te voy a cuidar."* ("I am sorry my love. I am sorry. Mom is here. I am going to take care of you, my love. I am going to take care of you.") The therapist's ability to uphold the Dyadic Relational Fidelity strand by responding simultaneously to the mother's and the child's experience was a key ingredient in helping Aurelia and Marianna to heal as individuals and to develop a closer and more satisfying relationship.

In the case of 25-month-old Susan, the child's progress increased significantly when Susan's father, Arthur, joined the family in treatment and the therapeutic focus was expanded to a triadic approach. He had stopped drinking and had met alone with the therapist to complete the CPP assessment, where he reflected both on how this experience had affected Susan and Nancy and how his own history of witnessing domestic violence as a child might be linked to his violent behavior. He did not want to attend individual therapy, but he was a member of a Chinese Catholic church and was receiving counseling from a priest there. In his first CPP session with Susan, he apologized to her for pushing her and scaring her. He said he got angry and hurt her mom, and that was not right. He talked about how he was trying to change and not be scary. Susan listened attentively but again showed a pattern of avoiding any negative feelings. Susan's mother and father both agreed that it might be helpful to slowly help Susan learn that it was OK both to talk about what had happened and to develop the capacity to tolerate feelings of sadness, anger, and fear. Her father was particularly instrumental in helping her. The therapist and father found moments to bring up very briefly the violent episode and talk about feelings. Susan invariably responded by moving away or asking to go the bathroom or to get water. The therapist helped the father and mother tell Susan that it was hard to remember scary things, but now she and her mother were safe. They then allowed Susan to change activities. By interspersing bouts of talking and playing about the violence with regulating activities that included blowing bubbles, rolling a ball back and forth, and drawing, they hoped to help Susan learn at a body-based level that she could feel negative emotions without becoming overwhelmed. A particularly poignant moment that demonstrated Susan's and her parents' growing ability to manage strong negative feelings came at the end of treatment. Susan, now 3 years old, was drawing pictures with her father. "Draw a mad face, Daddy" she instructed. He did it. "I was scared, Daddy," she said. Her dad looked down and then drew a sad face. "I am sorry, Susan. I am so sorry I scared you." "Yes," Susan said and sighed, and then she slowly leaned on him. The father looked at the mother and said, "I am sorry I scared you, too." The mother responded, "I know, and I am glad you are learning not to do that anymore." Together, the mother and father were able, in this moment, to create a circle of protection around Susan that the therapist very much hoped would become the new norm for the family.

Strand 4: Trauma Framework Fidelity

> "On knowing what you're not supposed to know and feeling what you're not supposed to feel." (Bowlby, 1988)

The three interconnected fidelity strands described in the previous sections—Reflective Practice Fidelity, Emotional Processing Fidelity, and Dyadic Relational Fidelity—represent the historical roots of CPP. Within the original model, there were ghosts in the nursery, but trauma was not mentioned explicitly. Perhaps this was because in the 1970s, when Selma Fraiberg developed infant–parent psychotherapy, the diagnosis of PTSD was new and had not yet been widely applied to women and children, most particularly not to children under 6 years old. Trauma Framework Fidelity reflects CPP's commitment to implement Bowlby's call to action to identify and clinically address real-life experiences of violence. As Bowlby noted, "An early therapeutic task is to identify the real-life experiences lying close behind the deceptive camouflage" (Bowlby, 1988, p. 117). Young children often show what they have experienced through story, play, and behavior. When it is story or play, we may see it as purely fantasy. When they behave in ways that are disturbing, we may feel compelled to banish the behavior without considering its meaning. TJ communicated through both fantasy and action. He told stories of a terrifying monster who would destroy the house and take him away. "You have to fight the monster," he would repeatedly say. Sometimes, it seemed like he was joyfully playing. At other times, he seemed truly terrified. TJ also choked other children at school. The school administration demanded immediate intervention. "What's wrong with him?" the teachers asked. As we are learning, this was not the right question. To truly understand TJ, his therapist, aunt, and teachers needed to understand his history. They needed to understand not what was wrong with him, but what had happened to him.

TJ's aunt didn't know, but his mother told her the following story. It was just a small part of TJ's experience, but it helped his aunt to understand what he had been through. When TJ was around 13 months old, at Halloween, TJ's parents got in a huge fight while they were both sitting in the front seat of their car. The mother told TJ's father that she would leave him, and the father started choking her. She got out of the car and tried to get TJ, but the father drove off while the door was open, yelling that he would kill her if she tried to get TJ. In that one scene, the therapist saw links to both TJ's play about monsters and his aggressive behavior. The aunt responded that TJ was so little—was it truly possible that he could remember? It was a horrible scene, one that everyone wished that TJ did not know, and yet, as his therapist and aunt came to understand, he did know what he was not supposed to know. The key to reducing his re-experiencing symptoms and aggressive behaviors lay in conveying to him that his caregivers also knew, that they appreciated how scary and overwhelming things had been, and that they were trying to ensure that these frightening things did not happen again. As we work with children like TJ, we need to think about how fantasy and actions may be linked to real-life experience. To do this, we must prepared to ask about, hear, and remember traumatic and violent experiences that are unfortunately much too common in the lives of many children.

The crux of Trauma Framework Fidelity is as follows: When either the child or caregiver has experienced at least one traumatic event, the treatment includes helping the parent and child understand and process how the trauma affected each of the family members and to use this knowledge as a vehicle to regulate affect, correct misperceptions, and restore momentum toward health. Core components of Trauma Framework Fidelity include the following:

1. Assessing the child's and family's trauma history.
2. Developing a therapeutic agreement with the caregiver about how to address the trauma history in treatment.
3. Keeping in mind how the trauma history may affect current functioning and responses to intervention.
4. Tailoring interventions to help the child and parent incorporate a more adaptive response to trauma reminders and put the traumatic experience in the broader context of their lives.

The work involves "speaking the unspeakable" but doing so in ways that uphold the importance of safety and of trusting, protective relationships. The trauma framework conveys the conviction that a trauma history should not suppressed or ignored but neither should it define or overwhelm a person. It should be integrated as an experience that was painful but can become part of one's growth.

Embedded in Trauma Framework Fidelity is the importance of assessing for and keeping in mind not only the child's but also the caregiver's trauma history. As discussed before, Jaylen's therapist was able to support the father's reactions during treatment by keeping the father's history in mind. At 7 years old, James witnessed his cousin's murder. At 11 years old, he saw a serious bus accident in which people were killed. From 14 to 16 years old, he witnessed severe community violence and moved out of the area after a gang threatened his brother. When James was 25 years old, his father, who was a big source of support, passed away from a sudden heart attack, and at 26, he and Jaylen witnessed the event that brought them to treatment—namely, the shooting of a child in their community. Although James requested psychotherapy with the sole goal of helping Jaylen recover from this last event, progress toward this goal was supported by the therapist's understanding of the cumulative impact of James' trauma history on his ability to be emotionally present for his child. James had tried to banish these memories from his mind, but with the therapist's help, he realized that these unwelcome memories continued to be present and to wield power over his reactions. He found that by talking about them with the therapist, he was able to both normalize and make meaning of his response, regain his sense of competence, be kinder to himself, and become better able to support his son.

Integrating Trauma Framework Fidelity into the therapeutic work can challenge the therapist's ability to hold onto the first three strands of fidelity because of the power of trauma—including vicarious trauma—to dysregulate and fragment. These challenges were illustrated in many of the examples throughout this section. Challenges to Reflective Practice Fidelity take place when the family's traumatic stress responses and dysregulated behavior derail the therapist's ability to monitor and regulate her own responses. Challenges to Emotional Process Fidelity occur when the family's strongly expressed emotions render the therapist helpless and incapable of helping the parent and child regulate their feelings and behavior. Challenges to Dyadic Relational Fidelity may occur when parent and child become traumatic triggers for each other and the therapist becomes aligned with either the parent's or the child's experience, overlooking the perspective, motivations, and feelings of the other.

During our 18-month CPP trainings, many participants remarked that they found it difficult to initiate talking with parents and children about the frightening events that had happened to them and how those events affected them. Participants also said that once they learned to speak the language of trauma, they realized that they were working with the same families as before, with the difference that now they were hearing and holding their stories. Although this opened new pathways for intervention that led to remarkable changes for families, it also meant that the therapists needed to learn how to hold these stories within their own minds and bodies. Many of them had come to the work to help children and to strengthen children's relationships with their caregivers. The therapists had not planned to become trauma therapists. As they saw it now, when these relationships and the child's development were threatened by traumatic experiences, someone needed to address the trauma with the family. It was important work that many of them wanted to do, but it was different, and it was hard.

To facilitate conversation on this important issue during trainings, we used a metaphor that many participants found helpful. We described ourselves as firemen and firewomen. Firefighters do the very counterintuitive move of walking toward fire. Most people would not do it. As trauma therapists, we do the counterintuitive move of speaking directly about trauma. Again, most people would not do it. How to do it holds the key to determining whether this counterintuitive move is more likely to be life-saving than life-threatening. Firefighters know that they do not send a rookie into a fire alone and without support. Rookies need training, lots of drills, special equipment, and the support of a veteran firefighter and a team. If a rookie is sent in alone to fight a fire, she might get hurt. The same is true for therapists. As they learn to walk toward trauma, "rookies" (therapists who are new to working with trauma and/or new to psychotherapy in general) are at the greatest danger of experiencing vicarious traumatization, burnout, or compassion fatigue. With good training and supervision, the trauma therapy version of "drills" (learning to ask supportively about trauma, practice handling difficult ports of entry), and the support of a team, the risk for these harmful effects lessens, and the satisfaction with the work increases. Many trauma therapists feel as passionately committed to this work as firefighters feel to theirs. As they become more competent at helping families in great jeopardy and witness the well-being that is often brought about by therapists' efforts, they gain a new understanding of the enormous potential for psychological and spiritual growth that may reside in creating meaning out of suffering. The emotional burden for the therapists of hearing the stories is still present and needs to be addressed, but the therapists carry this burden differently, and, as they walk toward the fire, they see not only destruction but hope and light.

Strand 5: Procedural Fidelity

> "CPP fidelity is guided by reflection, not by rigid adherence to what might be perceived as perfection." (Ghosh Ippen et al., 2014)

Within each phase of CPP (Foundational, Core Intervention, and Recapitulation and Termination), there are key procedures that guide and organize the work. These procedures are listed within the Procedural Fidelity section of the CPP fidelity measure for each phase. The Foundational Phase Fidelity measure (see Appendix A) tracks Assessment and Engagement Procedural Fidelity (pages 7–10) and Feedback Session Procedural Fidelity (pages 11–12). The Core Intervention Phase Fidelity measure (see Appendix B) tracks Procedural Fidelity for the session where the child is introduced to CPP (pages 2–3), and the Recapitulation and Termination Phase Fidelity measure (see Appendix C) tracks Procedural Fidelity for this phase (page 2). Within the Procedural Fidelity sections are key tasks, core topics for dialogue, and reminders to track affective processes.

Within the CPP Procedural Fidelity Assessment and Engagement section, it is not mandatory to use specific measures, but it is important to assess core domains.

Different screening instruments can be used for this purpose. Parents have been receptive to instruments that contain a range of stressful and traumatic events and begin with non-interpersonal traumas such as accidents, natural disasters, and medical traumas before asking about interpersonal violence such as domestic violence and child abuse. Across cultures and countries, people recognize that it is normal to have reactions following accidents or natural disasters. As parents acknowledge the impact of noninterpersonal traumas on themselves and on their children, the therapist is able to help them appreciate that exposure to other events, including interpersonal violence, can also affect both children and adults. Noninterpersonal traumas may be "safer" for caregivers to talk about because these traumas typically do not lead to child abuse reports and may be less guilt-inducing than experiences where the child has witnessed violence or has been directly harmed. From a relatively modulated affective state (Emotional Process Fidelity), caregivers may be better able to take in psychoeducation, hear the therapist's efforts to normalize the traumatic response, and learn core trauma concepts including the concept of trauma and loss reminders. Moreover, although the reason for referral may involve interpersonal trauma in telling their story, children may begin by processing less charged events, or they may play out a car accident, medical procedure, and a domestic violence incident within the same story. Although not linked in time, these incidents may be linked by theme.

> EXAMPLE.
>
> Anthony Craft was in the NICU for 1 month and was fed via a nasogastric tube. He had numerous medical procedures shortly after being born. For a young baby, it would be natural that this experience would teach him that the world was a dangerous place where people did things to you that hurt. This may have made him less responsive and connected to adults. His later experiences of abuse and violence would have confirmed his theory. Understanding Anthony's full history, including the ages when events happened, helped his therapist and caregiver to reflect on how these events shaped his sense of danger.

A core part of Procedural Fidelity during the Foundational Phase is that the therapist provides the caregiver with a rationale for completing a trauma screening instrument and asks the caregiver to jointly complete a trauma screening instrument. In some cases, such as Jaylen Fisher's, this may seem unnecessary because he was being referred for a specific trauma. Yet, as we saw in Section II, Jaylen's father and therapist were able to have important dialogues during the trauma screening process that lay the foundation for the rest of treatment. The therapist learned that Jaylen's grandfather had passed away 1 year earlier—an important fact, as it helped the father and therapist think about Jaylen's prior experience with death.

Sometimes, therapists hesitate to screen for trauma when a caregiver is mandated because they worry that it might negatively affect rapport, and the parent may not provide accurate information. For example, if the therapist working with TJ Bishop were to begin working with TJ's mother, the mother might not be ready to talk about what TJ went through. She also might not provide an accurate response if she were in the process of reunification and if admitting to reportable events could jeopardize reunification with her son. However, in going through the questionnaire, she may understand that these were events that may have affected TJ. Moreover, the therapist would be able to consider what it might mean to TJ to be seen in CPP treatment with his mother if she could not acknowledge documented experiences of violence that he had undergone.

In other cases, such as Anthony and Alyssa Craft, where the caregiver is a foster parent, it may seem unproductive to screen for trauma because the foster parent is not likely to know the children's full history, and the therapist may worry that it may take a long time to do the assessment, particularly when the child is in critical need of intervention. As noted in the descriptions of the therapist's work with TJ and the aunt, when the caregiver is not fully aware of the child's trauma history, the therapist and caregiver meet alone and use the instrument to talk about what the caregiver knows, what the caregiver fears the child's behavior may mean, and what the therapist knows from other sources, provided that appropriate permissions have been obtained.

In any of these cases, a caregiver may choose to refuse to complete an instrument. Fidelity is not assessed by the caregiver's response but, rather, by the therapist's ability to describe the rationale for the importance of talking about stressful events and to ask caregivers to complete the trauma screening.

EXAMPLE.

When Anthony and Alyssa Craft's caregivers, Gina and Kerri, entered treatment, they were focused on the children's problems and were willing to be a part of treatment. They agreed to complete the child trauma screening instrument but were unsure as to why they needed to answer questions about their own history. "I get why you'd want to know all this stuff if you were working with their mom," Kerri said, "but I don't know why you need to know about me." The therapist agreed that it might seem confusing, as they had not been involved in any way in what had happened to the kids, but then added, "Sometimes, when children have extreme behavior problems, they can push our buttons. They can remind us of people from our past or things that have happened that we'd rather not think about. It can also be very stressful to care for children who have been through what they have been through. They have lots of fears that people may hurt them or leave them, and they have lots of problems calming themselves down when they get upset. I don't know that we always give foster parents enough support, and you are doing very important work. I would like to be able to support you." Gina thought about it and then said that Anthony did push her buttons, but she could manage. Given the severity of Anthony's behavior problems, she wanted to get started with treatment. She decided not to share her history at that time, but she seemed to appreciate the therapist's comments. Much later in treatment, as she continued to be frustrated with Anthony, she did open up to the therapist. She noted that sometimes Anthony was really sweet, but when he was aggressive, he reminded her of her own mother, who had been diagnosed with bipolar disorder. She had also heard that Anthony's mother had also been diagnosed with bipolar disorder, and she worried about what might happen as he grew up— and if she could deal with him. Treatment seemed to shift after Kerri began sharing her past and connecting it to the way she responded to Anthony.

As illustrated in the vignette, the sheer act of providing a rationale and asking to talk about traumatic experiences opens a door. The caregiver may choose not to walk through it initially, but in opening the door, the therapist has been faithful to CPP. Because the door has been opened, it remains a viable path during future intervention efforts.

During the Core Intervention Phase there are relatively few prescribed procedures with the exception of the session where the child is introduced to CPP. Treatment is guided by the therapist's conceptualization of the needs of the family, attention to timing, and response to core domains of intervention. A common question that arises in training is whether, in working with a caregiver and infant, it is necessary to explain the reason for treatment to the infant. Clinical experience has shown that clearly describing the reason for why the caregiver, infant, and therapist are meeting together in the infant's presence and highlighting the different sides of the triangle creates a shared understanding for the caregiver and therapist in a way that supports and focuses future efforts.

EXAMPLE.
Marianna, 9 months old, had been present during many of the assessment sessions with her mother Aurelia, but to mark the start of the Core Intervention Phase, the therapist who was working with them decided to name the CPP triangle at the end of the feedback session. The work with Marianna and her mother was done in Spanish, and so it is shared first in Spanish and then in English.

"Hola, Marianna. Tú te ves tan tranquila en los brazos de tu mamá mientras que mamá y yo hablamos de como ayudarte. Sabemos que te dolió mucho. No sabemos lo que pasó, pero sabemos que tu cuerpo muchas veces te duele. Fue espantoso para tí estar dolida y estar en el hospital sin tu mamá. Tu mamá quería estar contigo, pero tuvo que trabajar. A veces lloras y no quieres acurrucarte por el dolor que sientes en tu cuerpo. Tu mami y yo queremos ayudarte a aprender que puedes relajarte y sentirte segura en los brazos de tu mamá. Así como estás ahora. Las cosas eran tan duras para tu mamá cuando ella era chiquita, y ella quiere que sea diferente para tí. Verdad, Aurelia?" "Sí," dice Aurelia. "Quiero que sepa que yo siempre voy a estar a su lado, y que la quiero tanto." Con estas palabras, Mariana volteó la cabeza y miró a su mamá. "Creo que nos escucha," dijo la terapeuta.

"Hello, Marianna. You look so peaceful in your mommy's arms while Mommy and I are talking about how to help you. We know you were hurt really badly. We don't know what happened, but we know that you often feel a lot of pain in your body. It was very scary for you to be in pain and then to be in the hospital without your mommy. Your mommy wanted to be with you, but she had to work. Sometimes you cry and you don't want to cuddle because of the pain you feel in your body. Your mommy and I want to help you to learn that you can relax and feel safe in your mommy's arms. Just like you are now. Things were hard for your mom when she was little, and she wants things to be different for you. Isn't that right, Aurelia?" "Yes," says Aurelia. "I want her to know that I am always at her side, and I love her so much." With these words, Mariana turns her head and looks at her mother. "I think she is listening to us," says the therapist.

As treatment comes to a close, core procedures once again become important. These are described in detail under "Phase 3: Recapitulation and Termination: Promoting Sustainability of Gains." Meetings with the caregiver and posttreatment evaluations are used to highlight improvements in functioning and to identify any ongoing challenges. Structured termination procedures—including reviewing the family's story, counting down sessions, and planning and carrying out a good-bye session—help the therapist and family members to consolidate the work so that treatment gains are more likely to be maintained and to have a good-bye that may be different from unplanned good-byes of the past.

Strand 6: Content Fidelity

How can you write a measure that is faithful?

To history, authenticity,

the evolving needs of each child and family?

The last line of this verse is a reminder that the overarching goals of treatment remain the same across families, but treatment is tailored to the evolving needs of each child and family. As treatment unfolds, families change in their needs and capacities, and the therapist's conceptualization of the family must remain flexible, with the goals of treatment and the therapist's intervention changing in tandem with the family's needs. Content Fidelity tracks the therapist's conceptualization of the family's needs, the specific CPP goals that are the primary targets of intervention, and the degree to which there is a match between the therapist's conceptualization and interventions.

The next section describes specific treatment objectives and provides examples from the treatments with Jaylen, TJ, Susan, Marianna, and Alyssa and Anthony. Objectives are presented in the order that they appear on the CPP Intervention Fidelity section, which is part of the CPP Fidelity Instruments for each phase.

1. *Convey hope.* As discussed throughout this manual, hope—rooted in realistic knowledge of the family's capacities and situation—is a critical element of treatment. The therapist offers benevolent reframes, reminds the parent that small changes can make a big difference, and highlights positive steps that the family has taken. Depending on the family's values and traditions, the therapist may also help the family connect to spiritual resources. Through rituals, prayers, and connection with others who share similar spiritual values, families often derive a deep sense of peace and hope.

    EXAMPLE.
    Susan's father spoke to the therapist about how he regularly attended church. He had confessed to the priest what he had done and had felt tremendously relieved when the priest had reminded him that we could "hate the sin but love the sinner." In extended conversations with the priest, Susan's father felt that there was hope that he could change, that he did not need to lose his family, and that perhaps this was God's way of ensuring that he addressed the issues that were tearing his family apart. He brought a book, *Chicken Soup for the Soul,* to treatment and said it inspired him to be a better parent.

    The gradual and often nonlinear nature of change can be a helpful reminder for parents not to lose hope when progress is not as quick as they would like. Many caregivers grew up in dangerous circumstances that led to the development of significant symptoms and risky behaviors. When they came to the attention of service providers, they were often labeled as having attention-deficit/hyperactivity disorder, bipolar disorder, and substance abuse problems. Although they may have met criteria for some of these diagnoses, parents often mentioned that they never realized and were never helped to understand that traumatic experiences may have contributed to their difficulties. They believed that the issue was rooted in their genes (the ever-popular theory of the "bad seed") and that somehow they had passed this on to their children so that they, in turn, were doomed to the same fate. Knowing that the problem did not reside within the person's inalterable genetics, but instead was a result of what happened to the parent or the child, can be freeing and inspire hope for the next generation.

EXAMPLE.

The therapist working with TJ's mother initially had difficulty appreciating the steps that the mother was taking. As treatment unfolded, the mother met a few times with the therapist. The mother was fighting a battle against her traumatic past and her addiction to alcohol and heroin. It was a battle that she unfortunately lost frequently, and yet she loved her son. She wanted him to know it was not his fault that he was angry and aggressive. It was not his fault that she could not be in his life. For now, the best that she could do was to make sure that he had a stable home and a loving caregiver. For now, that person was Rosa. TJ's mom showed up when she could, and then she disappeared unexpectedly, leaving TJ to melt down in tears in Rosa's arms. She openly described TJ's history to Rosa so that Rosa could better understand TJ and so that as TJ grew, Rosa could help him understand why his parents could not be the people who raised him. It was less than ideal, the therapist thought, and yet, TJ was freed from negative attributions from his aunt. She knew that he would melt down when his mother left. She appreciated that his behaviors were at times challenging, but this was to be expected given what he had been through. It was not the outcome the therapist wanted, but it involved a growing acceptance on TJ's part that his mother's love could be real and deeply flawed at the same time.

The parent's view of the child is sometimes impaired by the traumatic event. The parent asks, "How will my child ever be the same?" Normative developmental challenges (e.g., separation anxiety, tantrums) become worrisome indications that the child might be damaged. Even when these worries are warranted, such as when the child has sustained an injury that may negatively affect the child's development, a pessimistic outlook can constitute an additional risk factor that may jeopardize the child's improvement. An accurate but forward-looking appraisal of the child's potential for growth is a critical focus of treatment.

EXAMPLE.

In early sessions with Marianna and Aurelia, Aurelia was devastated by her infant's head injury and feared she had brain damage. Instilling hope was essential to Marianna's development. During the assessment, the therapist noticed Marianna reach for a small toy that she had brought and then lightly babble. "Do you see what she is doing?" she said. Aurelia turned and looked. "Look at the way she is reaching for the toy and making little noises. She wants it." "Ah ah ah," said Marianna. "Ah ah ah," said the therapist. "Look at her," said the therapist. "She was hurt really badly, and we have been so worried about how she is, but she is wanting to play and communicate. This is good to see." Aurelia smiled faintly, a flicker of hope flashing over her face.

2. *Develop an empathic relationship with family members.* Family members come to treatment with varying degrees of openness to engaging with the therapist and the therapeutic process. Jaylen's father, James, initially attended treatment at the insistence of his wife, Tiana. He was uncertain as to whether he actually wanted to talk about what he and Jaylen had been through. He thought it was strange to bring a 2½-year-old to therapy, and he worried that his friends would laugh at him if they found out he had been to therapy. After all, they had all seen shootings. Arthur, Susan's father, was initially apprehensive that he would be judged by the therapist and would be viewed only as a violent man rather than as a father who missed his child. TJ's Aunt Rosa was concerned that some young therapist was going to tell her how to parent TJ. The child was out of control, and she needed help, but she didn't want anyone telling her what to do. Marianna's mother, Aurelia, felt unsure of her own ability to parent her child. She watched as other providers, the home-visiting nurse, and the occupational therapist competently cared for Marianna, and she wondered why she could not help Marianna. She was also concerned that using multiple services might jeopardize her ability to one day obtain legal immigration status. Foster parents Kerri and Gina were overwhelmed by the twins' behavior problems and were furious at a system that

was providing inadequate care to the children, had not told them about the children's difficulties before placement, and was now suggesting that the children might be returned to their mother in spite of the foster mothers' strenuous efforts to help them progress.

The development of an empathic relationship goes beyond simply being warm and involves empathically listening to the parents as they describe their prior experience with service providers and their anger, apprehension, or ambivalence regarding participating in treatment. The therapist also seeks to understand historical factors including caregiver and child trauma history, prior interactions with systems, cultural beliefs about therapy, and many other variables that shape current interactions and responses. The therapist holds that behavior has meaning and that to truly understand the perspective of different family members, we have to open ourselves to understanding and keeping in mind their experience. In each of the cases described previously, it was important that the therapist listen first, prior to intervening, because change is only possible within the context of a safe therapeutic relationship.

3. *Enhance safety.* The expression "safety first" highlights the priority of addressing safety when working with families who have experienced trauma. The goal of enhancing safety can be further broken down into subgoals, which are described next.

   - Physical safety: The therapist addresses serious risks to physical safety, including risks related to placement instability.

     EXAMPLE.
     In Jaylen's case, although there was ongoing community violence, both the therapist and the parents felt that they could manage this risk, and physical safety was not a focus of treatment.

     EXAMPLE.
     At intake, Susan's mother was separated from Susan's father, and the therapist was not initially concerned about safety, although Susan was having visits with her father. However, approximately 1 month into the Foundational Phase, Susan's mother raised the possibility of returning to him. At this point, physical safety became an important focus of the intervention given his history of having recently choked

Susan's mother and pushed Susan. The therapist met alone with Susan's mother to address these concerns, listened to her wishes to reunite her family, and then said, "I understand that you and Susan both miss Arthur and are hoping he is truly trying to change. I am still very concerned about you. Have you and Arthur been able to talk about what he is doing so that this does not happen again?" The therapist's task here was to acknowledge hope while thinking clearly and openly about risk.

EXAMPLE.

Anthony's placement was in serious jeopardy. After a particularly difficult visit with his biological mother, he went into a rage, and when Kerri tried to contain him, he kicked and hit her so badly that she had bruises. She called the therapist, threatening to drop him off to child protective services then and there. The therapist listened to Kerri and then worked with the child welfare worker to develop a plan to limit Anthony's visits with his mother, make the visits more predictable, and provide Kerri and Gina with some respite. This intervention enabled Kerri to feel that the therapist was responsive to her concerns and gave her the freedom to tell the therapist that she and Gina might not be able to keep Anthony. The therapist opened herself to this possibility without blaming the mothers and suggested that, if this happened, they could plan in advance how to move Anthony to another home in the most supportive way possible. Kerri, Gina, and the therapist acknowledged that leaving their home would be hard for Anthony, but a thoughtful plan would be preferable to his experiencing another abrupt move.

- Safety in the environmental context: The therapist works jointly with the caregiver to identify ecological risks including poverty, community violence, immigration related-risks, inadequate or unsafe housing, inadequate access to services, and the experience of racism and oppression. Then, in a manner consistent with the family's needs and beliefs, the therapist acknowledges the role that these contextual risks play in child and family functioning; integrates them into the therapist's and caregiver's understanding of the family's needs, strengths, and challenges; and develops interventions that incorporate an understanding of ecological risk factors and address these risks when possible.

EXAMPLE.

During the time that Martín worked with Jaylen and James, the news was filled with stories of African-American men and boys who had been killed by police officers. Martín and James spoke about how these incidents represented additional traumas experienced collectively by James and his community. After each new incident, James had nightmares, overwhelming anger, and fear for himself and Jaylen. He said he was not sleeping, felt irritable, and had less patience with Jaylen as a result of the strong feelings these incidents evoked. As he spoke with Martín, James was able to feel supported in the appropriateness of his indignation in the face of social ills and felt better able to differentiate between his anger at the social circumstances surrounding him and his unmodulated responses to everyday parenting stressors.

EXAMPLE.

During a home visit, as Aurelia cared for Marianna's wound, she remarked to the therapist, "They sent her home from the hospital after only 1 week. She needed more care." The therapist echoed her view that she had not been in the hospital long given the severity of her injuries. "Do you think it is because I have no papers and speak no English?" she asked. The therapist was unsure how to respond but finally said, "It is hard to think that, but it does sometimes happen." "Yes," said Aurelia, "It does happen. Another girl was in the hospital, and they let her stay even though she was not hurt as badly as my Marianna, and I feel so much anger because I love my daughter. I want her to have the best. Even if they do not want to help me, my daughter was born here. I wanted her to have a better life." Little Marianna made a small noise, and the therapist turned to her and said, "Your mommy is angry. Sometimes in this country people do not treat immigrants well, and your mommy wants the very best for you. It makes her so sad and angry to think that you did not get the very best care." The therapist paused and added, "but you are getting such good care from your mommy. Carolina (the nurse) has been showing Mommy how to take good care of you, and your mommy is so good at learning." "Carolina is a good person" noted the mom. "Yes," said the therapist, and added, "I know it is hard when people treat you differently because of your immigration status."

- Stabilization: The therapist supports the family in obtaining basic needs and access to services, and helps the caregiver to reflect on root causes of recurrent crisis and ongoing instability.

EXAMPLE.

Aurelia's job was threatened because she had to stay home and care for Marianna. Although people at the church had volunteered to help her, she was reluctant to take their help because Marianna had been harmed by a church member. The therapist helped Aurelia access food stamps and Women, Infants, and Children (WIC) and connected her to an organization that provided her with 1 month of emergency rent. She also helped Aurelia consult with an immigration lawyer because she was eligible for a U-Visa given that a child protective services report and a police report had been filed related to her child's injuries. Through a U-Visa, she later received legal papers so that she could stay and work in the United States.

- Safety and consistency in therapy: The therapist creates a reliable, safe, and consistent environment by openly discussing safety risks related to participating in therapy (e.g., mandated reporting) and by encouraging consistent weekly therapy sessions.

EXAMPLE.

When the therapist initially met with Arthur, Susan's father, she asked him how he felt about coming for treatment related to domestic violence. She told him that children are better off when they have the support of both parents and acknowledged how much Susan loved and missed him. She also went carefully over the limits of confidentiality, noting that, in her state, she did not need to report past incidents of domestic violence. In addition, because there had already been a child protective services report filed related to the incident where Susan was pushed, he could talk openly about what had happened. The therapist noted that violence in families was unfortunately too common, and that it was a shame that more people did not come to treatment to get help. She drew a model on a piece of paper showing how stresses outside the family (work problems, financial pressures, community violence) often affect the adults and sometimes lead to problems within the family. This model resonated with Arthur and helped him feel safe speaking with the therapist about what had happened.

- Safety within caregiver–child relationships: The therapist helps establish the caregiver as a protective, benevolent, legitimate authority figure and supports the caregiver's ability to socialize the child in ways that are consistent with the family's cultural values and the family's context.

EXAMPLE.

During a challenging session with Anthony, Alyssa, and Kerri, Kerri instructed Anthony to go sit on a chair after he threw a large toy truck at his sister. Anthony went over and turned the chair over and began screaming, "You're not my mom. You're not my mom." The therapist was not in favor of time-outs and thought that Anthony needed more adult assistance to help him regulate, but she supported Kerri and her instructions, saying, "You are trying to help him calm down." Then she turned her attention to Anthony, stating, "Anthony, Kerri is not your mother, but she is taking care of you. It is her job to keep you and Alyssa safe. She wants you to see that it's not safe to throw toys."

4. *Strengthen family relationships: Promote emotional reciprocity.* When the parent–child relationship is severely impaired and the parent has negative attributions toward the child (e.g., "he is bad"; "she bugs me on purpose"), it becomes challenging for the caregiver to serve as a regulatory partner for the child. The child's behavior may serve as a trauma trigger, leading the parent to respond with automatic fight, flight, or freeze reactions. In such cases, a core therapeutic task is to help the parent come to see how current expectations or beliefs about the child may be shaped by past experiences and may interfere with the caregiver's capacity to respond to the child in benevolent and growth-promoting ways.

EXAMPLE.

A therapeutic door opened in the therapist's work with Kerri and Anthony after Kerri mentioned that Anthony reminded her of her mother, who had a diagnosis of bipolar disorder. Kerri's mother had unpredictable rages that terrified Kerri. As Kerri grew up, she coped with her terror by developing defenses against strong negative affect. She said laughingly that this is why she fell in love with Gina, who was very even-keeled. Anthony, she said, took her back to her childhood. She wanted to protect Alyssa from him just as she wished someone would have protected her from her mother. The therapist remarked, "I wonder if Anthony had a similar experience to yours. His mother and her boyfriend were unpredictable and scary." "Wow," said Kerri. "I never would have thought that Anthony and I had anything in common, but maybe we both had out-of-control mothers." As Kerri linked her past to Anthony's, she became better able to respond to his needs for regulation and to be interested about the meanings and needs behind his behavior.

5. *Coordinate care.* As therapists begin working with a family, it is often helpful to identify and connect with the other care providers involved in the family's life to understand their different roles and their points of view, to determine whether additional services are needed, and if so, who might help obtain them. Sometimes, the other care providers should be included as core members of the team to protect the child's safety. The treatments involving Jaylen Fisher, Susan Chan, and Travis Bishop Jr. (TJ) involved little care coordination. Their parents were resourceful, and there were few service providers involved with the families. TJ's therapist had a single call with TJ's child protective services worker, who reiterated that the plan was for TJ's aunt to retain legal guardianship. The mother was in substance abuse treatment, the ongoing visits with TJ were arranged with the aunt, and there was no current plan for reunification. In contrast, care coordination was a primary target in the therapists' work with Marianna and with Anthony and Alyssa Craft.

EXAMPLE.

The therapist working with Marianna requested a team meeting that included the hospital social worker, the occupational therapist, and the home nurse. Together they considered Marianna's prognosis,

Aurelia's depression, and their substantial need for basic resources. The hospital social worker was able to provide Aurelia with additional case management. The home-visiting nurse began focusing on Aurelia's depression, and the providers integrated a trauma-informed perspective in understanding both Marianna's and Aurelia's challenges. Throughout the course of treatment, the providers checked in with each other so that they could monitor treatment gains across multiple perspectives.

EXAMPLE.

As noted before, the therapist reached out to the child protective services worker to stabilize Anthony's placement. They discussed what the visits with his mother looked like and his response afterwards. The worker pulled the records from the supervised visitation and noted that the mother was telling Anthony and Alyssa that they were going to come live with her, and she was saying negative things about his foster mothers. Given that she had also hit Anthony during a visit, the worker decided to request therapeutic visits where the person supervising the visits worked with the dyad to help them interact more positively and to ensure safety during visits. Throughout the course of treatment, the therapist remained in touch with the child protective services worker to obtain respite for the caregiver, to better understand the current status of the reunification plan, and to advocate that child protective services obtain speech and language therapy and occupational therapy services for Anthony. The worker also sent the therapist the court reports detailing the reasons for removal, and the therapist was able to go over the children's history with their foster mothers after a judge ruled that information from children's records could be shared if it stabilized their placement.

6. *Strengthen dyadic affect regulation capacities.* It is natural for children who experienced traumatic events to have strong feelings about these experiences. They may become easily overwhelmed by these emotions because their regulatory capacities are not yet fully developed. A core treatment objective is to help children and their caregivers learn to safely experience and tolerate strong emotions, knowing, for example, that anger does not destroy the people they love.

EXAMPLE.

As the therapist continued to work with Anthony and Kerri, she observed that when Anthony became dysregulated and started tantruming, Kerri often told him that he needed to calm down and then come back and talk to her nicely. At other times, she purposefully ignored him, and he escalated and became increasingly disorganized. By now, the therapist and Kerri had established a more solid relationship, and the therapist was able to empathically ask what Kerri was trying to teach Anthony. Kerri noted that she had learned that one should ignore negative behavior because it will only increase with attention. The therapist agreed that this was a common belief. Kerri told her that Anthony had a skills worker, and she had taught Kerri to ignore negative behaviors. Although the therapist acknowledged with Kerri that the technique may be useful for some children, she said that it might not be effective for Anthony given his history and may interfere with Anthony's capacity to use Kerri as a regulatory partner. She offered two core pieces of psychoeducation. First, these techniques assume that the child has the capacity to calm himself down. Anthony had never had a regulatory partner and had not developed the capacity to self-regulate. Second, they knew that Anthony's mother often locked him in a closet when she could not deal with him. The therapist wondered whether removal of caregiver attention in moments of distress might remind him of those times, making it ultimately more difficult for him to calm down. Kerri asked, "What should I do, then?" The therapist suggested that she might listen to his cry and think about what his distress might be about as a first step in responding in soothing ways and help him return to a regulated state. Once he was calmer, it would be possible to teach him to interact in more positive ways because then he would be able to listen.

EXAMPLE.

At first, Anthony's behaviors were so disruptive that it was hard for the caregiver and therapist to turn their attention to Alyssa. Anthony's behaviors derailed the therapist's ability to think in an integrated way and to consider the perspective of all those in the room (Reflective Practice Fidelity), her ability to track and support relationships and notice that Alyssa often seemed stranded (Dyadic Relational Fidelity), and her ability to recognize and respond to Alyssa's strong emotions (Emotional Process Fidelity). As she made a concerted effort to notice Alyssa's reactions, the therapist noticed that as Anthony tantrumed, Alyssa looked distressed, and she too was unable to turn to her mothers for help with regulation. Instead, she wandered aimlessly around the room while touching her private parts in a repetitive way. The therapist pointed this out to Kerri and Gina. It was disturbing but important to address this behavior, and together they thought about how the chaos of Anthony's tantrums triggered Alyssa. They attempted to find ways to give voice to her affect and to let her know that they were there to keep her safe. Over time, Alyssa was able to run over to the mothers and motion that she wanted one of them to pick her up when she became distressed. When one of them did, she nuzzled into the foster mother's chest, and her body visibly relaxed.

7. *Strengthen body-based regulation.* The previous example is also connected to body-based regulation. Young children learn to regulate in the arms of their caregivers. Through subtle movements, stroking, and the warm physical connection, Alyssa learned to feel safe and to regulate. Another aspect of body-based regulation involves helping children and caregivers become aware of how the body becomes the site for both stress and regulation.

   EXAMPLE.

   TJ's aunt noticed that when TJ's mother was around for a while or when she left unexpectedly, "TJ was a wreck." The stress associated with fearing that his mother would leave—and then the feelings that he experienced when she actually *did* disappear—were more than his body could bear. His aunt recognized how it affected him. In her words, he became "hyperactive," and he had really bad stomachaches. She was unable to set limits on TJ's mom because she valued family connections, loved her niece, and wanted her to feel welcome in her house when she was sober, but she saw that TJ needed help. She took him to the park so he could run, and she decided to enroll him in a soccer class so he would have regular physical activity. As she thought about her own body, her mind returned to the metaphor of the lidded pot, and she decided to take a Zumba class, so she too could begin to let out some steam.

EXAMPLE.

In play, TJ reminded us of another way that the body remembers. The Department of Child and Family Services (DCFS) report contained information that the therapist disclosed to the aunt during the assessment. When TJ was 15 months old, DCFS removed him from his father's care in response to an anonymous call from a neighbor. He was malnourished, had bruises on his legs, his knee was swollen, and he had a leg fracture. The father, Travis Sr., was arrested. TJ was sent to a series of foster homes, and the full nature of his removal was forgotten until his therapist read about it in the report. One day, TJ asked to play with a baby doll. At first, he played nicely and fed the baby. He used a doctor's kit to check the baby out, and then he took the reflex hammer and banged it on the baby doll's knee. He did this again and again. His aunt and therapist looked at each other, silently sharing the knowledge that he had been hurt in the leg. TJ dragged the baby doll around the room by the leg and then dropped it. This theme of babies and hurt legs was repeated several times in the play, and the therapist and aunt decided to give voice to the pain in the baby's legs. "Ouch, it hurts," they said over and over, and then they told him that when he was little, he was hurt in the leg.

8. *Support the child's relationship with other important caregivers.* In the introduction to treatment for Susan, her mother acknowledged how much Susan loved and missed her father. Even immediately following the incident where Arthur had choked her and she was fighting for custody of Susan, Nancy remained firm in her mind that Arthur was Susan's father and was important to her. Nancy said that perhaps she felt this way because, growing up, she knew that her own father suffered from the atrocities he witnessed in Cambodia. As a result, he was often quiet and distant, but she understood that this was because of what he had been through. She applied this thinking to Susan. The child had seen her daddy who she loved behave in such a scary way, and she wanted Susan to have help in understanding what happened. She also wanted Susan to know that her father had problems, needed help, and was

not safe, but he was still the same man who made her bunny pancakes for breakfast and who had sat patiently drinking tea with Susan and her stuffed animals. In the case of Susan and Nancy, the mother was able to support her child's relationship with her father from the beginning. With other families, this might be an ongoing goal.

This was the case for Anthony and Alyssa. As Kerri and Gina came to care about both children, they found it harder to allow the children's mother to have any claim to them. They did not want pictures of her in their house. They became tense when the children told stories about their life with her, even when the stories were positive. They were very angry with her for what she let happen when the children were in her care. The therapist was angry, too, but she recognized that Anthony and Alyssa needed their caregivers' help to know that their mommy had problems and could not raise them. If their caregivers supported them in holding on to angel memories, they would grow up knowing that there were times when their biological mother saw them as precious and worthy of love.

9. *Enhance understanding of the meaning of behavior.* When Jaylen's parents brought him to treatment, they understood that he feared separations both because he was 2½ years old and separation anxiety is normal at that age and because he had seen that people sometimes die and don't return. He now feared that something bad might happen to him or his parents when they were not together. His parents' understanding of the meaning of his behavior allowed them to respond in soothing ways to him when he clung to them and asked them not to leave.

Over the course of treatment, TJ's aunt came to understand that he communicated through his behavior. She began by understanding, with the therapist's help, the scenes in his play, and then she applied what she learned to TJ's reactions at home and at school. She told his teachers that TJ got scared and then wild when he felt that someone was denying him food. She realized this as she watched TJ play with baby dolls. At first, his play seemed sadistic to her. He instructed the aunt and the therapist to hold the baby dolls and make them cry. Then he brought out the food toys. "You want food?" he said. "Yes, yes," they would say. "Well," he replied. "You can't have some." Then he would laugh in an odd voice. "I don't know," TJ's aunt said. "TJ's dad was kind of like that. He told TJ's mom that she was fat after she had TJ. Said he didn't want any fat women. I wonder if he would have kept food from them." The therapist never knew if the aunt's interpretation was right, but it changed the way she responded to TJ around food. She understood the broader meaning that not having food made TJ scared and then wild, and she helped other caregivers to understand this too.

10. *Support the child in returning to a normal developmental trajectory.* Often, in the treatments with Jaylen, Susan, TJ, Marianna, Anthony, and Alyssa, there were moments when they were simply playing, delighting in blowing bubbles and popping them not because this was a good way to regulate emotions but simply because it was fun. Jaylen came in one day dressed like a pirate. He wanted to show the therapist his Halloween costume. Jaylen, James, and Martín (the therapist) spent a good part of the treatment hour pretending to be pirates on the high seas. Martín kept on the lookout for themes related to Jaylen's experience. There were themes of danger related to being pirates, but they seemed more like regular play than trauma processing. The next session, Jaylen came in and wanted to draw. He drew a very crude picture of his family (he was only 3 years old) and focused hard on drawing a figure in his mother's belly. "It's my baby sister," he said. His father smiled and nodded. They had just found out that they were having a girl. The therapist and Jaylen's father supported Jaylen in playing in these normal ways. Helping Jaylen return to a normal developmental trajectory and engage in healthy nontrauma play was both a goal of treatment and a sign that he was ready to begin ending.

At one point toward the end of the treatment, TJ became upset when he couldn't put together a small puzzle. "Do you think he's triggered?" asked the aunt. The therapist watched TJ and then lightly joked with the aunt. "It's a good question, but I wonder if maybe he's just 4. It's frustrating when you're 4, and you can't do everything you want to do." The aunt laughed, and then the therapist said, "Seriously, TJ is lucky you're always thinking about how what he's doing may be connected to what he's been through. He is doing so much better thanks to you. There may be things that trigger him, but there may also be challenges he faces just because it's part of growing up, and we'll have to let him face those challenges and grow from them." The aunt smiled and finished the sentence, "Just like any other normal kid."

11. *Normalize the traumatic response.* The process of normalizing the traumatic response begins during the assessment process and continues throughout treatment. In going through a listing of symptoms of PTSD, depression, and behavior problems, the therapist helps the caregiver to understand that these are common reactions to traumatic events. For some dyads, such as Jaylen Fisher and his father, the objective of helping to normalize the traumatic response is achieved during the Foundational Phase. For others, such as TJ, Anthony and Alyssa, and their caregivers, the work continues in the Core Intervention Phase as the therapist helps the caregivers to understand the ways in which the child's behavior and response are connected to what they have been through.

12. *Support the dyad in acknowledging the impact of trauma.* The construction of the triangle of explanation helps the caregiver to begin the Core Intervention Phase by acknowledging the impact of the trauma. It is a good beginning, but many young children show that they need adults to repeatedly witness their story. TJ told the story of a monster that raged and hurt babies and babies who were hurt over and over on their leg. Alyssa continually showed us babies left alone who were crying. Often, the child's story continues and the violence gets worse until the meaning—the communication behind the play—is received by the caregiver. It is as if they truly need the caregiver to acknowledge how awful and scary it was before they can trust that they are safe. For caregivers who have also experienced trauma, a core part of the work is to acknowledge the ghosts, help the caregiver to meet them, and then place them firmly in the past, as illustrated in Kerri's discussions with the therapist about her mother.

13. *Help the dyad differentiate between then and now.* In simple ways, the therapist helps the family members talk about real-life changes they have made toward establishing safety and compare the current situation with the scary way things used to be.

    EXAMPLE.
    Susan's dad read the book, *Moody Cow Meditates* (MacLean, 2009), with her. In the book, the characters make a meditation jar—a jar full of glitter and water. When upset, Moody Cow shakes the jar up and then breathes and meditates as the glitter falls to the bottom. This

book provided a lovely dyadic affect regulation exercise that enhanced mindfulness and body-based regulation and, at the same time, helped Susan see that her father was trying to be different. Each day, they would have meditation time, shake the jar up, and breathe to show that they were all learning new ways of dealing with difficult feelings.

EXAMPLE.

TJ's aunt realized that his mother's presence in the house was scary for him. At home, by herself, the aunt openly told him that she had not known how bad things were for TJ when he was little. She told him she never would have let it happen if she had known. Now she knew, and now TJ was big enough to tell her whether anything happened to him. The aunt also said that when his mommy came, she wanted them to have fun because his mommy was like her own little girl and she loved her, but she would not let anything bad ever happen again. Now she was watching. The aunt commented to the therapist that saying and doing this was different for her, too. She was developing new family patterns of protection that were different from what she had grown up with.

14. *Help the dyad put the traumatic experience in perspective.* Little Marisol's story has not yet been told in the manual, but it is a striking example of a child who has put her experience in perspective. When she was 3, Marisol was sexually molested repeatedly by her day care provider's son. She told her mother that he had touched her "pipi" and readily identified him as bad. When she was 4 years old, she insisted that her mother and therapist go to the police station so that she could tell the police what the bad man had done and they could arrest him. She was worried because her day care provider sometimes also cared for a baby, and she was afraid the baby was also being hurt. The police took her report and gave her a sticker as an award. Marisol was not satisfied. She knew that her molester had not been arrested because they sometimes saw him on the street. "He is a bad man, and he should be punished," she said. One day, she asked her mother during a session, "Mama, isn't it true that when he goes to see God at the gate, God will say that he cannot come through because he hurt Marisol?" "Yes," her mother acknowledged, "that is true." Marisol took comfort in this. Little Marisol grew in her ability to use

her voice and her sense of right and wrong. Her mother told the therapist with a mixture of shame and pride that Marisol had talked to her preschool teacher when she had yelled at the class. "You shouldn't yell," she said. "I think it scares the children." Fortunately, her teacher had a kind heart and agreed that Marisol was right. The following year, Marisol went to kindergarten, and at graduation, she was chosen as kindergarten valedictorian. She stood up in front of everyone and gave a speech. Marisol did not let her sexual abuse define her. She grew from her experience because of her parents' support and developed a strong voice that she has used and will likely continue to use to advocate for justice.

IMPLICATIONS FOR SUPERVISORS

The supervisor is the therapist's partner in CPP. *Reflective supervision* is a relationship-based endeavor with the primary goal of immersing oneself in the emotional and interpersonal experiences of the child, caregivers, and therapist in order to understand the therapeutic pathways that would be most helpful to this family. Clinical authenticity is key, and supervision should not become a place where therapist and supervisor meet solely to monitor fidelity.

Nevertheless, the fidelity strands may be useful as the supervisor and supervisee jointly consider ways to support both the therapist and the family. Next we list core tasks of supervision related to each strand of fidelity.

REFLECTIVE PRACTICE FIDELITY

The supervisor helps the therapist . . .

- Consider his or her emotional reactions to the family or the work
- When needed, understand factors that may contribute to the practitioner's emotional response
- Think about how these reactions may affect the way the therapist intervenes
- Regulate strong emotions
- Consider the perspective of the family as influenced by current context, cultural beliefs, and family history

EMOTIONAL PROCESS FIDELITY

The supervisor helps the therapist . . .

- Consider the emotional responses of individual family members
- Understand how different family members may respond when they have strong emotions (e.g., shutting down, becoming active, needing to be held)
- Consider ways to foster dyadic emotion regulation
- Learn specific emotion regulation techniques appropriate for both young children and caregivers

DYADIC RELATIONAL FIDELITY

The supervisor helps the therapist . . .

- Consider the degree to which interventions held the perspective of different family members
- Consider the degree to which the intervention involved the different family members in the room
- Consider the degree to which interventions strengthened the caregiver–child relationship and other family relationships
- Develop interventions that help caregiver and child to better see each other's perspective

TRAUMA FRAMEWORK FIDELITY

The supervisor helps the therapist . . .

- Remember and hold the family's trauma history
- Understand the connection between the child's and/or the caregiver's trauma history and their behavior in session
- Process emotional reactions (therapist's, caregiver's, child's) related to addressing the trauma
- Consider ways to address the trauma

PROCEDURAL FIDELITY

The supervisor . . .

- Thinks with the practitioner about how to carry out CPP procedures at different phases of treatment

- Helps the practitioner become more comfortable and skilled in completing CPP procedures
- As needed, teaches the practitioner skills and provides opportunities for the practitioner to practice (e.g., via role play) specific CPP procedures (e.g., explaining the rationale for screening for child trauma, screening for trauma, helping the caregiver to understand the concept of trauma reminders, providing feedback)
- Helps the practitioner identify and think of any challenges related to completing CPP procedures

CONTENT FIDELITY

The supervisor helps the therapist . . .

- Conceptualize the needs of the family and identify, after the Foundational Phase, core goals that will be addressed during treatment
- Consider ways in which his or her interventions are addressing the core goals
- Develop interventions that address core goals

IMPLICATIONS FOR SYSTEMS

> "What will change when a system becomes trauma informed . . . . everything." (Epstein et al., 2014)

It is beyond the scope of this manual to discuss all the implications that adopting a treatment like CPP may hold for systems. The questions listed here are meant to guide reflection.

STAFF SELECTION AND SUPPORT

- At your agency, how will staff be selected for training in CPP?
- What might be the specific learning challenges for each of these individuals? For example, learning how to . . .
  - Hold the perspective of a caregiver
  - Work with challenging caregivers
  - Share personal reactions in supervision
  - Understand early childhood development

- – Work with young children and help them make meaning of their experience
- – Translate the meaning of a child's behavior and/or play to a caregiver
- – Feel comfortable talking about and directly addressing trauma
- How will your agency support each of these individuals as they learn CPP?

REFLECTIVE PRACTICE FIDELITY

- How many hours of supervision a week does a supervisee typically receive?
- To what degree is supervision focused on clinical versus administrative issues?
- While a therapist is learning CPP (or any new practice), how does the agency accommodate his or her learning needs in terms of . . .
  - – Additional supervision?
  - – Outside trainings to gain core knowledge and core competencies that are foundational to CPP?

EMOTIONAL PROCESS FIDELITY

- Do agency policies support emotional process fidelity? For example, does the agency understand that therapists need to . . .
  - – Meet alone with caregivers who are having strong emotional reactions that interfere with their capacity to help their child process their experience?
  - – Be able to link caregivers to therapy services as needed?
  - – Configure treatment (e.g., have family sessions that include siblings, or hold separate sessions for different siblings) based on the emotional needs of different family members?
  - – Determine the number of sessions needed based, in part, on family members' emotional responses to intervention?
- Does your agency offer any child care to facilitate a therapist's being able to meet alone with a caregiver or to meet with just the caregiver and one child in a family with multiple children?

DYADIC RELATIONAL FIDELITY

- Can the agency bill for a variety of treatment configurations that may be used in CPP?
  - Joint dyadic sessions and family sessions
  - Individual caregiver sessions
  - Joint caregiver sessions (when there are multiple caregivers involved in treatment)
  - Individual child sessions
- As the agency evaluates treatment outcomes, does the agency and system recognize family-level outcomes in addition to child outcomes?

TRAUMA FRAMEWORK FIDELITY

- How does the agency think about and respond to vicarious trauma that therapists may experience as they learn to do trauma-informed work?
- Does the agency think about how trauma affects the work when they assign cases to therapists?
- Does the agency think about . . .
  - Variability in terms of the number of trauma cases a therapist feels capable of seeing?
  - Involving therapists in a discussion related to the number of trauma cases and types of trauma cases they feel comfortable seeing?
  - Factors that may affect a therapist's ability to see many trauma cases? For example:
    - Whether a therapist is learning the model or has established some competence in the model
    - Amount of agency support
    - Level of challenge to reflective practice that certain cases may present
  - Types of trauma cases that may require more reflective supervision/consultation
  - The importance of variability in terms of caseload
    - For example, not all sexual abuse or traumatic bereavement cases
    - For example, not all cases with significant systems issues
    - For example, not all cases with significant safety issues

- For example, ensuring that some cases within a therapist's caseload have a higher likelihood of treatment success because the caregiver acknowledges and wants to address the child's trauma history
  - Other treatment models a therapist might do jointly with CPP in order to meet caseload or billing requirements
- Are the agency's policies and practices consistent with a trauma framework?
  - Are agency policies responsive to the fact that individuals with a trauma history may be difficult to engage in treatment?
  - Is the agency and system aware of how policies and practices around reporting issues (e.g., domestic violence) may affect a family's ability to engage fully and openly in treatment?
  - Does the agency understand that termination is an important phase of treatment in trauma work because it often brings up key issues for those with a history of trauma and loss?

PROCEDURAL FIDELITY

- How consistent are CPP procedures with current agency practices?
- In what ways are they different?
- Do therapists typically do the assessment?

CONTENT FIDELITY

- Is the agency aware that when practitioners work with families who have experienced multiple, chronic traumas, safety, affect regulation, and the development of trusting relationships are critical targets of intervention? The primary goal of treatment is not always symptom reduction.
- Is the agency aware that when practitioners work with families who have experienced multiple, chronic traumas, safety issues may emerge during the course of treatment and may alter the course of treatment?

INTRODUCTION TO THE MEASURES

In the Appendices, we share the following CPP Fidelity packets and tools:

- Foundational Phase: Assessment and Engagement fidelity packet (Appendix A), which consists of the following:
  - Client Registration Form

- Intervention Fidelity (the core measure tracking adherence to the six strands of CPP fidelity)
- Contact Log
- Assessment and Engagement Procedures (assessing completion of procedures specific to this phase)
- Feedback Fidelity (tracking procedures specific to the feedback session)

- Core Intervention Phase fidelity packet (Appendix B), which includes:
  - Registration Form
  - Introducing Child to CPP (assessing procedures specific to the session where the child is formally introduced to treatment)
  - Contact Log
  - Intervention Fidelity
- Recapitulation and Termination Phase fidelity packet (Appendix C), which includes
  - Closing Form
  - Procedural Fidelity (tracking procedures specific to this phase)
  - Contact Log
  - Intervention Fidelity

These tools are meant to serve as a guide as the therapist progresses through the different phases of treatment.

SECTION IV

CASE MANAGEMENT

CASE MANAGEMENT, DEFINED MOST SUCCINCTLY as concrete assistance with problems of living, is an integral component of Child–Parent Psychotherapy (CPP) when working with families facing socioeconomic hardship. This is a natural extension of the model's emphasis on the importance of the ecological/transactional context in supporting child development. Child–parent psychotherapists utilize their intimate knowledge of the family circumstances to identify areas where additional support is needed, to link the family with the appropriate resources, and to monitor the integration of the different services.

The goal of concrete assistance with problems of living is not only to resolve problems in the moment but also to provide a learning opportunity so that parents can learn to solve similar problems on their own. The clinician informs the parent about community resources, models for the parent how to contact these resources, guides the parent in taking the initiative in making use of the resources, and provides feedback on additional steps that might be needed to maximize the usefulness of the services. This model can be used, for instance, to help the parent make appropriate use of medical care, to secure good-quality child care, to work out transportation problems, to resolve problems at work, and to improve the quality of housing.

For some families, the concrete needs are so continuous and pervasive that the child–parent psychotherapist cannot at the same time provide mental health intervention and case management without an unrealistic drain on his or her time and energy. In these cases, it is important to connect the family to community resources whose mission is to provide these services.

Some programs have case managers and child–parent psychotherapists performing their services separately within the program. This model is feasible when both service providers have compatible views of what the family needs and when they communicate well with each other about the actions they are taking on behalf of the family. Regular meetings between the service providers are recommended as a way of ensuring that there is a unified plan of action to address the family's needs.

Working with families who are exposed to violence often calls for extensive involvement with child protective services and with the family court system. The following describes the model's approach to involvement with these systems.

WHEN POSSIBLE CHILD ABUSE OCCURS: REPORTING TO CHILD PROTECTIVE SERVICES

Marital violence tends to overlap with a high incidence of child abuse, which might be perpetrated by either parent whether they are living together or not. The child abuse episode might be witnessed by the clinician in the course of a session, or the child or the parent might describe during the session a past incident that may qualify as child abuse.

This is invariably a very difficult therapeutic situation because, no matter how thoughtfully and competently it is handled, it threatens the viability of the treatment. Even in situations where the perpetrator is not the parent but a third party, the parent might feel burdened and threatened by the intervention of child protective services and the legal system. Nevertheless, the clinician cannot refrain from making a child abuse report due to fear that the treatment will be damaged or terminated. Clinicians are legally obligated to report suspected abuse, and the investigation to confirm or disconfirm child abuse is not within their power but is the province of child protective services.

Nevertheless, a clinician can and should explore what happened in order to make a useful report. For example, seeing a bruise on a child's forehead is not, by itself, sufficient grounds for a report if the parent and the child provide a clear and cogent explanation that the child bumped her head against a hard surface and there is no reason to suspect otherwise (such as previous reports of similar incidents, a history of abuse, parental neglect, or lack of impulse control toward the child). Conversely, vague and contradictory explanations in the context of other risk factors call for making a report.

When the clinician decides to make a report, every effort should be made to inform the parent before actually making the report. Optimally, the parent should be told privately and in person, even if this means having to speak on the phone or schedule an additional session. It is essential that sufficient time be allotted so that there is an opportunity to process and bring temporary closure to the strong feelings that will emerge. In order to be constructive and protect the treatment, a report should optimally follow the six steps described here:

1. The clinician explains to the parent that she or he (the clinician) has a legal obligation to report the incident, and stresses that this report in no way implies a lessened commitment to working with the family. It is often helpful to explain that the abuse incident is a sign that the intervention is not helping enough to keep the child safe, and that additional services are needed to make sure that this happens.

2. The clinician tells the parent that, although it is not possible to know how child protective services will proceed (i.e., whether a case will be opened or not, and what placement decisions will be made), the clinician is willing to meet jointly with the child protective services worker and the parent, and to participate collaboratively in drawing up a plan of action that will simultaneously protect the child's safety and support the parent in protecting the child. The clinician also assures the parent that no information will be provided to the child protective services worker without first discussing it with the parent, and that information not directly related to the abuse incident will remain confidential unless the parent requests otherwise.

3. The clinician encourages the parent to take the initiative in phoning child protective services to make the report during the session, and offers support in helping the parent to do so. If the parent declines to make the call, the clinician offers to make the phone call during the session and in the parent's presence. This enables the parent to hear the clinician's report as it takes place, and increases her confidence in the clinician's good will.

4. After the report is made, the clinician elicits the parent's reactions, including the fear that the child will be placed in foster care. Whenever plausible, and consistent with the child's safety, the clinician reassures

the parent that she or he (the clinician) will make every effort to ensure that the child is not removed from the home, including testifying in court if necessary. If foster placement might be indicated, the clinician discusses with the parent the reasons for this possibility, eliciting the parent's reactions. Feelings of anger toward the clinician for making the report are acknowledged and legitimized. A plan is made for keeping in touch over the telephone before the next session, and the date for the following session is scheduled.

5.   If the child protective services worker requests a written report, the clinician informs the parent, eliciting her input about the content of the report. Before mailing it, the clinician shows the report to the parent, asks for approval, and makes the changes suggested by the parent if appropriate.

6.   Throughout the steps outlined here, the clinician keeps in mind what the child's involvement in the reporting process should be and discusses this with the parent. Depending on the child's age and developmental level, a simplified explanation might be necessary to prepare the child for the possibility of an individual interview with the child protective services worker. During this explanation, the emphasis should be kept on the wish of the parent and the clinician to make sure that the child is safe, and on the need for help to make sure that this happens.

Although the six steps are optimal in maximizing the chances that the parent will not be alienated by the referral to child protective services, circumstances are often such that an orderly child protective services referral cannot be made. Sometimes, the report to child protective services is made by someone outside the treatment, and the parent suspects the clinician. The clinician is then in the awkward position of having to deny her involvement but at the same time probe about the events leading to the referral in order to decide on a plan of action. At other times, the parents respond explosively and refuse further contact when the clinician informs them that a child protective services report must be made. It can also happen that the child protective services intervention is conducted in a way that is deeply offensive to the parents, and in their anger at the child welfare worker, the parents also become suspicious and angry with the clinician. In all of these circumstances, the clinician must strive to keep personal emotions contained and not overidentify with any of the parties involved. This stance will allow the clinician to play a useful role as a caring but objective broker between the parent and the legal system.

There are cases where the parent is so unpredictable and dangerous that the clinician fears for his or her personal safety in telling the parent that a report will be made. In these circumstances, the clinician must place personal safety above other considerations. This might involve informing the parent over the phone that a report was made, discontinuing home visits, and substituting office visits, if appropriate, until the situation is considered to be safe.

WHEN CUSTODY PROBLEMS OCCUR: WORKING WITH THE FAMILY COURT SYSTEM

High-conflict divorce and bitter custody disputes often follow the termination of a marriage or live-in relationship due to domestic violence. One common configuration is that the battered woman fears that unsupervised visitation or overnight visits with the violent father will endanger the child's safety. The father, however, frequently denies that the violence took place or that it was as severe as portrayed by the mother, and argues that his parental rights should not be jeopardized. Charges and countercharges of child endangerment and of parental alienation can lead to protracted legal disputes in which both sides try to muster evidence to support their respective positions.

Child therapists are often placed at the center of these legal disputes because of their intimate knowledge of the child's emotional experience. Child–parent psychotherapists are in a particularly difficult situation because they have knowledge not only of the child's functioning but also of the emotional status of the parent with whom they work. As a result, that parent may ask the therapist to provide testimony about his or her adequacy as a parent or about the impact of domestic violence on the child. The other parent may seek access to clinical material to support his or her position to the court.

There are no simple solutions to the clinical dilemmas posed by complex legal situations. However, there are some working principles that may guide the therapist's thinking in deciding on a course of action that will protect the therapeutic process from becoming prey to legal disputes. These principles are listed here. To make the use of gender-linked pronouns easier to follow, these principles are written as if the mother is the battered parent and is the one seeking CPP, and the father is the violent parent. Clearly, the principles apply also if the situation is reversed.

1. At the beginning of treatment, clarify with the participating parent whether the other parent (e.g., the father) has legal custody of the child and maintains regular contact with the child. If he does, ask whether the father knows about the planned treatment and approves of it. If he does not know, encourage the mother to notify him of her decision to seek treatment for the child. The knowledge and support for treatment of both parents gives the child the clear message that both parents are important and participate jointly in making decisions on the child's behalf. If the father opposes the treatment, explain to the mother that treatment cannot be provided without the consent of a parent who has legal custody. If the mother desires to keep the treatment secret from the parent, explain to the mother that this plan is not workable because it would place an emotional burden on the child by having to keep secrets from the father. The mother can be advised that, in some situations, the court orders treatment for the child in spite of a parent's opposition, and that this is a possibility that can be pursued in consultation with the mother's attorney.

2. At the beginning of treatment, explain to the mother that the therapist will not provide information to the attorneys for the purpose of supporting petitions to the court regarding custody or visitation. The only information that will be provided involves participation in treatment. Explain that divulging therapeutic information can be damaging to the child and the mother for at least three reasons. First, it opens the possibility that the other party will subpoena clinical records and misuse the information. Second, it diverts time and energy from the therapeutic process. Third, it may limit what the mother feels free to tell the therapist for fear that the therapist will form a negative opinion that will contaminate possible court testimony. During this conversation, the therapist should be careful not to make any statements that can give the impression that she or he is taking sides in the parents' dispute over custody and visitation.

3. It is possible that, in the course of treatment, situations will emerge where

the therapist needs to provide information to an attorney, a mediator, or a judge that contravenes the initial indication to the mother that no such information will be made available. Each one of these exceptions needs to be carefully thought out because it can have important ramifications in setting precedents about the limits of confidentiality and about what the attorneys and the court expect from the therapist.

4. Therapists must make a clear differentiation between clinical assessment and treatment and forensic evaluation. The lines between the clinical activities and the forensic activities should not be blurred. Confidentiality and improvement in mental health functioning are the hallmarks of clinical assessment and treatment. Forensic evaluations have the goal of providing information to the court for the purposes of decision making, and these are not covered by confidentiality constraints. A clinical assessment should not become a forensic tool for the sake of convenience or for financial reasons.

5. Therapists must remember that it contravenes ethical standards to make clinical recommendations about child custody or visitation schedules without first conducting an objective assessment of all the parties involved and without prejudging what is in the best interests of the child. By the very nature of the therapeutic alliance, a therapist cannot be a neutral, objective party. The therapist's views and opinions are influenced by the nature and content of the clinical process. If the therapist decides to provide information to the legal system about this process, the testimony needs to be carefully crafted to clarify the limitations of the sources of information available to the therapist and to describe the implications of these limitations for the conclusions that the therapist is able to make.

SECTION V

SIMILARITIES AND DIFFERENCES ACROSS TREATMENTS

A. ITEMS THAT ARE ESSENTIAL BUT NOT UNIQUE TO CHILD–PARENT PSYCHOTHERAPY

ALL MENTAL HEALTH INTERVENTIONS SHARE some basic principles that are essential to their effectiveness. One principle is the reliance on a predictable and reliable schedule of meetings that are focused on the client's experience. Another principle is the use of emotional support, warmth, and empathy as essential adjuncts to therapeutic intervention.

Other principles are shared across some approaches but not others. Child–Parent Psychotherapy (CPP) and psychodynamic psychotherapies share the view that mental health disturbances can be an expression of internal conflict and that internal conflict may originate in early experience. In common with intervention approaches based on attachment theory, CPP seeks to promote secure attachments by stressing the importance of security and protection in the child–parent relationship and by encouraging parental sensitive responsiveness to the child's emotional experience and signals of need. It shares with developmental approaches the use of developmental guidance and parenting education to increase parental knowledge of age-appropriate behaviors and child-rearing strategies. Social learning theory and cognitive–behavioral theory contribute intervention strategies that emphasize practicing new forms of behaving and thinking to overcome maladaptive patterns of functioning. Elements of trauma-related intervention are incorporated to promote modulation of affective arousal and to foster realistic responses to threat and danger. Items that CPP has in common with other approaches are described as follows.

Items Geared to Building a Safe and Supportive Therapeutic Frame and Daily Environment

1. The clinician is punctual and reliable in attending the sessions.
2. The clinician makes sure that the sessions take place in a safe place.
3. The clinician receives regular supervision geared to his or her level of experience.
4. Staff members have regularly scheduled meetings to discuss therapeutic issues and to provide mutual consultation and support.
5. The clinician makes statements that convey positive regard for the individual client.
6. The clinician is respectful of the individual's point of view.
7. The clinician shows empathy for the individual's distress.
8. The clinician encourages the parent to make explicit statements of loving commitment to the child.
9. The clinician helps the individual client practice realistic appraisals of whether a situation is dangerous or safe.
10. The clinician promotes a sense of safety by helping the individual differentiate between re-experiencing frightening events and experiencing actual danger in the moment.
11. The clinician makes referrals for additional services as needed, including psychotropic medication, individual or group psychotherapy, substance abuse services, and developmental intervention such as speech and language therapy or occupational therapy.

Items That Focus on Emotion, Cognition, and Action

12. The clinician normalizes the individual's responses to trauma by explaining the universality of the response.
13. The clinician encourages the individual to use words to name feelings.
14. The clinician helps the individual recognize and change self-defeating and destructive thoughts.
15. The clinician helps the individual recognize and find alternatives to behaviors that make others angry.
16. The clinician demonstrates nondestructive ways of coping with anger and sadness.

17. The clinician demonstrates and helps the individual practice ways of managing anxiety, including turning to others for help, exercising, breathing, praying, meditating, or engaging in other spiritual practices or relaxing or pleasurable activities.
18. The clinician helps the individual find a larger meaning in the feelings of the moment by linking the experience with other emotionally relevant events.
19. The clinician helps the individual manage despair and place painful experiences in a larger context by reminding him or her of areas of strength and satisfaction.
20. The clinician promotes an integration of emotional polarities by helping the individual realize that good and bad aspects of a person coexist, and that love and hatred can be felt for the same person.
21. The clinician responds nondefensively and noncritically when the individual expresses negative feelings toward the clinician.
22. The clinician helps the individual find and engage in behaviors that promote a feeling of well-being.

Items That Emphasize Developmental Progress

23. The clinician makes available developmentally appropriate toys, books, and other materials as vehicles for the intervention.
24. The clinician encourages developmentally appropriate play between parent and child.
25. The clinician encourages the parent to use books, toys, pleasurable activities, and games to provide developmentally appropriate experiences to the child.
26. The clinician provides the parent with information about the developmental meaning of the child's behavior.
27. The clinician encourages the individual to persevere in efforts to achieve developmentally appropriate milestones.

B. ITEMS THAT ARE INCOMPATIBLE WITH CHILD–PARENT PSYCHOTHERAPY

The forms of intervention that are incompatible with CPP have in common the use of techniques that allow the clinician to control what will happen during the session. These techniques do not foster reciprocity in relationships because they do not model it in the therapeutic relationship between parent and therapist or between child and therapist. Examples of incompatible strategies are given here:

1. Use of "bug-in-the-ear" approaches to guide the parent's behavior toward the child.
2. Use of "bug-in-the-ear" approaches to guide the therapist's interventions.
3. "Flooding" interventions, in which the individuals are encouraged to immerse themselves in the traumatic experience.
4. Desensitization techniques in which the individuals are systematically exposed to reminders of the traumatic experience.
5. Curriculum-driven didactic instruction.
6. Use of aversive stimuli to change behavior.
7. Didactic instruction that is not based on developmental principles or that is not responsive to the child's individual characteristics or subjective experience.

APPENDIX A: FOUNDATIONAL PHASE: ASSESSMENT AND ENGAGEMENT FIDELITY PACKET

ChildParent PSYCHOTHERAPY

CPP FIDELITY

FOUNDATIONAL PHASE: ASSESSMENT AND ENGAGEMENT

Client Registration

v.09.2015
Completed by: Therapist
Reviewed with Supervisor

CPP Training Name: _____

Therapist Name: _____   Client Nickname: _____   Client ID: automatically generated

TREATMENT INFORMATION

Date CPP Treatment Started	Language Treatment Conducted in (indicate all)	Will a Translator be Used?
		☐ No ☐ Sometimes ☐ Yes

TARGET CHILD INFORMATION

Age in months	Gender	Ethnicity (check all that apply)	Language(s) spoken
	☐ male ☐ female	☐ African American ☐ Asian* ☐ Caucasian ☐ Latino/a*	☐ Spanish ☐ English ☐ Other (specify)
	☐ other, specify: _____	☐ Native American ☐ Other*	Specify: _____
		*Specify(Asian, Latino, Other)	

SIBLING INFORMATION

Age in Years	Gender (M/F/O)	Relation to Child (e.g. full sibling, half sibling)	Where Resides (e.g. w/ child, w/dad)	In treatment with Child?
				☐ No ☐ Sometimes ☐ Yes
				☐ No ☐ Sometimes ☐ Yes
				☐ No ☐ Sometimes ☐ Yes
				☐ No ☐ Sometimes ☐ Yes
				☐ No ☐ Sometimes ☐ Yes
				☐ No ☐ Sometimes ☐ Yes
				☐ No ☐ Sometimes ☐ Yes
				☐ No ☐ Sometimes ☐ Yes

CAREGIVER #1 INFORMATION

Age in Years	Ethnicity (check all that apply)	Relationship to Child (select one)	Language(s) spoken:
	☐ African American ☐ Asian* ☐ Caucasian ☐ Latino/a*	☐ Biological mother ☐ Caregiver's female partner (girlfriend) ☐ Uncle	☐ Spanish ☐ English ☐ Other (specify)
	☐ Native American ☐ Other*	☐ Biological father ☐ Caregiver's male partner (boyfriend) ☐ Great aunt	Specify: _____
	*Specify(Asian, Latino, Other)	☐ Adoptive mother ☐ Grandmother ☐ Great uncle	
		☐ Adoptive father ☐ Grandfather ☐ Other relative, please specify	
		☐ Step-mother ☐ Great grandmother ☐ Other non-relative, please specify	
		☐ Step-father ☐ Great grandfather	
		☐ Foster mother ☐ Aunt Specify: _____	
		☐ Foster father	

Years of Education (1st grade=1, Graduated High school=12; Graduated college=16) _____

Involved in child's treatment? ☐ Yes   ☐ Partially   ☐ No   ☐ UNK

USE AS NEEDED

CAREGIVER #2 INFORMATION

☐ Not applicable – no other caregiver

Age in Years

Years of Education (1st grade=1, Graduated High school=12; Graduated college=16)

Involved in child's treatment?
☐ Yes ☐ Partially ☐ No ☐ UNK

Ethnicity (check all that apply)
☐ African American ☐ Asian* ☐ Caucasian ☐ Latino/a*
☐ Native American ☐ Other*
*Specify(Asian, Latino, Other)

Relationship to Child (select one)
☐ Biological mother
☐ Biological father
☐ Adoptive mother
☐ Adoptive father
☐ Step-mother
☐ Step-father
☐ Foster mother
☐ Foster father
☐ Caregiver's female partner (girlfriend)
☐ Caregiver's male partner (boyfriend)
☐ Grandmother
☐ Grandfather
☐ Great Grandmother
☐ Great Grandfather
☐ Aunt
☐ Uncle

Language(s) spoken
☐ Spanish ☐ English ☐ Other (specify)
Specify:_____

☐ Great aunt
☐ Great uncle
☐ Other relative, please specify
☐ Other non-relative, please specify
Specify:_____

CAREGIVER #3 INFORMATION

☐ Not applicable – no other caregiver

Age in Years

Years of Education (1st grade=1, Graduated High school=12; Graduated college=16)

Involved in child's treatment?
☐ Yes ☐ Partially ☐ No ☐ UNK

Ethnicity (check all that apply)
☐ African American ☐ Asian* ☐ Caucasian ☐ Latino/a*
☐ Native American ☐ Other*
*Specify(Asian, Latino, Other)

Relationship to Child (select one)
☐ Biological mother
☐ Biological father
☐ Adoptive mother
☐ Adoptive father
☐ Step-mother
☐ Step-father
☐ Foster mother
☐ Foster father
☐ Caregiver's female partner (girlfriend)
☐ Caregiver's male partner (boyfriend)
☐ Grandmother
☐ Grandfather
☐ Great grandmother
☐ Great grandfather
☐ Aunt
☐ Uncle

Language(s) spoken
☐ Spanish ☐ English ☐ Other (specify)
Specify:_____

☐ Great aunt
☐ Great uncle
☐ Other relative, please specify
☐ Other non-relative, please specify
Specify:_____

CAREGIVER #4 INFORMATION

☐ Not applicable – no other caregiver

Age in Years

Years of Education (1st grade=1, Graduated High school=12; Graduated college=16)

Involved in child's treatment?
☐ Yes ☐ Partially ☐ No ☐ UNK

Ethnicity (check all that apply)
☐ African American ☐ Asian* ☐ Caucasian ☐ Latino/a*
☐ Native American ☐ Other*
*Specify(Asian, Latino, Other)

Relationship to Child (select one)
☐ Biological mother
☐ Biological father
☐ Adoptive mother
☐ Adoptive father
☐ Step-mother
☐ Step-father
☐ Foster mother
☐ Foster father
☐ Caregiver's female partner (girlfriend)
☐ Caregiver's male partner (boyfriend)
☐ Grandmother
☐ Grandfather
☐ Great grandmother
☐ Great grandfather
☐ Aunt
☐ Uncle

Language(s) spoken
☐ Spanish ☐ English ☐ Other (specify)
Specify:_____

☐ Great aunt
☐ Great uncle
☐ Other relative, please specify
☐ Other non-relative, please specify
Specify:_____

REFLECTIVE PRACTICE FIDELITY

POTENTIAL SOURCES OF CHALLENGE

	Level (select one)			
	No	Low	Moderate	Significant
Family is difficult to engage or work with	☐	☐	☐	☐
Family trauma history is likely to provoke negative reactions in any clinician	☐	☐	☐	☐
Systems are involved in complicated and/or conflictual ways with family/treatment	☐	☐	☐	☐
Therapist and caregiver have significantly different perspectives or cultural beliefs	☐	☐	☐	☐
Therapist knowledge and skill level (e.g. new therapist, new to the model or trauma work)	☐	☐	☐	☐
Limited access to safe reflective supervision or reflective consultation	☐	☐	☐	☐

THERAPIST REFLECTIVE PRACTICE CAPACITY

	Therapist Capacity (select one)		
	Requires Development	Emerging	Acquired
Awareness of own emotional reactions			
In the moment (in session)	☐	☐	☐
Upon self-reflection (outside session)	☐	☐	☐
In supervision/consultation	☐	☐	☐
Awareness of own personal and/or cultural biases			
In the moment (in session)	☐	☐	☐
Upon self-reflection (outside session)	☐	☐	☐
In supervision/consultation	☐	☐	☐
Ability to consider multiple perspectives (caregiver's, child's, own)			
In the moment (in session)	☐	☐	☐
Upon self-reflection (outside session)	☐	☐	☐
In supervision/consultation	☐	☐	☐
Ability to recognize and regulate strong emotions prior to intervening (in the moment)	☐	☐	☐
Use of self-care practices to enhance ability to regulate	☐	☐	☐

USE OF EXTERNAL SUPPORTS

Appropriately uses supervision and/or consultation with colleagues to:

	Requires Development	Emerging	Acquired
Process emotional reactions	☐	☐	☐
Consider alternative perspectives	☐	☐	☐
Seek new knowledge & new skills	☐	☐	☐

(Foundational Phase: Intervention Fidelity)

EMOTIONAL PROCESS FIDELITY

POTENTIAL SOURCES OF CHALLENGE

Degree to which in sessions. . .	Level (select one)			
	No	Low	Moderate	Significant
Caregiver is dysregulated or triggered	☐	☐	☐	☐
Caregiver is avoidant or shut down	☐	☐	☐	☐
Child is dysregulated or triggered	☐	☐	☐	☐
Child is avoidant or shut down	☐	☐	☐	☐

CAPACITY TO HANDLE EMOTIONAL CHALLENGES

Therapist is able to . . .	Therapist Capacity (select one)			
	Requires Development	Emerging		Acquired
Identify when caregiver is not regulated	☐	☐		☐
Tolerate caregiver's strong emotional reactions	☐	☐		☐
Intervene in ways to help caregiver become regulated	☐	☐		☐
Identify when child is not regulated	☐	☐		☐
Tolerate child's strong emotional reactions	☐	☐		☐
Create a context where child's emotional response is understood	☐	☐		☐
Create a context where child is helped to regulate	☐	☐		☐

DYADIC-RELATIONAL FIDELITY

POTENTIAL SOURCES OF CHALLENGE

Degree to which in the sessions. . .	Level (select one)			
	No	Low	Moderate	Significant
Caregiver and child have conflictual, competing agendas	☐	☐	☐	☐
Caregiver has difficulty understanding or tolerating child's behavior or temperament	☐	☐	☐	☐
Caregiver and/or child serve as trauma reminders to the other	☐	☐	☐	☐
Caregiver has unrealistic expectations of the child	☐	☐	☐	☐
Child has sensorimotor or affect regulation challenges	☐	☐	☐	☐

CAPACITY TO ADDRESS THE NEEDS OF CAREGIVER AND CHILD

Therapist is able to . . .	Therapist Capacity (select one)			
	Requires Development	Emerging		Acquired
Balance attention between caregiver and child (tracking both)	☐	☐		☐
Hold/support child and caregiver perspectives	☐	☐		☐
Bridge/translate between caregiver & child (help them understand each other)	☐	☐		☐
Intervene in ways that strengthen the caregiver-child relationship	☐	☐		☐
Think about and support child's relationship with other important caregivers (e.g. father)	☐	☐		☐

TRAUMA FRAMEWORK FIDELITY

POTENTIAL SOURCES OF CHALLENGE
Challenges related to. . .

	No	Level (select one)		
		Low	Moderate	Significant
Child's history being unknown	☐	☐	☐	☐
Caregiver's history being unknown	☐	☐	☐	☐
Caregiver not fully acknowledging child's history or not agreeing to talk about it	☐	☐	☐	☐
Caregiver not having a trauma framework (does not view child behavior in light of history)	☐	☐	☐	☐
Caregiver being triggered and having difficulty thinking about child's past experience	☐	☐	☐	☐

CAPACITY TO INTERVENE WITHIN A TRAUMA FRAMEWORK
Therapist is able to. . .

	Therapist Capacity (select one)		
	Requires Development	Emerging	Acquired
Keep child's and caregiver's trauma history in mind	☐	☐	☐
Think about how the child's and caregiver's history may be affecting interactions with each other and with the therapist	☐	☐	☐
Frame interventions (e.g. affect regulation, improving relationships) within the broader context of the family's traumatic experiences (in addition to other contributing factors)	☐	☐	☐
Directly talk about and bring up the family's trauma history when relevant	☐	☐	☐

PROCEDURAL FIDELITY

POTENTIAL SOURCES OF CHALLENGE

	No	Level (select one)		
		Low	Moderate	Significant
Scheduling challenges due to family illness, work, competing needs, or irregular visitation schedule make it difficult for family to attend weekly sessions	☐	☐	☐	☐
Scheduling challenges due to therapist illness, work schedule or competing needs make it difficult for therapist to hold weekly sessions	☐	☐	☐	☐
Family structure (e.g. multiple children) makes it difficult for therapist and caregiver to hold sessions focusing on the needs of individual children when clinically indicated	☐	☐	☐	☐
Home visiting environment often chaotic	☐	☐	☐	☐

CAPACITY TO CARRY OUT PROCEDURES
Therapist is able to. . .

	Response (check one)		
	No	Yes, But They Did Not Attend Regularly	Yes, Attended
Schedule sessions on a regular basis (generally 1x per week)	☐	☐	☐
Give appropriate notice for vacation	☐	☐	☐
Propose caregiver collateral sessions when. . .	Not needed ☐		
• Caregiver is triggered by child or child's play or in need of psychoeducation	☐	☐	☐
• Caregiver does not understand trauma as a potential cause of child's behaviors	☐	☐	☐
• Caregiver needs to share information with therapist (e.g. new traumatic events)			

(Foundational Phase: Intervention Fidelity)

PROCEDURAL FIDELITY: CPP CONTACT LOG

COMPLETE FOR ANY CONTACT

COMPLETE FOR SCHEDULED SESSIONS (NOT PHONE CONTACTS)

Date	Contact Type Assessment Case management Feedback Dyadic Treatment* Individual caregiver* Individual child* Cgiver phone – conversation Cgiver phone – message Collateral – meeting Collateral – phone Collateral – other Team meeting Other	Minutes	Session Status Show Cancel No Show	Reason for Not Attending Childcare problem Conflicting appointment Forgot Illness Therapist cancelled Transportation Weather Other	Who Attended (check all that apply) Target child Caregiver 1 Sibling 1 Caregiver 2 Sibling 2 Caregiver 3 Sibling 3 Caregiver 4 Sibling 4 Collateral: specify	Where Held Home Clinic Community Other	Session Counter (#)

*Typically during the Foundational Phase, most sessions are coded as assessment, case management, or feedback

MAKE ADDITIONAL COPIES OF PAGE AS NEEDED

PROCEDURAL FIDELITY: ASSESSMENT AND ENGAGEMENT

This is a suggested order; items do not need to be done in this order but do need to be done before the CPP core intervention phase begins. This checklist should be completed for each caregiver involved in treatment, with attempts made to engage all primary caregivers. Trauma and symptom screening should occur without the child present unless the child is a young infant (e.g. < 6 months) and the caregiver has no source of childcare.

#	ITEM	Caregiver Response	Done
1	**Elicited Caregiver Perception of Need for Treatment** Met alone and discussed with caregiver the reason for referral, referral source, and how caregiver feels about treatment		☐
2	**Elicited Caregiver Description of Family Circumstances, Challenges, and Strengths** Met alone and discussed caregiver's concerns about child, self, and other family members		☐
3	**Provided a Sense of Positive Expectations About Improvement** Noticed protective actions, conveyed realistic hope, provided emotional support, and acknowledged that coming to treatment is an important first step		☐
4	**Shared with Caregiver Rationale for Screening for Child Trauma** (for this specific child or in general)		☐
5	**Asked Caregiver to Jointly Complete a Child Trauma Screening Instrument**		☐
	5a. Is caregiver aware of child's history?	☐No ☐In part ☐Yes	
	5b. Select one to describe how you and caregiver discussed child's experience of trauma a) Child has no known history of trauma (e.g. newborn baby) b) Met <u>alone</u> with caregiver and screened for child's trauma history using a comprehensive trauma screening instrument to discuss what the caregiver knows and what is known from other sources (e.g. court reports, past therapists) c) Caregiver is not aware of child's trauma history. Met alone with caregiver and used a comprehensive trauma screening instrument or trauma history summary to talk to caregiver about child's history (facts and hypotheses) gathered from other sources (e.g. social worker, prior caregivers & therapists, court reports) Note: get appropriate releases prior to sharing information d) Caregiver refused to complete trauma screening, but did provide details regarding child's trauma history e) Caregiver refused to complete trauma screening, and refused to talk about child's trauma history	☐a (NA) ☐b ☐c ☐d ☐e	
	5c. Indicate instrument used to screen for child trauma history ☐TESI-PRR ☐Other, specify: Click here to enter text.		
6	**Considered Caregiver's Response to Child's Trauma History** Considered the quality of the way the caregiver thinks about the child's traumatic experiences (NA child has no trauma hx)		☐ ☐NA

6a. Factual response: Select one to describe caregiver's factual response to child's trauma history
   a) Child has no known history of trauma
   b) Acknowledged traumatic event(s) and impact on child
   c) Acknowledged traumatic event(s) but may be unsure of impact on child
   d) Acknowledged event but denied impact
   e) Denied child's experience of documented traumatic events

☐a (NA) ☐b ☐c ☐d ☐e

6b. Emotional response: Select one to describe caregiver's emotional response to child's trauma history
   a) N/A Child has no known history of trauma
   b) Integrated: Emotionally integrated, able to talk about experience without being overwhelmed
   c) Triggered: Overwhelmed or flooded by thinking about child's experience
   d) Avoidant: Avoids thinking about child's experience, blocks or pushes away experience
   e) Mixed Avoidant & Triggered: Overwhelmed by child's experience and actively avoids thinking about it

☐a (NA) ☐b ☐c ☐d ☐e

Note: Caregivers can refuse to answer any questions that make them feel uncomfortable. However, if a caregiver completely refuses to talk about a child's potential history of trauma, or if a caregiver denies the child's experience of trauma, and the child has a known history of trauma, a fundamental goal of the Foundational Phase is to determine if the caregiver can talk about and acknowledge the child's history once s/he forms a relationship with you and feels safer. If not, it may be contraindicated to engage in trauma-informed CPP.

7 **Assessed Child Symptoms** (May be done prior to screening for trauma)
Met alone with caregiver and obtained caregiver report of child's symptoms and areas of concern
☐

7a. Method for assessing child's symptoms (select one)
☐a) Clinical interview
☐b) Standardized questionnaire (check all used)
   (Below are optional instruments. It is recommended that you use one of them, but none are required)
   ☐CBCL ☐DECA-I/T ☐DECA-C ☐ITSEA ☐BITSEA ☐SDQ ☐ECBI ☐Other: Click here to enter text.

8 **Assessed Child Trauma Symptoms** (Ideally done after screening for trauma)
Met alone with caregiver and obtained caregiver report of child's trauma symptoms using a standardized instrument or clinical interview (check NA if child has no history of trauma exposure)
☐ ☐NA

8a. Method for assessing child's trauma symptoms (check all that apply)
☐TSCYC ☐DIPA ☐PAPA ☐P.I.E. ☐Interview ☐None ☐Other, specify:

9 **Assessed Child Developmental Functioning**
Assessed child's developmental functioning (regulatory capacity, achievement of age appropriate skills)
☐

9a. Method for assessing child's developmental functioning (check all that apply)
☐ASQ ☐Clinical observation ☐Other:Click here to enter text.

#		
10	**Discussed Connection Between Child's Symptoms and Child's History** Talked to caregiver about how child's symptoms or functioning may be related to the child's trauma history (including any history of separations). Note: This may be repeated at different times in the treatment but needs to happen in the beginning as part of setting the trauma frame (check NA if child has no history of trauma exposure)	☐ ☐NA
11	**Discussed Trauma Reminders** Helped the caregiver understand the concept of a trauma reminder and begin to identify possible trauma reminders for the child and caregiver (check NA if child and caregiver have no history of trauma exposure)	☐ ☐NA
12	**Assessed for Child Safety Risks to Engaging in Trauma-Informed Treatment** (check NA if child and caregiver have no history of trauma exposure)	☐ ☐NA
	12a. Code any safety risks (check one) ☐ No risks, it seems safe to talk about the child's experience of trauma with the child ☐ Yes, there are potential safety risks (check all potential risks) ☐ Child has contact with violent caregiver who is unaware that child is participating in trauma treatment ☐ Child has contact with violent caregiver who denies the child's experience of trauma ☐ Other safety risk, specify Click here to enter text.	
	Note: If there are safety risks that cannot be resolved, conducting trauma-informed CPP with the child may be contraindicated. You can help the caregiver think about how to support the child and ensure safety, or engage in relationship-based CPP to strengthen their relationship, but it would not be safe to involve the child in trauma treatment.	
13	**Observed Child and Caregiver Interaction** Observed child and caregiver together to obtain information regarding quality of their relationship, the way child and caregiver typically play and interact	☐
14	**Discussed Impact of Child Trauma Treatment on Caregivers** Met alone with caregiver and discussed how talking about/processing a child's traumatic experiences can affect caregivers, highlighting both risks and benefits (check NA if child has no history of trauma exposure)	☐ ☐NA
15	**Shared Rationale for Asking About Caregiver Trauma History** Examples: • It may be helpful to know caregiver's trauma history, so you can support him/her with any reactions that may arise as you both talk about and process child's trauma history with child • When caregivers have experienced trauma, especially as children, this can affect the way they raise their children in positive and negative ways. It may be good to talk about this in treatment to break the cycle of trauma and violence	☐
16	**Asked Caregiver to Jointly Complete a Caregiver Trauma Screening Instrument** Met alone with caregiver and discussed using a trauma screening instrument to think about caregiver history	☐

(Assessment and Engagement Procedures)

16a. Caregiver response (select one)
a) Reports s/he has not experienced any traumatic events □a
b) Agreed to complete screening instrument □b
c) Did not agree to screening instrument but did describe his/her history □c
d) Did not want to talk about own trauma history now but is open to talking about it later □d
e) Did not want to talk about own trauma history □e

16b. Indicate instrument used to screen for caregiver trauma history
□ LSC-R □Other, specify: Click here to enter text.   □

17 Shared Rationale for Asking About Caregiver Symptoms
Examples:
• It is common for caregivers to be strongly affected when their children experience trauma, especially if they experienced the same event
• Caregiver's mood and functioning can affect the child
• In CPP, the therapist supports the caregiver and family in addition to the child   □

18 Introduced Caregiver Symptom Measures
Discussed using questionnaires or interviews to better understand the caregiver's symptoms

18a. Caregiver response (select one)
a) Agreed to complete questionnaires regarding his/her symptoms □a
b) Did not agree to questionnaire but did describe symptoms □b
c) Did not want to talk about own symptoms now but is open to maybe talking about it later □c
d) Did not want to talk about own symptoms □d

18b. Indicate method used to assess caregiver PTSD
□ NA No Trauma Hx □ None □ PSSI □ Clinical Interview □Other, specify:

18c. Indicate method used to assess caregiver depression
□ None □ CES-D □ Clinical Interview □Other, specify: Click here to enter text.

18d. Describe other instruments used to assess caregiver mood or functioning
Click here to enter text.

19 Processed Information Gathered During Assessment/Engagement with Supervisor/Colleague
• For supervisees: reviewed the checklist and discussed the assessment results and treatment conceptualization with a supervisor
• For supervisors and other licensed staff: As needed, processed assessment with a colleague to conceptualize treatment and reflect on emotions brought up by the dyad. Check done if reflected alone and no additional support was needed.   □

PROCEDURAL FIDELITY: FEEDBACK SESSION

After completing the assessment, therapist and caregiver meet alone to discuss what they have learned, plan treatment, and talk about how to introduce the child to treatment, including how to bring up the child's trauma history. Other caregivers may be present, but the child should not be present unless the child is an infant.

#	ITEM	Caregiver Response	Done
1	**Elicited Caregiver Perception About Assessment Process and Foundational Phase** Engaged caregiver in a conversation about what s/he learned, positive experiences, concerns, ideas for future steps		☐
2	**Described Therapist Perspective and Recommendations**		☐
3	**Provided Other Referrals as Needed for Child, Caregiver, or Other Family Members**		☐
4	**Provided Rationale for Dyadic Treatment** Examples • We work with caregivers to think about how trauma may affect the child's development and relationships and how caregivers can help them heal from this experience • For older toddlers and preschoolers: We help very young children talk/play about and process experiences with their caregivers • If a caregiver's trauma history is affecting perceptions of or interactions with the child, treatment can help the caregiver consciously think about how his or her history affects parenting and develop new ways to change intergenerational patterns		☐
5	**Processed Cultural Beliefs About Talking About Trauma** Discussed with caregiver how CPP's view of talking about and processing trauma may be different from the way they were raised or from typical cultural beliefs. Elicited caregiver's view on this. (check NA if child and caregiver have no history of trauma exposure)		☐ ☐NA
6	**Discussed Play in CPP** Spoke with caregiver about how we use play in CPP (e.g. to process experience and build relationships) and how this may differ from how people typically interact with young children in the caregiver's family/culture or in the broader culture.		☐
7	**Requested Permission to Introduce Trauma-Related Toys** (for children old enough to use play to process experience) Discussed with caregiver the toys you might bring to help the child process his/her experience. Obtained permission to introduce trauma-related toys (e.g. dolls especially for boys, police cars, knives). Highlighted that young children often benefit from having "props" to tell their "story" (check NA if child is too young or has no history of trauma exposure)		☐ ☐NA
8	**Discussed Child's Need for Emotion Regulation while Processing Trauma** (for children old enough to process trauma) Helped caregiver understand that child may need "emotion regulation breaks" when processing traumatic experiences. Helped caregiver think about the way this child may do this and how the caregiver will support the child in doing this.		☐ ☐NA
9	**Discussed with Caregiver the Need for Regular Weekly Sessions**		☐
10	**Asked About Caregiver's Perspective of CPP**		☐
	10a. Is caregiver in agreement about the need to address child's trauma history (either directly or at least if the child brings it up)? Code in part if there are aspects of a child's trauma history the caregiver is willing to bring up, and there are aspects that the caregiver prefers not be discussed.	☐No ☐In part ☐Yes	

		☐No ☐In part ☐Yes
	10b. Does caregiver understand why CPP is conducted jointly with child and caregiver?	
	If the caregiver does not agree with the treatment model or has serious concerns, it will be important to explore this further. CPP may be contraindicated and in this case a referral to an alternate treatment should be considered	
11	**Thought About the Appropriateness of Beginning CPP with Child** Considered items assessing: Caregiver's Response to Child's Trauma History, Safety Risks to Engaging in Trauma-Informed Treatment, and Caregiver's Perspective of CPP and decided whether to include child in CPP.	☐

	11a. Therapist assessment of appropriateness of CPP (select one)
	☐ a) It seems safe/appropriate to include child in CPP even if treatment includes a focus on child's trauma history
	☐ b) It is not safe and/or appropriate to begin trauma-informed CPP with the child
	  Given concerns, the treatment plan will focus on the following (check all that apply)
	  ☐ 1. Work with caregiver alone to enhance safety and provide case management
	  ☐ 2. Work with caregiver alone to help caregiver begin to acknowledge child's history
	  ☐ 3. Conduct CPP with caregiver and child to strengthen the relationship but not address the trauma
	  ☐ 4. Develop alternate CPP plan, (describe) Click here to enter text.
	  ☐ 5. Refer family to alternate treatment Click here to enter text.	

12	**Developed CPP Triangle of Explanations with Caregiver**	☐
	12a. Describe the components of the CPP triangle Experience: Feelings/Behavior: How Treatment will Help: Protective and Growth Promoting Factors: Modality: Way this will be shared with the child (e.g. discussion, using toys)	

(Foundational Phase: Feedback Fidelity)

CPP CASE CONCEPTUALIZATION AND CONTENT FIDELITY

- Clinical Focus: Throughout the phase, degree to which the therapist's interventions addressed the objective:
  0=not at all a focus; 1=minor, 2=moderate; 3=significant
- Appropriateness: Under=Therapist should have focused more on this objective; Appropriate=Amount of therapeutic focus seems appropriate; Over=Therapist may have overly focused on this objective, to the detriment of other important objectives
- Progress Towards Objective (Referral=Upon Referral; Current=At the end of the Foundational Phase)
  3 = Established: Good enough to support development
  2 = Present but Unstable: Good under some conditions. Not fully consolidated. Lost in response to internal or external stress.
  1 = Emerging: Early manifestations
  0 = Primary Target/Urgent Concern: Immediate risk to development, relationship and/or therapeutic alliance

CPP OBJECTIVES	Clinical Focus (0-3)	Appropriateness (check one)			Progress Referral (0-3)	Progress Current (0-3)
		Under	Appropriate	Over		
CONVEY HOPE						
• Highlighted that change and growth are possible given positive steps the family has made	—	☐	☐	☐	—	—
• Provided realistic examples of potential pathways for healing, noting ways that caregiver efforts and treatment may lead to improved caregiver and child functioning						
• Helped the family connect to spiritual resources consistent with family traditions						
DEVELOP EMPATHIC RELATIONSHIP WITH FAMILY MEMBERS						
• Empathically listened to concerns: ☐ caregiver ☐ child's	—	☐	☐	☐	—	—
• Understood difficult behavior given past history & current context: ☐caregiver ☐child						
• Made warm supportive comments or recognized accomplishments: ☐ caregiver ☐child						
• Understood caregivers' mistrust of providers and reluctance to engage in treatment in light of their past history and current experiences with potentially punitive systems						
ENHANCE SAFETY						
Safety - Physical Safety (chart all safety risks separately)						
• Helped caregiver reflect on his/her history of physical endangerment and how it shapes current expectations regarding danger and safety	—	☐	☐	☐	—	—
• In a supportive, non-confrontational manner, directly addressed safety issues with caregiver with the goal of increasing caregiver awareness and mobilizing protective action						
• Balanced respect for the caregiver's psychological vulnerabilities with the need to address lapses in safety and destructive or self-destructive behavior						
• Encouraged the caregiver to develop an attitude that prioritizes safety as a core value for the caregiver, child, and family						
• Supported caregiver in engaging other family members in addressing risks to safety (including partners who may have been violent)						
• Focused on and addressed serious risks to physical safety, including risks within family relationships and permanency of placement						
• Engaged in safety planning						
• Assessed for and filed appropriate DCF reports for suspected abuse						

CPP OBJECTIVES	Clinical Focus (0-3)	Appropriateness (check one)			Progress Referral (0-3)	Progress Current (0-3)
		Under	Appropriate	Over		
Safety - Environmental Context						
• Discussed ways that contextual risks (e.g. poverty, community violence, immigration related-risks, inadequate or unsafe housing, and inadequate access to services) affect child and family functioning	—	☐	☐	☐	—	—
• Considered the impact of racism and historical trauma on child and family functioning						
Safety – Stabilization						
• Discussed provision/maintenance of basic needs						
• Provided case management to help family obtain basic needs		☐	☐	☐	—	—
• Helped caregiver develop the capacities to obtain services and needs independently (to overcome barriers, communicate about needs, and collaborate with service providers)						
• Helped caregiver identify and address root causes of recurrent crisis and ongoing instability						
Safety & Consistency in Therapy						
• Acknowledged safety risks to participating in therapy: reporting, mandated nature, etc.		☐	☐	☐	—	—
• Encouraged consistent, on-time participation in therapy						
• Created a consistent environment for treatment						
Perceived Safety						
• Identify misperceptions of danger or safety: ☐caregiver ☐child		☐	☐	☐	—	—
• Foster accurate perceptions of danger and safety						
Safety within Caregiver-Child Relationships						
• Acknowledged past history of risks to safety: ☐ caregiver ☐ child						
• Highlighted the need for safe behavior while legitimizing feelings (e.g. child cannot hit others even though child is angry)						
• Fostered caregiver's ability to socialize child in ways that are consistent both with the caregiver's cultural values and beliefs and the family's context						
• Identified factors that may interfere with caregivers capacity to socialize child, including environmental circumstances, strong emotions (e.g. guilt, fear, feelings of worthlessness), and prior history						
• Support caregiver's development of routines to enhance safety						
• Helped establish caregiver as a protective, benevolent, legitimate authority figure						

CPP OBJECTIVES	Clinical Focus (0-3)	Appropriateness (check one)			Progress Referral (0-3)	Progress Current (0-3)
		Under	Appropriate	Over		
STRENGTHEN FAMILY RELATIONSHIPS: PROMOTE EMOTIONAL RECIPROCITY						
• Helped caregiver reflect on how current expectations about relationships (child's or caregiver's) are shaped by past experience	—	☐	☐	☐	—	—
• Helped caregiver identify and explore origins of negative views/representations of the child						
• Helped caregiver think about how perceptions may affect behavior or interactions with child						
• Helped caregiver and child notice and respond supportively to each other's relational bids						
• Helped caregiver reflect and respond benevolently to the child's challenging behavior						
• Helped identify negative perceptions child may have about caregiver						
• Helped child understand and appreciate caregiver's efforts on the child and family's behalf						
• Helped caregiver and child learn ways to repair and connect after conflict						
• Helped caregiver and child consciously explore new ways of relating that promote trust, continuity, reciprocity, and pleasure						
COORDINATE CARE						
• Engaged in systematic efforts to obtain all relevant information about child history (e.g. CPS reports related to placement history)	—	☐	☐	☐	—	—
• Helped family members obtain needed referrals to other services						
• Communicated and coordinated care as needed with other service providers						
• Reflected on the needs of the entire family and prioritized services according to immediacy of needs						
• Took steps to ensure that risks to the child's safety were known and addressed effectively by the team of service providers involved with the family						
• Fostered a climate of transparency in communicating to caregiver the way that service providers are working together to ensure child safety						
STRENGTHEN DYADIC AFFECT REGULATION CAPACITIES						
• Fostered caregiver's ability to respond in soothing ways when child is upset	—	☐	☐	☐	—	—
• Fostered child's ability to use caregiver as a secure base						
• Provided developmental guidance around typical early childhood fears/anxieties						
• Acknowledged and helped find words for emotional experiences: ☐caregiver ☐child						
• Provided developmental guidance around emotional reactions: ☐caregiver ☐child						
• Taught, developed, or fostered strategies for regulating affect: ☐caregiver ☐child						
• Explored with caregiver links between emotional responses to past experiences and current emotional responses to child's behavior						

CPP OBJECTIVES	Clinical Focus (0-3)	Appropriateness (check one)			Progress Referral (0-3)	Progress Current (0-3)
		Under	Appropriate	Over		
STRENGTHEN DYADIC BODY-BASED REGULATION	—	☐	☐	☐	—	—
• Fostered body-based awareness, including awareness of physiological responses, particularly as they relate to stress ☐caregiver ☐child						
• Fostered understanding and identification of body-based trauma reminders						
• Helped caregiver learn/engage in body-based regulation techniques to regulate affect						
• Helped caregiver & child learn or use body-based regulation techniques to soothe child						
• Helped caregiver and child exchange physical expressions of care						
• Enhanced understanding of safe body-based boundaries						
SUPPORT CHILD'S RELATIONSHIP WITH OTHER IMPORTANT CAREGIVERS	—	☐	☐	☐	—	—
• Helped caregivers understand the child's perspective and need for positive representations of alternative caregivers (e.g. father, step-parent, foster parents)						
• Helped caregiver support the child in integrating the positive and negative aspects of other caregivers						
• Shared the concept of angel moments and the importance of helping the child hold on to positive memories involving alternative caregivers, even when relationships between caregivers are strained						
• Supported child in developing an age-appropriate understanding of the family history						
• Supported the child in understanding that different family members have different points of view and different ways of relating to each other and to the child						
ENHANCE UNDERSTANDING OF THE MEANING OF BEHAVIOR	—	☐	☐	☐	—	—
• Helped caregiver notice behavior (child's, caregiver's, or another caregiver's)						
• Provided developmental guidance regarding age appropriate behavior and developmental meaning of behavior						
• Provided developmental guidance around how children learn and develop						
• Helped caregiver consider (reflect on) the meaning of child and/or caregiver behavior (thinking about developmental stage, past experiences, cultural beliefs)						
• Helped enhance reflective functioning in caregivers and child						
SUPPORT CHILD IN RETURNING TO A NORMAL DEVELOPMENTAL TRAJECTORY	—	☐	☐	☐	—	—
• Supported adaptive behavior and normative developmental activities						
• Supported healthy non-trauma play						
• Supported positive identity development						
• Fostered caregiver's efforts to engage in age appropriate activities						
• Provided case management to help engage child in age appropriate activities (e.g. school)						

CPP OBJECTIVES	Clinical Focus (0-3)	Appropriateness (check one)			Progress Referral (0-3)	Progress Current (0-3)
		Under	Appropriate	Over		
NORMALIZE THE TRAUMATIC RESPONSE						
• Acknowledged effects of child's and caregivers' experience of trauma and historical trauma						
• Provided psychoeducation: Impact of trauma, including common symptoms & PTSD, trauma reminders and how they affect child and caregiver	—		☐	☐	—	—
• Helped caregiver anticipate developmental changes in child's processing of the trauma						
SUPPORT DYAD IN ACKNOWLEDGING THE IMPACT OF TRAUMA						
• Promoted a deep emotional acknowledgement of the impact of trauma while attending and responding to dysregulated (over or under) affective states						
• Helped caregiver acknowledge what child has witnessed & remembers						
• Helped caregiver and child understand each other's reality (with regards to the trauma)	—		☐	☐	—	—
• Helped caregiver & child identify and cope with trauma reminders						
• Helped caregiver think about his/her own trauma history (ghosts in the nursery) and ways this history may affect her/him and the way s/he parents						
HELP DYAD DIFFERENTIATE BETWEEN THEN AND NOW						
• Highlighted difference between past and present circumstances						
• Helped dyad understand that they can make new choices						
• Helped child and caregiver become aware of the difference between reliving and remembering by helping them identify traumatic triggers and pointing out the different circumstances in the past and the present	—		☐	☐	—	—
HELP DYAD PUT THE TRAUMATIC EXPERIENCE IN PERSPECTIVE						
• Supported caregiver and child in making meaning (e.g. creating a story, using ritual, connecting with spiritual beliefs)						
• Integrate historical trauma as part of the family and personal narrative						
• Worked with beliefs (existential challenges) around why the traumatic events happened (e.g. that they are bad, being punished)						
• Helped caregiver and child see trauma as something that happened to them but that does not define them	—		☐	☐	—	—
• Supported family's advocacy work or work to help others						
• Fostered acceptance around how these experiences have shaped the caregiver and child's sense of self						
• Helped the family find pathways to post trauma growth and joy						
• Encouraged appreciation of goodness, beauty, and hope						

APPENDIX B: CORE INTERVENTION PHASE FIDELITY PACKET

ChildParent
PSYCHOTHERAPY

v.09.2015
Completed by: Therapist
Reviewed with Supervisor

CPP FIDELITY
CORE INTERVENTION PHASE

CPP Training Name: _____

Therapist Name: _____   Client Nickname: _____   Client ID: _automatically generated_

Date Core Intervention Phase Began: _____

Typically the core intervention phase begins by introducing the child to CPP. In rare circumstances, where safety is a concern, treatment may begin with the caregiver alone. If for any reason the child will not be involved in treatment, please indicate this here. In this case, check "Not Done" in the "Procedural Fidelity: Introducing the Child to CPP" section

☐ Child will be involved in treatment

☐ Child will not be involved in treatment
  Please indicate reasons why: (check all that apply)
  ☐ Another caregiver has not given consent for child to participate
  ☐ Another caregiver is not aware that child will be participating in a trauma treatment and it would be unsafe to inform caregiver about treatment
  ☐ Core intervention phase will at least initially consist of individual meetings with the caregiver to enhance caregiver's capacity to acknowledge child's experience of trauma and/or to focus on safety
  ☐ Other (describe below)

Describe any reason for not holding dyadic sessions during core intervention phase:

(Core Intervention Phase: Registration Form)   Page 1 of 12

PROCEDURAL FIDELITY: INTRODUCING THE CHILD TO CPP

Instructions: Complete immediately after the session where the child is introduced to CPP.

☐ Not done (child initially not involved in CPP sessions)

#	ITEM	Done
1	**Prepared for Session: Selected Toys for Treatment** Ensured that toy bag or playroom had toys related to child's traumatic experience (see CPP toy list) as well as toys to help the child and caregiver regulate. • For infants, ensured access to toys/materials appropriate given treatment goals.	☐
2	**Explained the Reason for Treatment to Child** Had a session with the child and caregiver where you discussed the reason for treatment with the child using what was decided during the feedback session as a starting point. • If the child is an infant or young toddler, had an introductory session with the child present and discussed the reason for treatment with caregiver, referring back to the young child.	☐
	2a. Describe the Way the CPP Triangle of Explanations was Presented in Session Experience: Feelings/Behavior: How Treatment Will Help: Protective and Growth Promoting Factors:	

(Core Intervention Phase: Introducing Child to CPP Page 2 of 12)

3	Tracked Child Response to Introduction to Treatment	☐
	3a. Describe How Child Responded to Introduction to Treatment	
	(e.g. played out content of trauma, became aggressive, crawled into caregiver's lap. . .)	
	Click here to enter text.	
	3b. Code Emotional Response (check all that apply)	☐
	☐ Child is a young infant and does not show a response to the introduction	
	☐ Integrated: Emotionally integrated, remained connected to caregiver and/or intervener, able to talk about experience without being overwhelmed	
	☐ Triggered: Became overly active, overwhelmed, clingy	
	☐ Avoidant: Actively avoided topic, wanted to leave, turned back on intervener	
	☐ Mixed Avoidant & Triggered: Active and overwhelmed and actively avoids thinking about it	
	☐ Other, make sure you described this above	
4	Supported Caregiver During Introduction to Treatment	☐
	Checked in with caregiver to see how s/he understood child's response to the introduction to treatment. Provided any emotional support necessary.	
5	Benevolent Explanation for Any Negative Reactions/Behaviors	☐ ☐ NA
	During the opening session, provided a benevolent or developmentally-informed explanation to the caregiver for any reactions in the child or caregiver that may be perceived as negative (e.g. child who plays out an aggressive or violent scene)	
6	Processed Session with Supervisor/Colleague	☐
	• For supervisees: Processed session with supervisor	
	• For supervisors and other licensed staff: Processed session with colleague as needed given any feelings or confusion that may have arisen. Check done if reflected alone and no additional support was needed.	

PROCEDURAL FIDELITY: CPP CONTACT LOG

Instructions: Use to track treatment participation during the core intervention phase

	COMPLETE FOR ANY CONTACT			COMPLETE FOR SCHEDULED SESSIONS (NOT PHONE CONTACTS)			
Date	Contact Type Assessment Case management Feedback Dyadic Treatment* Individual caregiver* Individual child* Cgiver phone – conversation Cgiver phone – message Collateral – meeting Collateral – phone Collateral – other Team meeting Other	Minutes	Session Status Show Cancel No Show	Reason for Not Attending Childcare problem Conflicting appointment Forgot Illness Therapist cancelled Transportation Weather Other	Who Attended (check all that apply) Target child Caregiver 1 Sibling 1 Caregiver 2 Sibling 2 Caregiver 3 Sibling 3 Caregiver 4 Sibling 4 Collateral: specify	Where Held Home Clinic Community Other	Session Counter (#)

MAKE ADDITIONAL COPIES OF PAGE AS NEEDED

(Core Intervention Phase: Contact Log) Page 4 of 12

CPP CORE INTERVENTION FIDELITY

Instructions:
- For most agencies, pages 5-12 completed after every 12 CPP sessions to re-conceptualize the case unless termination has begun
- In clinics designated as CPP Agencies (with an endorsed CPP training team), complete paged 5-12 after every 20 sessions

Date Completed: _____   CPP Session #: _____

REFLECTIVE PRACTICE FIDELITY

POTENTIAL SOURCES OF CHALLENGE	No	Level (select one)		
		Low	Moderate	Significant
Family is difficult to engage or work with	□	□	□	□
Family trauma history is likely to provoke negative reactions in any clinician	□	□	□	□
Systems are involved in complicated and/or conflictual ways with family/treatment	□	□	□	□
Therapist and caregiver have significantly different perspectives or cultural beliefs	□	□	□	□
Therapist knowledge and skill level (e.g. new therapist, new to the model or trauma work)	□	□	□	□
Limited access to safe reflective supervision or reflective consultation	□	□	□	□

THERAPIST REFLECTIVE PRACTICE CAPACITY	Therapist Capacity (select one)		
	Requires Development	Emerging	Acquired
Awareness of own emotional reactions			
In the moment (in session)	□	□	□
Upon self-reflection (outside session)	□	□	□
In supervision/consultation	□	□	□
Awareness of own personal and/or cultural biases			
In the moment (in session)	□	□	□
Upon self-reflection (outside session)	□	□	□
In supervision/consultation	□	□	□
Ability to consider multiple perspectives (caregiver's, child's, own)			
In the moment (in session)	□	□	□
Upon self-reflection (outside session)	□	□	□
In supervision/consultation	□	□	□
Ability to recognize and regulate strong emotions prior to intervening (in the moment)	□	□	□
Use of self-care practices to enhance ability to regulate	□	□	□
USE OF EXTERNAL SUPPORTS			
Appropriately uses supervision and/or consultation with colleagues to:			
Process emotional reactions	□	□	□
Consider alternative perspectives	□	□	□
Seek new knowledge & new skills	□	□	□

EMOTIONAL PROCESS FIDELITY

POTENTIAL SOURCES OF CHALLENGE — Degree to which in sessions. . .	Level (select one)			
	No	Low	Moderate	Significant
Caregiver is dysregulated or triggered	☐	☐	☐	☐
Caregiver is avoidant or shut down	☐	☐	☐	☐
Child is dysregulated or triggered	☐	☐	☐	☐
Child is avoidant or shut down	☐	☐	☐	☐

CAPACITY TO HANDLE EMOTIONAL CHALLENGES — Therapist is able to . . .	Therapist Capacity (select one)		
	Requires Development	Emerging	Acquired
Identify when caregiver is not regulated	☐	☐	☐
Tolerate caregiver's strong emotional reactions	☐	☐	☐
Intervene in ways to help caregiver become regulated	☐	☐	☐
Identify when child is not regulated	☐	☐	☐
Tolerate child's strong emotional reactions	☐	☐	☐
Create a context where child's emotional response is understood	☐	☐	☐
Create a context where child is helped to regulate	☐	☐	☐

DYADIC-RELATIONAL FIDELITY

POTENTIAL SOURCES OF CHALLENGE — Degree to which in the sessions. . .	Level (select one)			
	No	Low	Moderate	Significant
Caregiver and child have conflictual, competing agendas	☐	☐	☐	☐
Caregiver has difficulty understanding or tolerating child's behavior or temperament	☐	☐	☐	☐
Caregiver and/or child serve as trauma reminders to the other	☐	☐	☐	☐
Caregiver has unrealistic expectations of the child	☐	☐	☐	☐
Child has sensorimotor or affect regulation challenges	☐	☐	☐	☐

CAPACITY TO ADDRESS THE NEEDS OF CAREGIVER AND CHILD — Therapist is able to . . .	Therapist Capacity (select one)		
	Requires Development	Emerging	Acquired
Balance attention between caregiver and child (tracking both)	☐	☐	☐
Hold/support child and caregiver perspectives	☐	☐	☐
Bridge/translate between caregiver & child (help them understand each other)	☐	☐	☐
Intervene in ways that strengthen the caregiver–child relationship	☐	☐	☐
Think about and support child's relationship with other important caregivers (e.g. father)	☐	☐	☐

(Core Intervention Phase: Intervention Fidelity) Page 6 of 12

TRAUMA FRAMEWORK FIDELITY

POTENTIAL SOURCES OF CHALLENGE Challenges related to . . .	No	Level (select one)		
		Low	Moderate	Significant
Child's history being unknown	☐	☐	☐	☐
Caregiver's history being unknown	☐	☐	☐	☐
Caregiver not fully acknowledging child's history or not agreeing to talk about it	☐	☐	☐	☐
Caregiver not having a trauma framework (does not view child behavior in light of history)	☐	☐	☐	☐
Caregiver being triggered and having difficulty thinking about child's past experience	☐	☐	☐	☐

CAPACITY TO INTERVENE WITHIN A TRAUMA FRAMEWORK Therapist is able to . . .	Therapist Capacity (select one)		
	Requires Development	Emerging	Acquired
Keep child's and caregiver's trauma history in mind	☐	☐	☐
Think about how the child's and caregiver's history may be affecting interactions with each other and with the therapist	☐	☐	☐
Frame interventions (e.g. affect regulation, improving relationships) within the broader context of the family's traumatic experiences (in addition to other contributing factors)	☐	☐	☐
Directly talk about and bring up the family's trauma history when relevant	☐	☐	☐

PROCEDURAL FIDELITY

POTENTIAL SOURCES OF CHALLENGE	No	Level (select one)		
		Low	Moderate	Significant
Scheduling challenges due to family illness, work, competing needs, or irregular visitation schedule make it difficult for family to attend weekly sessions	☐	☐	☐	☐
Scheduling challenges due to therapist illness, work schedule or competing needs make it difficult for therapist to hold weekly sessions	☐	☐	☐	☐
Family structure (e.g. multiple children) makes it difficult for therapist and caregiver to hold sessions focusing on the needs of individual children when clinically indicated	☐	☐	☐	☐
Home visiting environment often chaotic	☐	☐	☐	☐

CAPACITY TO CARRY OUT PROCEDURES Therapist is able to . . .	Response (check one)		
	No	Yes, But They Did Not Attend Regularly	Yes, Attended
Schedule sessions on a regular basis (generally 1x per week)	☐	☐	☐
Give appropriate notice for vacation	☐	☐	☐
Propose caregiver collateral sessions when . . .	Not needed		
• Caregiver is triggered by child or child's play or in need of psychoeducation	☐	☐	☐
• Caregiver does not understand trauma as a potential cause of child's behaviors	☐		
• Caregiver needs to share information with therapist (e.g. new traumatic events)	☐	☐	☐

CPP CASE CONCEPTUALIZATION AND CONTENT FIDELITY

- Clinical Focus: Throughout the phase, degree to which the therapist's interventions addressed the objective:
  0=not at all a focus; 1=minor; 2=moderate; 3=significant
- Appropriateness: Under=Therapist should have focused more on this objective; Appropriate=Amount of therapeutic focus seems appropriate; Over=Therapist may have overly focused on this objective, to the detriment of other important objectives
- Progress Towards Objective
  3 = Established: Good enough to support development
  2 = Present but Unstable: Good under some conditions. Not fully consolidated. Lost in response to internal or external stress.
  1 = Emerging: Early manifestations
  0 = Primary Target/Urgent Concern: Immediate risk to development, relationship and/or therapeutic alliance

CPP OBJECTIVES	Clinical Focus (0-3)	Appropriateness (check one)			Progress Current (0-3)
		Under	Appropriate	Over	
CONVEY HOPE					
• Highlighted that change and growth are possible given positive steps the family has made					
• Provided realistic examples of potential pathways for healing, noting ways that caregiver efforts and treatment may lead to improved caregiver and child functioning	___	☐	☐	☐	___
• Helped the family connect to spiritual resources consistent with family traditions					
DEVELOP EMPATHIC RELATIONSHIP WITH FAMILY MEMBERS					
• Empathically listened to concerns: ☐ caregiver ☐ child's					
• Understood difficult behavior given past history & current context: ☐caregiver ☐child					
• Made warm supportive comments or recognized accomplishments: ☐ caregiver ☐child	___	☐	☐	☐	___
• Understood caregivers' mistrust of providers and reluctance to engage in treatment in light of their past history and current experiences with potentially punitive systems					
ENHANCE SAFETY					
Safety - Physical Safety (chart all safety risks separately)					
• Helped caregiver reflect on his/her history of physical endangerment and how it shapes current expectations regarding danger and safety					
• In a supportive, non-confrontational manner, directly addressed safety issues with caregiver with the goal of increasing caregiver awareness and mobilizing protective action					
• Balanced respect for the caregiver's psychological vulnerabilities with the need to address lapses in safety and destructive or self-destructive behavior					
• Encouraged the caregiver to develop an attitude that prioritizes safety as a core value for the caregiver, child, and family	___	☐	☐	☐	
• Supported caregiver in engaging other family members in addressing risks to safety (including partners who may have been violent)					
• Focused on and addressed serious risks to physical safety, including risks within family relationships and permanency of placement					
• Engaged in safety planning					
• Assessed for and filed appropriate DCF reports for suspected abuse					

CPP OBJECTIVES	Clinical Focus (0-3)	Appropriateness (check one)			Progress Current (0-3)
		Under	Appropriate	Over	
Safety - Environmental Context					
• Discussed ways that contextual risks (e.g. poverty, community violence, immigration related-risks, inadequate or unsafe housing, and inadequate access to services) affect child and family functioning	——	☐	☐	☐	——
• Considered the impact of racism and historical trauma on child and family functioning					
Safety – Stabilization					
• Discussed provision/maintenance of basic needs	——	☐	☐	☐	——
• Provided case management to help family obtain basic needs					
• Helped caregiver develop the capacities to obtain services and needs independently (to overcome barriers, communicate about needs, and collaborate with service providers)					
• Helped caregiver identify and address root causes of recurrent crisis and ongoing instability					
Safety & Consistency in Therapy					
• Acknowledged safety risks to participating in therapy: reporting, mandated nature, etc.	——	☐	☐	☐	——
• Encouraged consistent, on-time participation in therapy					
• Created a consistent environment for treatment					
Perceived Safety					
• Identify misperceptions of danger or safety: ☐caregiver ☐child	——	☐	☐	☐	——
• Foster accurate perceptions of danger and safety					
Safety within Caregiver-Child Relationships					
• Acknowledged past history of risks to safety: ☐ caregiver ☐ child	——	☐	☐	☐	——
• Highlighted the need for safe behavior while legitimizing feelings (e.g. child cannot hit others even though child is angry)					
• Fostered caregiver's ability to socialize child in ways that are consistent both with the caregiver's cultural values and beliefs and the family's context					
• Identified factors that may interfere with caregivers capacity to socialize child, including environmental circumstances, strong emotions (e.g. guilt, fear, feelings of worthlessness), and prior history					
• Support caregiver's development of routines to enhance safety					
• Helped establish caregiver as a protective, benevolent, legitimate authority figure					

CPP OBJECTIVES	Clinical Focus (0-3)	Appropriateness (check one)			Progress Current (0-3)
		Under	Appropriate	Over	
STRENGTHEN FAMILY RELATIONSHIPS: PROMOTE EMOTIONAL RECIPROCITY					
• Helped caregiver reflect on how current expectations about relationships (child's or caregiver's) are shaped by past experience	___	☐	☐	☐	___
• Helped caregiver identify and explore origins of negative views/representations of the child					
• Helped caregiver think about how perceptions may affect behavior or interactions with child					
• Helped caregiver and child notice and respond supportively to each other's relational bids					
• Helped caregiver reflect and respond benevolently to the child's challenging behavior					
• Helped identify negative perceptions child may have about caregiver					
• Helped child understand and appreciate caregiver's efforts on the child and family's behalf					
• Helped caregiver and child learn ways to repair and connect after conflict					
• Helped caregiver and child consciously explore new ways of relating that promote trust, continuity, reciprocity, and pleasure					
COORDINATE CARE					
• Engaged in systematic efforts to obtain all relevant information about child history (e.g. CPS reports related to placement history)	___	☐	☐	☐	___
• Helped family members obtain needed referrals to other services					
• Communicated and coordinated care as needed with other service providers					
• Reflected on the needs of the entire family and prioritized services according to immediacy of needs					
• Took steps to ensure that risks to the child's safety were known and addressed effectively by the team of service providers involved with the family					
• Fostered a climate of transparency in communicating to caregiver the way that service providers are working together to ensure child safety					
STRENGTHEN DYADIC AFFECT REGULATION CAPACITIES					
• Fostered caregiver's ability to respond in soothing ways when child is upset	___	☐	☐	☐	___
• Fostered child's ability to use caregiver as a secure base					
• Provided developmental guidance around typical early childhood fears/anxieties					
• Acknowledged and helped find words for emotional experiences: ☐caregiver ☐child					
• Provided developmental guidance around emotional reactions: ☐caregiver ☐child					
• Taught, developed, or fostered strategies for regulating affect: ☐caregiver ☐child					
• Explored with caregiver links between emotional responses to past experiences and current emotional responses to child's behavior					

   (Core Intervention Phase: Intervention Fidelity)   Page 10 of 12

CPP OBJECTIVES	Clinical Focus (0-3)	Appropriateness (check one) Under	Appropriate	Over	Progress Current (0-3)
STRENGTHEN DYADIC BODY-BASED REGULATION					
• Fostered body-based awareness, including awareness of physiological responses, particularly as they relate to stress □caregiver □child	—	□	□	□	—
• Fostered understanding and identification of body-based trauma reminders					
• Helped caregiver learn/engage in body-based regulation techniques to regulate affect					
• Helped caregiver & child learn or use body-based regulation techniques to soothe child					
• Helped caregiver and child exchange physical expressions of care					
• Enhanced understanding of safe body-based boundaries					
SUPPORT CHILD'S RELATIONSHIP WITH OTHER IMPORTANT CAREGIVERS					
• Helped caregivers understand the child's perspective and need for positive representations of alternative caregivers (e.g. father, step-parent, foster parents)	—	□	□	□	—
• Helped caregiver support the child in integrating the positive and negative aspects of other caregivers					
• Shared the concept of angel moments and the importance of helping the child hold on to positive memories involving alternative caregivers, even when relationships between caregivers are strained					
• Supported child in developing an age-appropriate understanding of the family history					
• Supported the child in understanding that different family members have different points of view and different ways of relating to each other and to the child					
ENHANCE UNDERSTANDING OF THE MEANING OF BEHAVIOR					
• Helped caregiver notice behavior (child's, caregiver's, or another caregiver's)	—	□	□	□	—
• Provided developmental guidance regarding age appropriate behavior and developmental meaning of behavior					
• Provided developmental guidance around how children learn and develop					
• Helped caregiver consider (reflect on) the meaning of child and/or caregiver behavior (thinking about developmental stage, past experiences, cultural beliefs)					
• Helped enhance reflective functioning in caregivers and child					
SUPPORT CHILD IN RETURNING TO A NORMAL DEVELOPMENTAL TRAJECTORY					
• Supported adaptive behavior and normative developmental activities	—	□	□	□	—
• Supported healthy non-trauma play					
• Supported positive identity development					
• Fostered caregiver's efforts to engage in age appropriate activities					
• Provided case management to help engage child in age appropriate activities (e.g. school)					

CPP OBJECTIVES	Clinical Focus (0-3)	Appropriateness (check one) Under	Appropriate	Over	Progress Current (0-3)
NORMALIZE THE TRAUMATIC RESPONSE					
• Acknowledged effects of child's and caregivers' experience of trauma and historical trauma					
• Provided psychoeducation: Impact of trauma, including common symptoms & PTSD, trauma reminders and how they affect child and caregiver	—	☐	☐	☐	—
• Helped caregiver anticipate developmental changes in child's processing of the trauma					
SUPPORT DYAD IN ACKNOWLEDGING THE IMPACT OF TRAUMA					
• Promoted a deep emotional acknowledgement of the impact of trauma while attending and responding to dysregulated (over or under) affective states					
• Helped caregiver acknowledge what child has witnessed & remembers	—	☐	☐	☐	—
• Helped caregiver and child understand each other's reality (with regards to the trauma)					
• Helped caregiver & child identify and cope with trauma reminders					
• Helped caregiver think about his/her own trauma history (ghosts in the nursery) and ways this history may affect her/him and the way s/he parents					
HELP DYAD DIFFERENTIATE BETWEEN THEN AND NOW					
• Highlighted difference between past and present circumstances					
• Helped dyad understand that they can make new choices	—	☐	☐	☐	—
• Helped child and caregiver become aware of the difference between reliving and remembering by helping them identify traumatic triggers and pointing out the different circumstances in the past and the present					
HELP DYAD PUT THE TRAUMATIC EXPERIENCE IN PERSPECTIVE					
• Supported caregiver and child in making meaning (e.g. creating a story, using ritual, connecting with spiritual beliefs)					
• Integrate historical trauma as part of the family and personal narrative					
• Worked with beliefs (existential challenges) around why the traumatic events happened (e.g. that they are bad, being punished)	—	☐	☐	☐	—
• Helped caregiver and child see trauma as something that happened to them but that does not define them					
• Supported family's advocacy work or work to help others					
• Fostered acceptance around how these experiences have shaped the caregiver and child's sense of self					
• Helped the family find pathways to post trauma growth and joy					
• Encouraged appreciation of goodness, beauty, and hope					

APPENDIX C: RECAPITULATION AND TERMINATION PHASE FIDELITY PACKET

ChildParent PSYCHOTHERAPY

CPP FIDELITY
RECAPITULATION AND TERMINATION PHASE

CPP CLOSING FORM

v.09.2015
Completed by: Therapist
Reviewed with Supervisor

CPP Training Name: _____

Therapist Name: _____   Client Nickname: _____   Client ID: automatically generated

1. Please code when termination occurred: (check one & complete CPP logs as this will help us understand when family dropped)
   □ Foundational Phase   □ Core Intervention Phase   □ Termination Phase   □ Completed Termination Phase

2. Who initiated termination: (check one)
   □ Family   □ Therapist   □ Mutually agreed upon

3. Please code type of termination: (check one)
   □ Dropped (no termination process possible)
   □ Abrupt termination (informed of termination but full planned termination not possible)
   □ Planned termination

4. Change in functioning: (check one)
   □ Much worse   □ Slightly worse   □ No change   □ Slightly improved   □ Much improved

5. Prognosis: (check one)
   □ Poor   □ Fair   □ Good   □ Excellent   □ Unable to rate

6. Code reasons for closing below: (check all that apply)
   □ Completed treatment OR

Reason unknown	Caregiver challenges	Family did not want more treatment	Therapist left clinic or on leave
□ Moved	□ Mental illness	□ Felt not useful	□ Thought family better served by another treatment or agency
□ Too busy	□ Physical illness	□ Felt no more problems	□ Other, specify
□ Transportation problems	□ In drug treatment/residential	□ Other responsibilities	_____
□ Scheduling problems	□ In jail	□ Pressure from partner or other family	
□ Unexpected emergency	□ Lost custody of or visits w/ child	□ Unhappy with therapist	

7. Is part of the plan to transfer family to another CPP therapist?   □ No   □ Yes

© Ghosh Ippen, Van Horn & Lieberman, 2012 all rights reserved   DO NOT ALTER WITHOUT PERMISSION   (Termination Phase: Closing Form)   Page 1 of 11

PROCEDURAL FIDELITY: PLANNED TERMINATION

Instructions: Families often have great difficulty saying goodbye and may drop-out at any time during termination. This checklist is a guideline for termination planning when families are able to collaborate in the process. If treatment was abrupt, indicate which elements you were able to do.

☐ Not done (family dropped from treatment.)

		Done
1.	**Reflected on Termination** Before you began termination, remembered that goodbyes evoke profound feelings of rejection and loss no matter how well you prepare for and conduct them. Reviewed the caregiver and child's history of separation and loss to help you hypothesize about possible reactions they may have related to saying goodbye.	☐
2.	**Planned Termination with Caregiver** Began termination phase by talking alone w/ caregiver about ending treatment approximately 2 months before end date. If the child is an infant, this may be done with the child present. Rationale for 2 month period: Termination is integral to trauma treatment and a lot of "work" happens during this phase. In cases where a 2-month termination is not possible, try to incorporate the elements on the checklist and check the box for < 2 months.	☐ ☐ <2 mo
3.	**Planned Treatment Evaluation (Posttest)** As part of termination planning, scheduled treatment-outcome evaluation with caregiver.	☐
4.	**Completed Treatment Evaluation (Posttest)**	☐
5.	**Told Child About Termination** Let the child know treatment is ending at least one month before the end date. If child is an infant, had a session with the child present where you and the caregiver acknowledged that treatment will be ending.	☐ ☐ <1 mo
6.	**Jointly Planned Termination** Planned with caregiver and child (or caregiver alone if child is an infant) how treatment will end, how you will say goodbye.	☐
7.	**Processed the Goodbye** • Talked about how goodbyes can be hard and make you sad and angry • If appropriate, differentiated this goodbye from other goodbyes or separations • Allowed caregiver and child to be a part of the process and experience a range of feelings • Helped caregiver and child realize that they can feel connected to people even after they have said goodbye	☐
8.	**Counted Down the Sessions with Caregiver and Child** Every week reviewed how many more sessions until the end (e.g. with a calendar)	☐
9.	**Reviewed the Family's Story** Discussed the course of treatment and the family's treatment narrative • Where they were when they came here, whether things were hard, where things are now • The themes that emerged in treatment/play • If things are still not safe, how this affects them and how they can continue to talk about this and support each other	☐
10.	**Feedback: Treatment Evaluation** Met alone with caregiver and provided feedback from evaluation.	☐
11.	**Planned for the Future and Discussed Trauma Reminders with Caregivers** • Talked with caregivers about how symptoms may return with trauma reminders or when child is under stress (metaphor: posttraumatic stress reactions are like asthma, flare up from time to time when the person is under stress) • Helped caregivers reflect on how they have skills to help the child when this happens • Helped caregivers to recognize if child's symptoms are significant enough to perhaps warrant a return to treatment	☐
12.	**Held Last Session**	☐

(Termination Phase: Procedural Fidelity) Page 2 of 11

PROCEDURAL FIDELITY: CPP CONTACT LOG

Instructions: Use to track treatment participation during the termination phase

	COMPLETE FOR ANY CONTACT			COMPLETE FOR SCHEDULED SESSIONS (NOT PHONE CONTACTS)			
Date	Contact Type Assessment Case management Feedback Dyadic Treatment* Individual caregiver* Individual child* Cgiver phone – conversation Cgiver phone – message Collateral – meeting Collateral – phone Collateral – other Team meeting Other	Minutes	Session Status Show Cancel No Show	Reason for Not Attending Childcare problem Conflicting appointment Forgot Illness Therapist cancelled Transportation Weather Other	Who Attended (check all that apply) Target child Caregiver 1 Sibling 1 Caregiver 2 Sibling 2 Caregiver 3 Sibling 3 Caregiver 4 Sibling 4 Collateral: specify	Where Held Home Clinic Community Other	Session Counter (#)

MAKE ADDITIONAL COPIES OF PAGE AS NEEDED

CPP CORE INTERVENTION FIDELITY

Instructions:
Complete at the end of treatment to reflect on intervention fidelity during the termination phase.

REFLECTIVE PRACTICE FIDELITY

POTENTIAL SOURCES OF CHALLENGE	Level (select one)			
	No	Low	Moderate	Significant
Family is difficult to engage or work with	☐	☐	☐	☐
Family trauma history is likely to provoke negative reactions in any clinician	☐	☐	☐	☐
Systems are involved in complicated and/or conflictual ways with family/treatment	☐	☐	☐	☐
Therapist and caregiver have significantly different perspectives or cultural beliefs	☐	☐	☐	☐
Therapist knowledge and skill level (e.g. new therapist, new to the model or trauma work)	☐	☐	☐	☐
Limited access to safe reflective supervision or reflective consultation	☐	☐	☐	☐

THERAPIST REFLECTIVE PRACTICE CAPACITY	Therapist Capacity (select one)		
	Requires Development	Emerging	Acquired
Awareness of own emotional reactions			
In the moment (in session)	☐	☐	☐
Upon self-reflection (outside session)	☐	☐	☐
In supervision/consultation	☐	☐	☐
Awareness of own personal and/or cultural biases			
In the moment (in session)	☐	☐	☐
Upon self-reflection (outside session)	☐	☐	☐
In supervision/consultation	☐	☐	☐
Ability to consider multiple perspectives (caregiver's, child's, own)			
In the moment (in session)	☐	☐	☐
Upon self-reflection (outside session)	☐	☐	☐
In supervision/consultation	☐	☐	☐
Ability to recognize and regulate strong emotions prior to intervening (in the moment)	☐	☐	☐
Use of self-care practices to enhance ability to regulate	☐	☐	☐
USE OF EXTERNAL SUPPORTS			
Appropriately uses supervision and/or consultation with colleagues to:			
Process emotional reactions	☐	☐	☐
Consider alternative perspectives	☐	☐	☐
Seek new knowledge & new skills	☐	☐	☐

(Termination Phase: Intervention Fidelity)

EMOTIONAL PROCESS FIDELITY

POTENTIAL SOURCES OF CHALLENGE Degree to which in sessions. . .	No	Level (select one)		
		Low	Moderate	Significant
Caregiver is dysregulated or triggered	☐	☐	☐	☐
Caregiver is avoidant or shut down	☐	☐	☐	☐
Child is dysregulated or triggered	☐	☐	☐	☐
Child is avoidant or shut down	☐	☐	☐	☐

CAPACITY TO HANDLE EMOTIONAL CHALLENGES Therapist is able to . . .	Therapist Capacity (select one)		
	Requires Development	Emerging	Acquired
Identify when caregiver is not regulated	☐	☐	☐
Tolerate caregiver's strong emotional reactions	☐	☐	☐
Intervene in ways to help caregiver become regulated	☐	☐	☐
Identify when child is not regulated	☐	☐	☐
Tolerate child's strong emotional reactions	☐	☐	☐
Create a context where child's emotional response is understood	☐	☐	☐
Create a context where child is helped to regulate	☐	☐	☐

DYADIC-RELATIONAL FIDELITY

POTENTIAL SOURCES OF CHALLENGE Degree to which in the sessions. . .	No	Level (select one)		
		Low	Moderate	Significant
Caregiver and child have conflictual, competing agendas	☐	☐	☐	☐
Caregiver has difficulty understanding or tolerating child's behavior or temperament	☐	☐	☐	☐
Caregiver and/or child serve as trauma reminders to the other	☐	☐	☐	☐
Caregiver has unrealistic expectations of the child	☐	☐	☐	☐
Child has sensorimotor or affect regulation challenges	☐	☐	☐	☐

CAPACITY TO ADDRESS THE NEEDS OF CAREGIVER AND CHILD Therapist is able to . . .	Therapist Capacity (select one)		
	Requires Development	Emerging	Acquired
Balance attention between caregiver and child (tracking both)	☐	☐	☐
Hold/support child and caregiver perspectives	☐	☐	☐
Bridge/translate between caregiver & child (help them understand each other)	☐	☐	☐
Intervene in ways that strengthen the caregiver-child relationship	☐	☐	☐
Think about and support child's relationship with other important caregivers (e.g. father)	☐	☐	☐

(Termination Phase: Intervention Fidelity)   Page 5 of 11

TRAUMA FRAMEWORK FIDELITY

POTENTIAL SOURCES OF CHALLENGE Challenges related to. . .	No	Level (select one)		
		Low	Moderate	Significant
Child's history being unknown	□	□	□	□
Caregiver's history being unknown	□	□	□	□
Caregiver not fully acknowledging child's history or not agreeing to talk about it	□	□	□	□
Caregiver not having a trauma framework (does not view child behavior in light of history)	□	□	□	□
Caregiver being triggered and having difficulty thinking about child's past experience	□	□	□	□

CAPACITY TO INTERVENE WITHIN A TRAUMA FRAMEWORK Therapist is able to . . .	Therapist Capacity (select one)		
	Requires Development	Emerging	Acquired
Keep child's and caregiver's trauma history in mind		□	□
Think about how the child's and caregiver's history may be affecting interactions with each other and with the therapist	□	□	□
Frame interventions (e.g. affect regulation, improving relationships) within the broader context of the family's traumatic experiences (in addition to other contributing factors)		□	□
Directly talk about and bring up the family's trauma history when relevant	□	□	□

PROCEDURAL FIDELITY

POTENTIAL SOURCES OF CHALLENGE	No	Level (select one)		
		Low	Moderate	Significant
Scheduling challenges due to family illness, work, competing needs, or irregular visitation schedule make it difficult for family to attend weekly sessions	□	□	□	□
Scheduling challenges due to therapist illness, work schedule or competing needs make it difficult for therapist to hold weekly sessions	□	□	□	□
Family structure (e.g. multiple children) makes it difficult for therapist and caregiver to hold sessions focusing on the needs of individual children when clinically indicated	□	□	□	□
Home visiting environment often chaotic	□	□	□	□

CAPACITY TO CARRY OUT PROCEDURES Therapist is able to . . .	No	Response (check one)	
		Yes, But They Did Not Attend Regularly	Yes, Attended
Schedule sessions on a regular basis (generally 1x per week)	□	□	□
Give appropriate notice for vacation	□	□	□
Propose caregiver collateral sessions when . . . • Caregiver is triggered by child or child's play or in need of psychoeducation • Caregiver does not understand trauma as a potential cause of child's behaviors • Caregiver needs to share information with therapist (e.g. new traumatic events)	□ Not needed		

CPP CASE CONCEPTUALIZATION AND CONTENT FIDELITY

- Clinical Focus: Throughout the phase, degree to which the therapist's interventions addressed the objective:
  0=not at all a focus; 1=minor; 2=moderate; 3=significant
- Appropriateness: Under=Therapist should have focused more on this objective; Appropriate=Amount of therapeutic focus seems appropriate; Over=Therapist may have overly focused on this objective, to the detriment of other important objectives
- Progress Towards Objective
  3 = Established: Good enough to support development
  2 = Present but Unstable: Good under some conditions. Not fully consolidated. Lost in response to internal or external stress.
  1 = Emerging: Early manifestations
  0 = Primary Target/Urgent Concern: Immediate risk to development, relationship and/or therapeutic alliance

CPP OBJECTIVES	Clinical Focus (0-3)	Appropriateness (check one)			Progress Current (0-3)
		Under	Appropriate	Over	
CONVEY HOPE					
• Highlighted that change and growth are possible given positive steps the family has made	⸺	☐	☐	☐	⸺
• Provided realistic examples of potential pathways for healing, noting ways that caregiver efforts and treatment may lead to improved caregiver and child functioning					
• Helped the family connect to spiritual resources consistent with family traditions					
DEVELOP EMPATHIC RELATIONSHIP WITH FAMILY MEMBERS					
• Empathically listened to concerns: ☐ caregiver ☐ child's	⸺	☐	☐	☐	⸺
• Understood difficult behavior given past history & current context: ☐caregiver ☐child					
• Made warm supportive comments or recognized accomplishments: ☐ caregiver ☐child					
• Understood caregivers' mistrust of providers and reluctance to engage in treatment in light of their past history and current experiences with potentially punitive systems					
ENHANCE SAFETY					
Safety - Physical Safety (chart all safety risks separately)					
• Helped caregiver reflect on his/her history of physical endangerment and how it shapes current expectations regarding danger and safety	⸺	☐	☐	☐	⸺
• In a supportive, non-confrontational manner, directly addressed safety issues with caregiver with the goal of increasing caregiver awareness and mobilizing protective action					
• Balanced respect for the caregiver's psychological vulnerabilities with the need to address lapses in safety and destructive or self-destructive behavior					
• Encouraged the caregiver to develop an attitude that prioritizes safety as a core value for the caregiver, child, and family					
• Supported caregiver in engaging other family members in addressing risks to safety (including partners who may have been violent)					
• Focused on and addressed serious risks to physical safety, including risks within family relationships and permanency of placement					
• Engaged in safety planning					
• Assessed for and filed appropriate DCF reports for suspected abuse					

CPP OBJECTIVES	Clinical Focus (0-3)	Appropriateness (check one) Under	Appropriate	Over	Progress Current (0-3)
Safety - Environmental Context					
• Discussed ways that contextual risks (e.g. poverty, community violence, immigration related-risks, inadequate or unsafe housing, and inadequate access to services) affect child and family functioning	—	□	□	□	—
• Considered the impact of racism and historical trauma on child and family functioning					
Safety – Stabilization					
• Discussed provision/maintenance of basic needs					
• Provided case management to help family obtain basic needs	—	□	□	□	—
• Helped caregiver develop the capacities to obtain services and needs independently (to overcome barriers, communicate about needs, and collaborate with service providers)					
• Helped caregiver identify and address root causes of recurrent crisis and ongoing instability					
Safety & Consistency in Therapy					
• Acknowledged safety risks to participating in therapy: reporting, mandated nature, etc.					
• Encouraged consistent, on-time participation in therapy	—	□	□	□	—
• Created a consistent environment for treatment					
Perceived Safety					
• Identify misperceptions of danger or safety: □caregiver □child	—	□	□	□	—
• Foster accurate perceptions of danger and safety					
Safety within Caregiver-Child Relationships					
• Acknowledged past history of risks to safety: □ caregiver □ child					
• Highlighted the need for safe behavior while legitimizing feelings (e.g. child cannot hit others even though child is angry)					
• Fostered caregiver's ability to socialize child in ways that are consistent both with the caregiver's cultural values and beliefs and the family's context	—	□	□	□	—
• Identified factors that may interfere with caregivers capacity to socialize child, including environmental circumstances, strong emotions (e.g. guilt, fear, feelings of worthlessness), and prior history					
• Support caregiver's development of routines to enhance safety					
• Helped establish caregiver as a protective, benevolent, legitimate authority figure					

CPP OBJECTIVES	Clinical Focus (0-3)	Appropriateness (check one)			Progress Current (0-3)
		Under	Appropriate	Over	
STRENGTHEN FAMILY RELATIONSHIPS: PROMOTE EMOTIONAL RECIPROCITY					
• Helped caregiver reflect on how current expectations about relationships (child's or caregiver's) are shaped by past experience	—	☐	☐	☐	—
• Helped caregiver identify and explore origins of negative views/representations of the child					
• Helped caregiver think about how perceptions may affect behavior or interactions with child					
• Helped caregiver and child notice and respond supportively to each other's relational bids					
• Helped caregiver reflect and respond benevolently to the child's challenging behavior					
• Helped identify negative perceptions child may have about caregiver					
• Helped child understand and appreciate caregiver's efforts on the child and family's behalf					
• Helped caregiver and child learn ways to repair and connect after conflict					
• Helped caregiver and child consciously explore new ways of relating that promote trust, continuity, reciprocity, and pleasure					
COORDINATE CARE					
• Engaged in systematic efforts to obtain all relevant information about child history (e.g. CPS reports related to placement history)	—	☐	☐	☐	—
• Helped family members obtain needed referrals to other services					
• Communicated and coordinated care as needed with other service providers					
• Reflected on the needs of the entire family and prioritized services according to immediacy of needs					
• Took steps to ensure that risks to the child's safety were known and addressed effectively by the team of service providers involved with the family					
• Fostered a climate of transparency in communicating to caregiver the way that service providers are working together to ensure child safety					
STRENGTHEN DYADIC AFFECT REGULATION CAPACITIES					
• Fostered caregiver's ability to respond in soothing ways when child is upset	—	☐	☐	☐	—
• Fostered child's ability to use caregiver as a secure base					
• Provided developmental guidance around typical early childhood fears/anxieties					
• Acknowledged and helped find words for emotional experiences: ☐caregiver ☐child					
• Provided developmental guidance around emotional reactions: ☐caregiver ☐child					
• Taught, developed, or fostered strategies for regulating affect: ☐caregiver ☐child					
• Explored with caregiver links between emotional responses to past experiences and current emotional responses to child's behavior					

(Termination Phase: Intervention Fidelity)

CPP OBJECTIVES	Clinical Focus (0-3)	Appropriateness (check one) Under	Appropriateness Appropriate	Appropriateness Over	Progress Current (0-3)
STRENGTHEN DYADIC BODY-BASED REGULATION					
• Fostered body-based awareness, including awareness of physiological responses, particularly as they relate to stress ☐caregiver ☐child	—	☐	☐	☐	—
• Fostered understanding and identification of body-based trauma reminders					
• Helped caregiver learn/engage in body-based regulation techniques to regulate affect					
• Helped caregiver & child learn or use body-based regulation techniques to soothe child					
• Helped caregiver and child exchange physical expressions of care					
• Enhanced understanding of safe body-based boundaries					
SUPPORT CHILD'S RELATIONSHIP WITH OTHER IMPORTANT CAREGIVERS					
• Helped caregivers understand the child's perspective and need for positive representations of alternative caregivers (e.g. father, step-parent, foster parents)	—	☐	☐	☐	—
• Helped caregiver support the child in integrating the positive and negative aspects of other caregivers					
• Shared the concept of angel moments and the importance of helping the child hold on to positive memories involving alternative caregivers, even when relationships between caregivers are strained					
• Supported child in developing an age-appropriate understanding of the family history					
• Supported the child in understanding that different family members have different points of view and different ways of relating to each other and to the child					
ENHANCE UNDERSTANDING OF THE MEANING OF BEHAVIOR					
• Helped caregiver notice behavior (child's, caregiver's, or another caregiver's)	—	☐	☐	☐	—
• Provided developmental guidance regarding age appropriate behavior and developmental meaning of behavior					
• Provided developmental guidance around how children learn and develop					
• Helped caregiver consider (reflect on) the meaning of child and/or caregiver behavior (thinking about developmental stage, past experiences, cultural beliefs)					
• Helped enhance reflective functioning in caregivers and child					
SUPPORT CHILD IN RETURNING TO A NORMAL DEVELOPMENTAL TRAJECTORY					
• Supported adaptive behavior and normative developmental activities	—	☐	☐	☐	—
• Supported healthy non-trauma play					
• Supported positive identity development					
• Fostered caregiver's efforts to engage in age appropriate activities					
• Provided case management to help engage child in age appropriate activities (e.g. school)					

(Termination Phase: Intervention Fidelity)   Page 10 of 11

CPP OBJECTIVES	Clinical Focus (0-3)	Appropriateness (check one)			Progress Current (0-3)
		Under	Appropriate	Over	
NORMALIZE THE TRAUMATIC RESPONSE					
• Acknowledged effects of child's and caregivers' experience of trauma and historical trauma	___	☐	☐	☐	___
• Provided psychoeducation: Impact of trauma, including common symptoms & PTSD, trauma reminders and how they affect child and caregiver					
• Helped caregiver anticipate developmental changes in child's processing of the trauma					
SUPPORT DYAD IN ACKNOWLEDGING THE IMPACT OF TRAUMA					
• Promoted a deep emotional acknowledgement of the impact of trauma while attending and responding to dysregulated (over or under) affective states	___	☐	☐	☐	___
• Helped caregiver acknowledge what child has witnessed & remembers					
• Helped caregiver and child understand each other's reality (with regards to the trauma)					
• Helped caregiver & child identify and cope with trauma reminders					
• Helped caregiver think about his/her own trauma history (ghosts in the nursery) and ways this history may affect her/him and the way s/he parents					
HELP DYAD DIFFERENTIATE BETWEEN THEN AND NOW					
• Highlighted difference between past and present circumstances	___	☐	☐	☐	___
• Helped dyad understand that they can make new choices					
• Helped child and caregiver become aware of the difference between reliving and remembering by helping them identify traumatic triggers and pointing out the different circumstances in the past and the present					
HELP DYAD PUT THE TRAUMATIC EXPERIENCE IN PERSPECTIVE					
• Supported caregiver and child in making meaning (e.g. creating a story, using ritual, connecting with spiritual beliefs)	___	☐	☐	☐	___
• Integrate historical trauma as part of the family and personal narrative					
• Worked with beliefs (existential challenges) around why the traumatic events happened (e.g. that they are bad, being punished)					
• Helped caregiver and child see trauma as something that happened to them but that does not define them					
• Supported family's advocacy work or work to help others					
• Fostered acceptance around how these experiences have shaped the caregiver and child's sense of self					
• Helped the family find pathways to post trauma growth and joy					
• Encouraged appreciation of goodness, beauty, and hope					

REFERENCES

Achenbach, T. M. (1991). *Manual for the Child Behavior Checklist 4–18 and 1991 Profile*. Burlington: University of Vermont, Department of Psychiatry.

Achenbach, T. M., & Edelbrock, C. S. (1983). *Manual for the Child Behavior Checklist and Revised Child Behavioral Profile*. Burlington: University of Vermont, Department of Psychiatry.

Ainsworth, M. D. S. (1969). Object relations, dependency, and attachment: A theoretical review of the infant-mother relationship. *Child Development, 40*, 969–1025.

Ainsworth, M. D. S., Blehar, M. C., Waters, E., & Wall, S. (1978). *Patterns of attachment: A psychological study of the strange situation*. Hillsdale, NJ: Lawrence Erlbaum Associates.

American Academy of Child and Adolescent Psychiatry. (2010). Practice parameter for the assessment and treatment of children and adolescents with posttraumatic stress disorder. *Journal of the American Academy of Child & Adolescent Psychiatry, 49*, 414–430.

American Psychiatric Association. (1994). *Diagnostic and statistical manual of mental disorders* (4th ed.). Washington, DC: Author.

Bateson, G. (1972). Pathologies of epistemology. In W. P. Lebra (Ed.), *Transcultural research in mental health* (pp. 383–390). Oxford, England: University of Hawaii Press.

Bayley, N. (1969). *Scales of Infant Development manual*. New York, NY: The Psychological Corporation.

Beck, A. T., Ward, C. H., Mendelson, M., Mock, M., & Erbaugh, J. (1961). An inventory for measuring depression. *Archives of General Psychiatry, 4,* 561–571.

Benedek, T. (1959). Parenthood as a developmental phase: A contribution to the libido theory. *Journal of the American Psychoanalytic Association, 7,* 389–417.

Benjamin, J. (1988). *The bonds of love: Psychoanalysis, feminism and the problem of domination*: New York, NY: Pantheon.

Blake, D. D., Weathers, F., Nagy, L., Kaloupek, D. G., Klauminzer, G., Charney, D., & Keane T. M. (1990), Clinician Administered PTSD Scale. *Behavior Therapy, 18,* 12–14.

Bowlby, J. (1969/1982). *Attachment and loss: Vol. 1. Attachment* (2nd ed.). New York, NY: Basic Books.

Bowlby, J. (1973). *Attachment and loss, Vol. 2. Separation.* New York, NY: Basic Books.

Bowlby, J. (1980). *Attachment and loss, Vol. 3. Loss, sadness, and depression.* New York, NY: Basic Books.

Bowlby, J. (1988). *The secure base: Parent-child attachments and healthy human development.* New York, NY: Basic Books.

Bretherton, I., Oppenheim, D., Buchsbaum, H., Emde, R. N., & the MacArthur Narrative Group. (1990). *MacArthur Story Stem Battery.* Unpublished manual.

Briere, J. (2005). *Trauma Symptom Checklist for Young Children (TSCYC): Professional manual.* Odessa, FL: Psychological Assessment Resources.

Bronfenbrenner, U. (1979). Contexts of child rearing: Problems and prospects. *American Psychologist, 34,* 844–850.

Campbell, S., Shaw, D. S., & Gilliom, M. (2000). Early externalizing behavior problems: Toddlers and preschoolers at risk for early maladjustment. *Development and Psychopathology, 12*(3) , 467–488.

Cannon, W. B. (1932). *Effects of strong emotions.* Chicago, IL: University of Chicago Press.

Carrion, V. G., Weems, C. F., Ray, R., & Reiss, A. L. (2002). Towards an empirical definition of pediatric PTSD: The phenomenology of PTSD symptoms in youth. *Journal of the American Academy of Child & Adolescent Psychiatry, 41*, 166–173.

Chess, S., & Thomas, A. (1984). *Origins and evolution of behavior disorders: From infancy to early adult life.* Cambridge, MA: Harvard University Press.

Cicchetti, D., & Lynch, M. (1993). Toward an ecological/transactional model of community violence and child maltreatment: Consequences for children's development. *Psychiatry, 56*, 96–118.

Cicchetti, D., Rogosch, F. A., & Toth, S. L. (2000). The efficacy of toddler-parent psychotherapy for fostering cognitive development in offspring. *Journal of Abnormal Child Psychology, 28*, 135–148.

Cicchetti, D., Rogosch, F. A., & Toth, S. L. (2006). Fostering secure attachment in infants in maltreating families through preventive interventions. *Development and Psychopathology, 18*, 623–650.

Cicchetti, D., Rogosch, F. A., & Toth, S. L. (2011). The effects of child maltreatment and polymorphisms of the serotonin transporter and dopamine D4 receptor genes on infant attachment and intervention efficacy. *Development and Psychopathology, 23*, 357–372.

Cicchetti, D., Rogosch, F. A., Toth, S. L., & Sturge-Apple, M. L. (2011). Normalizing the development of cortisol regulation in maltreated infants through preventive interventions. *Development and Psychopathology, 23*, 789–800.

Cicchetti, D., Toth, S. L., & Rogosch, F. A. (1999). The efficacy of toddler-parent psychotherapy to increase attachment security in offspring of depressed mothers. *Attachment and Human Development, 1*, 34–66.

Cohen, J. A., Mannarino, A. P., & Deblinger, E. (2006). *Treating trauma and traumatic grief in children and adolescents.* New York, NY: Guilford Press.

Crusto, C. A., Whitson, M. L., Walling, S. M., Feinn, R., Friedman, S. R., Reynolds, J., ... Kaufman, J. S. (2010). Posttraumatic stress among young urban children exposed to family violence and other potentially traumatic events. *Journal of Traumatic Stress, 23*, 716–724.

Davidson, T. (1978). *Conjugal crime: Understanding and changing the wife beating pattern*. New York, NY: Hawthorne.

Derogatis, L. R. (1994). *Symptom Checklist-90-R: Administration, scoring, and procedures manual*. Minneapolis, MN: National Computer Systems.

Drell, M., Siegel, C., & Gaensbauer, T. (1993). Posttraumatic stress disorders. In C. Zeanah (Ed.), *Handbook of infant mental health* (pp. 291–304). New York, NY: Guilford Press.

Epstein, K., Dorado, J., Dolce, L., Loomis, B., Speziale, K., Aleman, N., & Marcin, M. (2014). *Transforming stress and trauma: Fostering wellness and resilience* [PowerPoint slides]. Training curriculum presented by the San Francisco Department of Public Health, Trauma Informed System Initiative, San Francisco, CA.

Erikson, E. H. (1964). *Childhood and society* (2nd ed.). Oxford, England: W. W. Norton.

Eth, S. E., & Pynoos, R. S. (1985). *Post-traumatic stress disorder in children*. Washington, DC: American Psychiatric Press.

Fairbairn, W. R. D. (1954). *An object relations theory of personality*. New York, NY: Basic Books.

Fantuzzo, J. W., & Fusco, R. A. (2007). Children's direct exposure to types of domestic violence crime: A population-based investigation. *Journal of Family Violence, 22*, 543–552.

Finkelhor, D., Ormrod, R., Turner, H., & Hamby, S. L. (2005). The victimization of children and youth: A comprehensive national survey. *Child Maltreatment, 10*(1), 5–25.

Fonagy, P. (2010). *Attachment theory and psychoanalysis*. New York, NY: Other Press.

Fonagy, P., Gergely, G., Jurist, E. L., & Target, M. (2002). *Affect regulation, mentalization, and the development of the self*. New York, NY: Other Press.

Fraiberg, S. H. (1959). *The magic years: Understanding and handling the problems of early childhood*. Oxford, England: Charles Scribners' Sons.

Fraiberg, S. (1980). *Clinical studies in infant mental health: The first year of life*. New York, NY: Basic Books.

Fraiberg, S. H., Adelson, E., & Shapiro, V. (1975). Ghosts in the nursery: A psychoanalytic approach to the problems of impaired infant-mother relationships. *Journal of the American Academy of Child and Adolescent Psychiatry, 14*, 387–422.

Freud, A. (1936/1966). *The ego and the mechanisms of defenses*. Madison, CT: International Universities Press.

Freud, S. (1923/1966). The ego and the id. In J. Strachey (Ed. & Trans.), *The standard edition of the complete psychological works of Sigmund Freud* (Vol. 19, pp. 12–66). London, England: Hogarth Press.

Freud, S. (1926/1959). Inhibitions, symptoms, and anxiety. In J. Strachey (Ed., & Trans.), *The standard edition of the complete psychological works of Sigmund Freud* (Vol. 20, pp. 87–156). London, England: Hogarth Press. (Original work published 1926).

Gaensbauer, T. J. (1994). Therapeutic work with a traumatized toddler. *The Psychoanalytic Study of the Child, 49*, 412–433.

Gaensbauer, T. J. (1995). Trauma in the preverbal period: Symptoms, memories, and developmental impact. *The Psychoanalytic Study of the Child, 50*, 122–149.

Ghosh Ippen, C., Ford, J., Racusin, R., Acker, M., Bosquet, K., & Rogers, C. (2002). *Trauma Events Screening Inventory–Parent Report Revised*. Unpublished measure, The Child Trauma Research Project of the Early Trauma Network and The National Center for PTSD Dartmouth Child Trauma Research Group. San Francisco, CA.

Ghosh Ippen, C., Harris, W. W., Van Horn, P., & Lieberman, A. F. (2011). Traumatic and stressful events in early childhood: Can treatment help those at highest risk? *Child Abuse and Neglect, 35*, 504–513.

Ghosh Ippen, C., Van Horn, P. J., & Lieberman, A. F. (2014). *Child–Parent Psychotherapy: Training manual* (Version 2). Unpublished manuscript, University of California, San Francisco.

Henggeler, S. W., Schoenwald, S. K., Borduin, C. M., Rowland, M. D., & Cunningham, P. B. (1998). *Multisystemic treatment of antisocial behavior in children and adolescents.* New York, NY: Guilford Press.

Herman, J. L. (1992). Complex PTSD: A syndrome of survivors of prolonged and repeated trauma. *Journal of Traumatic Stress, 5,* 377–391.

Horowitz, F. D., & O'Brien, M. (1986). Gifted and talented children: State of knowledge and directions for research. *American Psychologist, 41,* 1147–1152.

Kagan, J. (1981). *The second year: The emergence of self-awareness.* Cambridge, MA: Harvard University Press.

Kalmus, D. (1984). The intergenerational transmission of marital aggression. *Journal of Marriage and the Family, 46,* 11–19.

Kernberg, O. (1976). *Object relations theory and clinical psychoanalysis.* New York, NY: Aronson.

Klein, M. (1932). *The psycho-analysis of children.* New York, NY: W. W. Norton.

Lieberman, A. F. (1991). Attachment theory and infant–parent psychotherapy: Some conceptual, clinical, and research considerations. In D. Cicchetti & S. Toth (Eds.), *Rochester Symposium on Developmental Psychopathology, Volume 3: Models and Integrations* (pp. 262–287). Rochester, NY: University of Rochester Press.

Lieberman, A. F. (1992) Infant-parent psychotherapy with toddlers. *Development and Psychopathology, 4,* 559–575.

Lieberman, A. F. (1993). *The emotional life of the toddler.* New York, NY: The Free Press.

Lieberman, A. F. (1997). Toddlers' internalization of maternal attributions as a factor in quality of attachment. In L. Atkinson & K. J. Zucker (Eds.), *Attachment and psychopathology* (pp. 277–291). New York, NY: Guilford Press.

Lieberman, A. F. (1999). Negative maternal attributions: Effects on toddlers' sense of self. *Psychoanalytic Inquiry, 19,* 737–756.

Lieberman, A. F. (2004). Child–parent psychotherapy: A relationship-based approach to the treatment of mental health disorders in infancy and early childhood. In A. J. Sameroff, S. C. McDonough, & K. L. Rosenblum (Eds.), *Treating parent–infant relationship problems* (pp. 97–122). New York, NY: Guilford Press.

Lieberman, A. F., Chu, A., Van Horn, P., & Harris, W. M. (2011). Trauma in early childhood: Empirical evidence and clinical implications. *Development and Psychopathology, 23,* 397–410.

Lieberman, A. F., & Ghosh Ippen, C. (2014). *Introducing Child-Parent Psychotherapy to children and their caregivers.* Unpublished manuscript, University of California, San Francisco.

Lieberman, A. F., Ghosh Ippen, C., & Van Horn, P. J. (2006). Child–parent psychotherapy: Six-month follow-up of a randomized control trial. *Journal of the American Academy of Child & Adolescent Psychiatry, 45,* 913–918.

Lieberman, A. F., Padron, E., Van Horn, P., & Harris, W. (2005). Angels in the nursery: The intergenerational transmission of beneficial parental influences. *Infant Mental Health Journal, 26,* 504–520.

Lieberman, A. F., & Pawl, J. H. (1993). Infant–parent psychotherapy. In C. Zeanah (Ed.), *Handbook of infant mental health* (pp. 427–442). New York, NY: Guilford Press.

Lieberman, A. F., Silverman, R., & Pawl, J. H. (2000). Infant–parent psychotherapy: Core concepts and current approaches. In C. Zeanah (Ed.), *Handbook of infant mental health* (2nd ed., pp. 472–484). New York, NY: Guilford Press.

Lieberman, A. F., & Van Horn, P. (1998). Attachment, trauma, and domestic violence: Implications for child custody. *Child and adolescent psychiatric clinics of North America, 7,* 423–443.

Lieberman, A. F., & Van Horn, P. (2005). *Don't hit my mommy!: A manual for child–parent psychotherapy with young witnesses of family violence.* Washington, DC: ZERO TO THREE.

Lieberman, A. F., & Van Horn, P. (2008). *Psychotherapy with infants and young children: Repairing the effects of stress and trauma on early attachment.* New York, NY: Guilford Press.

Lieberman, A. F., Van Horn, P. J., & Ghosh Ippen, C. (2005). Toward evidence-based treatment: Child-parent psychotherapy with preschoolers exposed to marital violence. *Journal of the American Academy of Child & Adolescent Psychiatry, 44,* 1241–1248.

Lieberman, A. F., Weston, D. R., & Pawl, J. H. (1991). Preventive intervention and outcome with anxiously attached dyads. *Child Development, 62,* 199–209.

Lieberman, A. F., & Zeanah, C. H. (1995). Disorders of attachment in infancy. *Child and Adolescent Psychiatric Clinics of North America, 4,* 571–587.

Luborsky, L. (1984). *Principals of psychoanalytic psychotherapy.* New York, NY: Basic Books.

MacLean, K. L. (2009). *Moody cow meditates.* New York, NY: Simon and Schuster.

Mahler, M., Pine, F., & Bergman, A. (1975). *The psychological birth of the human infant.* New York, NY: Basic Books.

Main, M., & Hesse, E. (1990). Parents' unresolved traumatic experiences are related to infant disorganized attachment status: Is frightened and/or frightening parental behavior the linking mechanism? In M. T. Greenberg, D. Cicchetti, & M. Cummings (Eds.), *Attachment in the preschool years: Theory, research, and intervention* (pp. 161–182). Chicago, IL: University of Chicago Press.

Marans, S., & Adelman, A. (1997). Experiencing violence in a developmental context. In J. D. Osofsky (Ed.), *Children in a violent society* (pp. 202–223). New York, NY: Guilford Press.

Margolin, G. (1998). Effects of domestic violence on children. In P. K. Trickett & C. J. Schellenbach (Eds.), *Violence against children in the family and the community* (pp. 57–102). Washington, DC: American Psychological Association.

Marmar, C., Foy, D., Kagan, B., & Pynoos, R. (1993). An integrated approach for treating posttraumatic stress. In J. M. Oldham, M. B. Riva, & A. Tasman (Eds.), *American Psychiatric Press review of psychiatry* (vol. 12, pp. 238–272). Washington, DC: American Psychiatric Press.

Olds, D. L., & Kitzman, H. (1993). Review of research on home visiting for pregnant women and parents of young children. *The Future of Children: Home Visiting*, 3(3), 53–92.

Osofsky, J. D. (1995). The effects of exposure to violence on young children. *American Psychologist, 50*, 782–788.

Osofsky, J. D. (Ed.). (2004). *Young children and trauma: Intervention and treatment.* New York, NY: Guilford Press.

Osofsky, J. D. (2005). Professional training in infant mental health: Introductory overview. *Infants and Young Children, 18*, 266–268.

Osofsky, J. D., & Lederman, C. (2004). Healing the child in juvenile court. In J. D. Osofsky (Ed.), *Young children and trauma: Intervention and treatment* (pp. 221–241). New York, NY: Guilford Press.

Osofsky, J. D., & Scheeringa, M. S. (1997). Community and domestic violence exposure: Effects on development and psychopathology. In D. Cicchetti & S. L. Toth (Eds.), *Rochester Symposium on Developmental Psychopathology (Vol. 8, Developmental Perspectives on Trauma: Theory, Research, and Intervention*, pp. 155–180). Rochester, NY: University of Rochester Press.

Parson, E. R. (1995). Post-traumatic stress and coping in an inner-city child: Traumatogenic witnessing of interparental violence and murder. *The Psychoanalytic Study of the Child, 50*, 252–271.

Patterson, G. R. (1982). *Coercive family process* (Vol. 3). Eugene, OR: Castalia.

Pawl, J. (1995). On supervision. In L. Eggbeer & E. Fenichel (Eds.). *Educating and supporting the infant/family work force: Models, methods, and materials* (pp. 21–29). Arlington, VA: ZERO TO THREE.

Pawl, J. H., & St. John, M. (1998). *How you are is as important as what you do.* Washington, DC: ZERO TO THREE.

Peled, E. (2000). Parenting by men who abuse women: Issues and dilemmas. *British Journal of Social Work, 30,* 25–36.

Peltz, J. S., Rogge, R. D., Rogosch, F. A., Cicchetti, D., & Toth, S. L. (2015, July 20). The benefits of Child–Parent Psychotherapy to marital satisfaction. *Family, Systems, and Health.* Advance online publication. http://dx.doi.org/10.1037/fsh0000149

Piaget, J. (1959). Die relationale methode in der psychologie der wahrnehmung. [The method of relations in the psychology of perception.] *Zeitschrift fuer Experimentelle und Angewandte Psychologie, 6,* 77–94.

Pruett, K. D. (1979). Home treatment for two infants who witnessed their mother's murder. *Journal of the American Academy of Child & Adolescent Psychiatry, 18,* 647–657.

Pynoos, R. S. (1990). Posttraumatic stress disorder in children and adolescents. In B. Garfinkel, G. Carlson, & E. B. Weller (Eds.), *Psychiatric disorders in children and adolescents* (pp. 48–63). Philadelphia, PA: W. B. Saunders.

Pynoos, R. S. (1993). Traumatic stress and developmental psychopathology in children and adolescents. In J. M. Oldham, M. B. Riba, & A. Tasman (Eds.), *American Psychiatric Press Review of Psychiatry* (Vol. 12, pp. 205–238). Washington, DC: American Psychiatric Association.

Pynoos, R. S., & Eth, S. (Eds.). (1985). *Post-traumatic stress disorder in children.* Washington, DC: American Psychiatric Association Press.

Pynoos, R. S., & Nader, K. (1988). Children who witness the sexual assaults of their mothers. *Journal of the American Academy of Child & Adolescent Psychiatry, 27,* 567–572.

Pynoos, R. S., Steinberg, A. M., & Goenjian, A. (1996). Traumatic stress in childhood and adolescence: Recent developments and current controversies. In B. A. van der Kolk & A. C. McFarlane (Eds.), *Traumatic stress: The effects of overwhelming experience on mind, body, and society* (pp. 331–358). New York, NY: Guilford Press.

Pynoos, R. S., Steinberg, A. M., & Piacentini, J. C. (1999). Developmental psychopathology of childhood traumatic stress and implications for associated anxiety disorders. *Biological Psychiatry, 46*, 1542–1554.

Pynoos, R. S., Steinberg, A. M., & Wraith, R. (1995). A developmental model of childhood traumatic stress. In D. Cicchetti & D. Cohen (Eds.), *Manual of developmental psychopathology: Risk, disorder, and adaptation* (Vol. 2., pp. 72–95). New York, NY: Wiley.

Reid, J. B., & Eddy, J. M. (1997). The prevention of antisocial behavior: Some considerations in the search for effective interventions. In D. M. Stoff, J. Breiling, & J. D. Maser (Eds.), *Handbook of antisocial behavior* (pp. 343–356). Hoboken, NJ: John Wiley and Sons

Robins, L., Helzer, J., Orvaschel, H., Anthony, J., Blazer, D. G., Burnam, A., et al. (1985). The Diagnostic Interview Schedule. In W. Eaton & L. Kessler (Eds.), *Epidemiologic field methods in psychiatry* (pp. 143–170). New York, NY: Academic Press.

Robinson, J., Mantz–Simmons, L., Macfie, J., & the MacArthur Narrative Working Group. (1996). *The MacArthur narrative coding manual— Rochester revision.* Unpublished manuscript.

Rossman, B. B. R., Hughes, H. M., & Rosenberg, M. S. (2000). *Children and interparental violence: The impact of exposure.* Philadelphia, PA: Brunner/Mazel.

Roth, A., & Fonagy, P. (2014). *What works for whom? A critical review of psychotherapy research* (3rd ed.). New York, NY: Guilford Press.

Rozental, S. (1967). *My father Niels Bohr: His life and work as seen by his friends and colleagues.* Amsterdam, the Netherlands: North-Holland Publishing.

Sameroff, A., & Emde, R. N. (Eds.). (1989). *Relationship disturbances in early childhood: A developmental approach.* New York, NY: Basic Books.

Sapolsky, R. (1994). *Why zebras don't get ulcers: A guide to stress, stress-related diseases, and coping.* New York, NY: W. H. Freeman.

Scheeringa, M. S., & Zeanah, C. H. (1995). Symptom expression and trauma variables in children under 48 months of age. *Infant Mental Health Journal, 16*, 259–270.

Scheeringa, M. S., & Zeanah, C. H. (2001). A relational perspective on PTSD in early childhood. *Journal of Traumatic Stress, 14*, 799–815.

Scheeringa, M. S., Zeanah, C. H., Drell, M. J., & Larrieu, J. A. (1995). Two approaches to the diagnosis of posttraumatic stress disorder in infancy and early childhood. *Journal of the American Academy of Child & Adolescent Psychiatry, 34*, 191–200.

Scheeringa, M. S., Zeanah, C. H., Myers, L., & Putnam, F. W. (2003). New findings on alternative criteria for PTSD in preschool children. *Journal of the American Academy of Child and Adolescent Psychiatry, 42*, 561–570.

Segal, M. (1998a). *Your child at play: One to two years* (2nd ed.). New York, NY: Newmarket Press.

Segal, M. (1998b). *Your child at play: Two to three years* (2nd ed.). New York, NY: Newmarket Press.

Shalev, A. Y. (2000). Post-traumatic stress disorder: Diagnosis, history and life course. In D. Nutt, J. R. T. Davidson, & J. Zohar (Eds.), *Post-traumatic stress disorder: Diagnosis, management and treatment* (pp. 1–15). London, England: Martin Dunitz.

Sharfstein, S. (2006, February 3). New task force will address early childhood violence. *Psychiatric News, 41*(3). Retrieved from http://psychnews.psychiatryonline.org/doi/10.1176/pn.41.3.0003

Silverman, R. C., & Lieberman, A. F. (1999). Negative maternal attributions, projective identification, and the intergenerational transmission of violent relational patterns. *Psychoanalytic Dialogues, 9*, 161–186.

Slade, A. (1994). Making meaning and making believe: Their role in the clinical process. In A. Slade & D. Wolf (Eds.), *Children at play: Clinical and developmental approaches to meaning and representation* (pp. 81–110). New York, NY: Oxford University Press.

Slade, A. (2014). Imagining fear: Attachment, threat, and psychic experience. *International Journal of Relational Perspectives, 24*(3), 253–266.

Slade, A., & Wolf, D. (Eds.). (1994). *Children at play: Clinical and developmental approaches to meaning and representation.* New York, NY: Oxford University Press.

Stern, D. N. (1995). *The motherhood constellation: A unified view of parent-infant psychotherapy.* New York, NY: Basic Books.

Stern, D. N., Sander, L. W., Nahum, J. P., Harrison, A. M., Lyons-Ruth, K., Morgan, A. C., et al. (1998). Noninterpretative mechanisms in psychoanalytic therapy. The "something more" than interpretation. *International Journal of Psycho-Analysis, 79,* 903–921.

St. John, M. S., Thomas, K., & Norona, C. R., with the Irving Harris Foundation Professional Development Network Tenets Working Group. (2012). Infant mental health professional development: Together in the struggle for social justice. *Zero to Three, 33*(2), 13–22.

Stronach, P. E., Toth, L. S., Rogosch F., & Cicchetti, D. (2013). Preventive interventions and sustained attachment security in maltreated children. *Development and Psychopathology, 25,* 919–930.

Terr, L. C. (1981). Forbidden games: Post-traumatic child's play. *Journal of the American Academy of Child & Adolescent Psychiatry, 20,* 740–759.

Terr, L. C. (1991). Childhood traumas: An outline and overview. *American Journal of Psychiatry, 148,* 10–20.

Teti, D. M., Nakagawa, M., Das, R., & Wirth, O. (1991). Security of attachment between preschoolers and their mothers. Relations among social interaction, parenting stress, and mothers' sorts of the Attachment Q-Set. *Developmental Psychology, 27,* 440–447.

Toth, S. L., Gravener-Davis, J. A., Guild, D. J., & Cicchetti, D. (2013). Relational interventions for child maltreatment: Past, present, and future perspectives. *Development and Psychopathology, 25,* 1601–1617.

Toth, S. L., Manly, J. T., & Nilsen, W. J. (2008). From research to practice:

Lessons learned. *Journal of Applied Developmental Psychology, 29*, 317–325.

Toth, S. L., Maughan, A., Manly, J. T., Spagnola, M., & Cicchetti, D. (2002). The relative efficacy of two interventions in altering maltreated preschool children's representational models: Implications for attachment theory. *Developmental Psychopathology, 14*, 877–908.

Toth, S. L., Rogosch, F. A., Manly, J. T., & Cicchetti, D. (2006). The efficacy of toddler-parent psychotherapy to reorganize attachment in the young offspring of mothers with major depressive disorder: A randomized preventive trial. *Journal of Consulting and Clinical Psychology, 74*, 1006–1016.

U.S. Department of Health and Human Services. (2010). *Child maltreatment 2009.* Retrieved from www.acf.hhs.gov/programs/cb/stats_research/index.htm#can

van der Kolk, B. (1987). *Psychological trauma.* Washington, DC: American Psychiatric Press.

van der Kolk, B. (2014). *The body keeps the score: Brain, mind, and body in the healing of trauma.* New York, NY: Penguin.

van der Kolk, B. A. (1996). The body keeps score: Approaches to the psychobiology of posttraumatic stress disorder. In B. A. van der Kolk & A. C. McFarlane (Eds.), *Traumatic stress: The effects of overwhelming experience on mind, body, and society* (pp. 214–241). New York, NY: Guilford Press.

van IJzendoorn, M. H., & Kroonenberg, P. M. (1988). Cross-cultural patterns of attachment: A meta-analysis of the strange situation. *Child Development, 59*(1), 147–156.

Waltz, J., Addis, M. E., Koerner, K., & Jacobson, N. S. (1993). Testing the integrity of a psychotherapy protocol: Assessment of adherence and competence. *Journal of Consulting and Clinical Psychology, 61*, 620–630.

Waters, E. (1995). Appendix A: The Attachment Q set (version 3.0). *Monographs of the Society for Research in Child Development, 60*(2–3), 234–246.

Webster-Stratton, C. (1996). Early intervention with videotape modeling: Programs for families of young children with oppositional defiant disorder or conduct disorder. In E. D. Hibbs & P. S. Jensen (Eds.), *Psychosocial treatment research of child and adolescent disorders* (pp. 435–474). Washington, DC: American Psychological Association.

Wechsler, D. (1989). *Wechsler Preschool and Primary Scale of Intelligence—Revised manual.* San Antonio, TX: The Psychological Corporation.

Weiss, J. (1993). *How psychotherapy works: Process and technique.* New York, NY: Guilford Press.

Winnicott, D. W. (1962). Ego integration in child development. In M. M. Khan (Ed.), *The maturational processes and the facilitating environment* (pp. 56–63). London, England: Hogarth Press.

Winnicott, D. W. (1965). The theory of the parent-infant relationship. In D. W. Winnicott (Ed.), *The maturational processes and the facilitating environment* (pp. 37–55). New York, NY: International Universities Press.

Winnicott, D. W. (1971). *Playing and reality.* Oxford, England: Penguin.

Wolfe, J. W., Kimerling, R., Brown, P. J., Chrestman, K. R., & Levin, K. (1996). Psychometric review of The Life Stressor Checklist—Revised. In B. H. Stamm (Ed.), *Measurement of stress, trauma, and adaptation* (pp. 198–201). Lutherville, MD: Sidran Press.

Wolfenstein, M. (1966). How is mourning possible? *The Psychoanalytic Study of the Child, 21,* 93–123.

ZERO TO THREE. (2005). *Diagnostic classification of mental health and developmental disorders of infancy and early childhood (rev. ed.) (DC: 0-3R).* Washington, DC: Author.

ABOUT THE AUTHORS

Alicia F. Lieberman, PhD, is Irving Harris Endowed Chair in Infant Mental Health, professor at the University of California–San Francisco Department of Psychiatry, and director, Child Trauma Research Program, San Francisco General Hospital. She is the project director for the Early Trauma Treatment Network, a program of the SAMHSA-funded National Child Traumatic Stress Network (NCTSN) that has the mission of raising the standard of care and improving access to services for traumatized children and their families. Born in Paraguay, she received her BA degree at the Hebrew University of Jerusalem and PhD from The Johns Hopkins University. She is a member of the Board of Directors of ZERO TO THREE: National Center for Infants, Toddlers, and Families, She is the author of *The Emotional Life of the Toddler*, which has been translated to several languages; co-author with Patricia Van Horn of *Psychotherapy With Infants and Young Children: Repairing the Effect of Stress and Trauma on Early Attachment*, co-author with Nancy Compton, Patricia Van Horn, and Chandra Ghosh Ippen of *Losing a Parent to Death in the Early Years*; and editor, with Serena Wieder and Emily Fenichel, of *DC: 0–3 Casebook: A Guide to the Use of ZERO TO THREE's Diagnostic Classification of Mental Health and Developmental Disorders of Infancy and Early Childhood*. As a Jewish Latina, Dr. Lieberman has a special interest in cultural issues involving young children and their families.

Chandra Ghosh Ippen, PhD, is associate director of the Child Trauma Research Program at the University of California, San Francisco and the director of dissemination for Child-Parent Psychotherapy (CPP), an evidence-based treatment for young children who have experienced trauma. She is a clinician, researcher, and trainer and has co-authored more than 20 publications related to trauma and diversity-informed practice. Publications include a randomized trial documenting the efficacy of CPP, a study documenting the efficacy of CPP for children who have experienced four or more traumatic and stressful life events, *Guidelines for the Treatment of Traumatic Bereavement in Infancy and Early Childhood* (2003), and the Trinka and Sam storybooks. She has more than 14 years of experience training nationally and internationally in CPP and diversity-informed practice. As a first generation East Indian/Japanese American who is fluent in Spanish and past co-chair of the Culture Consortium of the National Child Traumatic Stress Network, she is committed to examining how culture and context affect perception and mental health systems.

Patricia Van Horn, JD, PhD, (d. January 2014) was clinical professor in the Department of Psychiatry at the University of California–San Francisco, director of the San Francisco General Hospital Division of Infant, Child, and Adolescent Psychiatry, and associate director of the Child Trauma Research Program. Dr. Van Horn received her JD in 1970 from the University of Colorado School of Law, and her PhD in 1996 from the Pacific Graduate School of Psychology. Dr. Van Horn was the co-developer of Child-Parent Psychotherapy and provided national and international trainings in the dissemination of this treatment. She was the lead planner for the San Francisco Safe Start Initiative and a consultant to San Francisco Safe Start in its implementation period. She was also a member of the steering committee of the Youth Family Violence Court in the San Francisco Unified Family Court. Dr. Van Horn co-authored *Losing a Parent to Death in the Early Years,* and *Psychotherapy with Infants and Young Children: Repairing the Effects of Stress and Trauma on Early Attachment.* She lectured widely on the subjects of early childhood development and the impact on young children of witnessing domestic violence.

The Child Trauma Research Program is a program of the University of California–San Francisco located at the San Francisco General Hospital. Its mission is to develop innovative intervention models and conduct treatment evaluation research for traumatized infants and young children. Since 2001 it has been a site of the SAMHSA-funded National Child Traumatic Stress Network (NCTSN), where it is the lead program for the Early Trauma Treatment Network (ETTN), a collaborative effort devoted to enhancing the quality and quantity of infancy and early childhood trauma services. In addition to the Child Trauma Research Program, the ETTN comprises the Child Witness to Violence Project at Boston Medical Center, the Child Violence Exposure Program at Louisiana State University Medical Center, and the Infant Team at Tulane University Medical Center.